Joseph Parker

Ecce Deus : Essays on the life and doctrine of Jesus Christ

With controversial notes

Joseph Parker

Ecce Deus : Essays on the life and doctrine of Jesus Christ
With controversial notes

ISBN/EAN: 9783337260200

Printed in Europe, USA, Canada, Australia, Japan

Cover: Foto ©Lupo / pixelio.de

More available books at **www.hansebooks.com**

ESSAYS ON THE

Life and Doctrine of Jesus Christ.

WITH CONTROVERSIAL NOTES

ON

"ECCE HOMO."

BOSTON:
ROBERTS BROTHERS.
1867.

PREFACE.

A CAREFUL consideration of the various points raised in ECCE HOMO induced the present writer to undertake a re-survey of the Life and Doctrine of Jesus Christ. He found, however, that he could not occupy the stand-point from which *Ecce Homo* had been written without, as it appeared to him, ignoring the mystery of the Incarnation, and thus putting himself into a false relation to all subsequent facts in Christian history. The following pages will show that on several points the writer finds himself in perfect coincidence with the author of *Ecce Homo ;* and he ventures to believe that on those points upon which the differences are irreconcilable he has not been betrayed into a tone which is inconsistent with the respect due to the finest genius and the frankest candor. In the following pages the writer proceeds upon four convictions: —

First: That it is not merely difficult, but absolutely impossible, rightly to survey the Life and Work of Jesus Christ without distinctly acknowledging the unprecedented conditions under which Jesus Christ became Incarnate.

Second: That those conditions can alone account for, and are essential to a true interpretation of, the entire doctrine and phenomena associated with the name of Jesus Christ.

Third: That those conditions and the whole course which they inaugurated (the miraculous conception, the doctrine, the miracle, the death and the resurrection), constitute a *unity* which *necessitates* the conclusion that Jesus Christ was God Incarnate. And —

Fourth: That the author of *Ecce Homo*, having overlooked or ignored those conditions, has worked from a wrong centre, and reached several sophistical and untenable conclusions.

It appears from his Preface that the author of *Ecce Homo* felt himself obliged to trace Christ's "biography from point to point, and accept those conclusions about him, not which Church doctors or even apostles have sealed with their authority, but which the facts themselves, critically weighed, appear to warrant." The present writer does not undertake to suggest that Church doctors and apostles did *not* critically weigh the facts themselves; but he does undertake to say that no weighing of the facts can be satisfactory which ignores the fact which lies at the base of the Christian structure. Nor does he see how the author of *Ecce Homo* can trace the biography of Jesus Christ "from point to point," when he only professes to "place himself in imagination at the time when he whom we call Christ bore no such name, but was simply .... a young man of promise, popular with those who knew him, and appearing to enjoy the Divine favor." How can a biography be traced "from point to point" when the "critical weighing of the facts themselves" does not begin until the subject of the biography has actually attained a "promising" and "popular position"? If a biography is to be traced from "point to point," how can it be done without referring to the birth, if not to the ancestry, of the person whose biography is traced? Suppose that a writer should undertake to trace from point to point the biography of the author of *Ecce Homo*, would the author, or would the public, be satisfied if the writer did not open the narrative earlier than the time of the appearance of that book? Yet this is what the author of *Ecce Homo* does with the biography of Jesus Christ, and with this disadvantage on his part, that he overlooks a fact without which all the succeeding facts never could have transpired. No "young man of promise, popular with those who knew him, and appearing to enjoy the Divine favor" (and there have been tens of thousands of such young men), ever did what Jesus Christ did; a fact which, "critically weighed," certainly suggests the necessity of going farther back than the time of "promise" and "popularity," in order to find out whether there was a reason explanatory of the whole series of phenomena.

The embarrassment of the present writer was considerably increased by another expression in the Preface to *Ecce Homo:*—"After reading a good many books on Christ, he felt still constrained to confess that there was no historical character whose motives, objects, and feelings remained so incomprehensible to him. The inquiry which has proved useful to himself may chance to be useful to others." How the author could diminish the incomprehensibleness of Christ's life by simply regarding Christ as "a young man of promise, popular with those who knew him, and appearing to enjoy the Divine favor," does not appear. The present writer is "constrained to confess" that, in proportion as he regards Jesus Christ in this light merely, the Life as narrated in the New Testament becomes utterly *in*comprehensible. Not until he realizes the fundamental fact of the Incarnation does he understand the sense in which Jesus Christ calls himself Son of God and Son of Man.

The present writer felt the difficulty of choosing a title for his book. It seemed to him that if the author of *Ecce Homo* intended to maintain the Godhead of Jesus Christ, it would not be unnatural for him to select the title of *Ecce Deus;* on this point, however, he was of course not informed, and he adopted the present name because it expresses most concisely the doctrine which is taught in the book.

Ecce Deus is not a reply to *Ecce Homo*. It claims to be an examination of the Life and Doctrine of Jesus Christ conducted on independent ground.

CONTENTS.

CHAP.		PAGE
I.	THE HOLY THING	13
II.	THE WRITTEN WORD	24
III.	THE WRITTEN WORD (*continued*)	38
IV.	THE INAUGURATION	46
V.	THE INAUGURATION: THE DIABOLIC PHASE	53
VI.	THE MIGHTY WORKS	66
VII.	THE CALLING OF MEN	84
VIII.	CHRIST REJECTING MEN	103
IX.	THE CHURCH	119
X.	THE CHURCH LEFT IN THE WORLD	140
XI.	CHRIST ADJUSTING HUMAN RELATIONS	156
XII.	CHRIST THE CONTEMPORARY OF ALL AGES	173
XIII.	THESE SAYINGS OF MINE	190
XIV.	ETERNAL PUNISHMENTS	207
XV.	THE CROSS OF CHRIST	228

CHAP.		PAGE
XVI.	RELATION OF THE CROSS TO THE LAW	250
XVII.	RELATION OF THE CROSS TO PRACTICAL MORALS	271
XVIII.	THE POSTHUMOUS MINISTRY OF JESUS CHRIST	306
XIX.	CONTROVERSIAL NOTES ON " ECCE HOMO "	318

ECCE DEUS.

CHAPTER I.

THE HOLY THING.

MANY false Christs have gone out into the world. The Christ that was born in Bethlehem has now to compete with the Christ born in the poet's fancy, carved out of an ideal humanity, or developed out of a benevolent sentiment. The noble, simple Nazarene has been left behind somewhere, probably in the Temple, or has passed through so many guises that the characteristic lineaments have been lost. This circumstance is a significant feature of the spiritual civilization of the day. Deepest and truest among its lessons is the doctrine that men must have a Christ. There has ever been a motion, a gravitation, more or less palpable, towards a man who should be the complement of every other man; and who, by the perfectness of his manhood, should be able to restore and preserve the equipoise which universal consciousness affirms to have been disturbed or lost.

The Incarnation is the radical mystery in the life of the Christ accepted by the Church. Without following the theologian into doctrine, we are bound to follow the historian into matters of fact. The historian introduces a man, under the name of Jesus, who was begotten as no other man was ever begotten. He does not represent the usual conditions of human birth, but stands alone among all men. The mysteriousness of his origin, even if it be but a supposition, will supply an easily available test of his entire life and teaching; the man who begins as no other man ever began, must continue as no other man ever continued.

In other senses than that of the procreation of human life, there have been miraculous conceptions in every age — conceptions by the overshadowing of the Holy Ghost too. Every foremost thought of God among men, every struggle of the soul in the direction in which God is supposed to have gone, has been an effect of divine operation upon the mind. In Jesus Christ alone have we a life which claims to have been produced immediately by a superhuman relation to the human body. Yet, though so produced, "the holy thing" born of the Virgin did not collide with the human race as an unexpected antagonistic element, but took his place in the human family by a process which, on one side, was fitted to awaken awe, and on the other, to excite sympathy. The world of the East had been accustomed to what may be termed miraculous conceptions in the intellectual sphere, as the world of the West has since become. Intellectual history presents a succession of births quite, in their degree and according to their nature, as inexplicable as any occurrence that could transpire in the merely material sphere. "The Holy Ghost has come upon, and the power of the Highest has overshadowed," all who have wrought upon the springs of civilization and enriched the resources of human life: poem and picture, book and statue, that have touched the world's soul, and given it any hint that there was a portion of the universe beyond the narrow visual line, or a deeper life in itself than could be sustained by bread alone, have been, notwithstanding the apparent irreverence of the expression, miraculous conceptions, fruits of the Spirit's strife with the human mind. The Spirit had to move upon intellectual chaos, and now all orderliness, or beauty, or music, is attributable to his power. The grim spectre of traditional orthodoxy may shudder at the notion, yet rather than pronounce the genius of civilization atheistic, it may be more reverent to describe it as a conception and production of the divine energy operating through human instrumentalities. The excess of difficulty is on the side of atheism, not of inspiration. On such a subject men are not required to be more orthodox than the Bible itself. Moses hesitated not to say that the Lord had called by name Bezaleel, the son of Uri, the son Hur, of the tribe of Judah, and had "filled him with the Spirit of God, in wisdom, in understanding, and in knowledge, and in all manner of workmanship, and to devise curious works; to work in gold and in silver and in brass, and in the cutting of stones to set them, and in carving of wood to make any manner of cunning work." Art is thus set among the miraculous conceptions, and civilization is robed as a worshipper in the outer court of the Temple. Still we have not a *man* who claims, in a peculiar sense, to have God's life in his veins. We have seen God in art; can we see God in blood?

It is important to remember, what one would have thought could never have been forgotten, that there is a document written by many scribes, which professes to be an authentic history of a Man who openly claimed to have been begotten by the Holy Ghost. How can we test the validity of such a claim? Without inquiring whether there are any other ways, there is certainly this simple and effectual plan: Is the mystery of the life consistent with the alleged mystery of the origin? Is the doctrine consistent with the birth? If the man be found to be in perfect accord with the mystery, — in proportion, so to speak, to it; if there be no break in the rhythm between the "sayings" of the teacher and the alleged revelation of the angel who foretold his birth, then this unity of mystery becomes itself an argument which compels certain conclusions. If, on the other hand, the phenomena of the birth and the tone of the doctrine be discrepant; if the cloud of mystery has been employed to conceal defect of stature, then the claim to have been begotten by the Holy Ghost is not only unsupported, but positively contradicted. The present inquiry will revert again and again to the consistency between the declared divinity of the fatherhood and the teaching of Him who was begotten.

Omnipotence covers the whole ground of difficulty as to the possibility of such a conception as is claimed on behalf of Jesus Christ. No argument, therefore, need be started in defence of that side of the question. Given the existence of God, and the power required to bring out the alleged result will be granted too; defect of power would be defect of Godhead, and defect of Godhead is an absurdity. Yet the entire Christ, so to speak, coming from God without human interposition, would have increased the difficulty of his acceptance among men. We can see how a union between the divine and human would have many advantages. If the Man spoke the language of earth with the accent of heaven; if he encouraged men by his common human nature to approach him, and then gave them assurance that the human enshrined the divine, he would complete by his power what he had begun by his weakness. This much we can see merely as an argument, without conceding that the facts which are yet to be collated bear it out. Are there any traces of duality in Christ's life and teaching? Anything that would confirm his claim to have descended from heaven? On the very face of the life there are many such traces; and in a more subtle and incidental way, there are hints and testimonies which should be scrutinized and estimated. We find Christ in the midst of a great multitude, and then he goes no man knowing whither; he sends his disciples to buy food, and then tells them that he has meat to eat which they know not of; in the very act of talking to a man, he says that he is in heaven; he is willing to be identified as the Son of Mary, yet never speaks of any father but God; he is known to have had no opportunities of technical learning, yet his wisdom is acknowledged by the doctors of the law; he submits to the fury of the ruffian band, yet talks of the legions of angels who wait but his prayer. All through we have these dualistic turns of speech — one part of the sentence plain, the other haloed with strange glory or lost in gloom.

This is a mere matter of fact, as found upon the face of the document which professes to contain the life of Jesus Christ. All this any sceptic would say, in common with any Christian. So far the matter is literary, not theological. Still there is an outline of an argument shaping itself from this view. The argument of consistency takes its inception at this point.

The so-called discrepancies on matters of fact, which some readers have professed to find upon a collation of the fourfold narrative, are less than nothing. History can never be written. It can only be hinted at, and most dimly outlined from the particular stand-point which the historian has chosen to occupy. It is only by courtesy that any man can be called an historian. Seldom do men so flatly contradict each other as upon points of fact. Incompleteness marks all narrations. No man can fully write even his own life. On reviewing the sheets which were to have told everything, the autobiographer is struck with their reticence and poverty. Two processes are synchronous in the act of writing, the process of the pen, and the process of the mind; and because the mind sees the subject in all its magnitude and bearings, it considers itself rather than the reader, who approaches the question from an outside point. Men cannot print tones, glances, sighs, or tears. The heart always suffers by being translated into speech. Readers bring their own methods of reading, and often the book which is essentially musical is dishonored by a vitiated articulation. The life of Christ has suffered much in the same way. It suffered by being written at all, and that it has outlived its suffering is one of the firmest proofs that there is a divine spirit in the earthly words. The life is before us in fragments only, and the most that we can do is to inquire whether the fragments lie in one direction, bear any evidence of having been cut out of the same rock, or testify to anything like unity of purpose.

It must be remembered that Jesus Christ had been the absorbing theme of all ages prior to his advent. This circumstance alone marks him off from all other men. The hope of his coming had kept society together, preserving it from intellectual and moral annihilation. When Christ came, long chapters of prophecy were to be closed like gates through which a king or conqueror had passed. In Christ the prayers of many ages were to be answered. The prophecies respecting him were marked by that strange dualism which attached to his life: taken separately as mere statements of fact they are contradictory, but looked at in the light of the dual nature which he claimed there is immediate and perfect reconciliation. The great paradoxes of prophecy were harmonized in the greater paradox of the life. Christ was " a root out of a dry ground," yet he was " the flower of Jesse and the plant of renown ; " he was " despised and rejected of men," yet he was " the desire of all nations ; " he was " without form and comeliness," yet he was " the fairest among ten thousand, and altogether lovely ; " he was "the Child," yet he was "the Ancient of Days." Thus we are detained on the same line of mystery. Prophecy and fulfilment are different phases of the same paradox. The range of evidence is thus extended, so that any man claiming to be Christ must be brought for judgment to the standard of prophecy.

This fact does much to clear the field of intruders, and to narrow the ground of competition. Christ distinctly threw himself upon prophecy, and challenged scribe and doctor and rabbi to "search the Scriptures." There was no wish to escape the test of written prediction, but a determination to abide by a careful search of the records which were regarded as having been received immediately from God. He began at Moses and all the prophets, and showed from all the Scriptures the things concerning himself. No challenge could be bolder. He stood at the close of the great prophetic dispensation and said, "the prophets wrote of me," and looking forward to the evolutions of time and tracing the course of religious education and development, he commanded that his name should be taught in "all nations." It was not, then, on some recondite and insignificant point that Christ claimed his position in the world, but on the broad ground of completed prophecy. He was the fruit which was to be produced by the roots of promise and hope which God had from the beginning put into the hearts of men. He closed the troubled era of prophecy, and opened a most gorgeous apocalypse, which took its power and glory entirely from his own name. If any challenge could have developed a rival, or brought into prominence the lawful heir of the heritage described by the prophets, this would have done so. An unlearned man addressing the sages of his time, who held the first literature of the world — not only unlearned but garbed as a peasant, poor in his known ancestry, and unsupported by any visible authority — said, 'Open your scrolls and read the prediction of my person and power; consult the prophets, and see if I bear not the hitherto mis-read signs of Messiahship; recall the music of the minstrels of Israel, and say whether my heart be not in accord with their rhythm.' This made it hard work for an impostor. The empiric may have brilliant visions of the future, but it is perilous for him to challenge his contemporaries to go far back in search of his ancestral roots. The case as laid down in the biographic document compels us to go beyond Bethlehem if we would understand the purpose of the birth. We have hardly turned the first page of the Bible until we feel that a new and marvellous element has been interjected into the history of man, which gives life and tone and purpose to the whole current of earthly affairs. The generations are centralized in one idea. From Abraham to David, from David to the carrying away into Babylon, and from Babylon until Herod reigned in Judea, there is a life far below the surface. From behind the prophetic veil, or through it, there glows the image of a man, stranger to everybody yet friendly to all. A marvellous image it is, so indistinct yet so positive; gentle, yet carrying awful power, as the summer cloud carries lightning; very near, yet distant as the unseen God. We feel this in coming along the biblical line; feel that almost at any moment a Man might stand up in the very likeness and majesty of God; and a strange, fascinating spell binds the reader, until having passed the prophecies he comes to the Star, and the Virgin, and the Child. That Child had been the mystery of all his reading; *there*, in infant life, lay the explanation, itself a mystery, of all the tumultuous events and hopeful promises which made up the sum of prophetic history. We cannot understand the Child without at least recognizing that it is *alleged* that he came up from unbeginning time to express, audibly and visibly, what otherwise could never have been known of God.

The opening chapter of the Gospels is more than a catalogue of names. It is the Old Testament summarized; it is human history in miniature; an assembly of the Past convened to witness the birth of " the holy thing, called the Son of God." We go through the list to the manger-cradle, and the heart saddens at more than one point in this illustrious succession; strange threads have been woven into this web; — the patriarch is here, and the king; the pure woman and the dissolute man; eldest sons, and sons younger than their brethren; names which make men proud of mankind, and names we would " willingly let die." Marvellous pedigree, indeed! It will surely be a great risk to attempt to get out of this mass a Man who will stand firm in all crises. The world has already lost one Adam, may it not lose another? In the case of the federal man the reading was brief and simple: we had the Creator and the creature in one sentence; we moved at one step from God to Adam. In this second case, we have to proceed from Adam to God. In Genesis, the work was easy; in Matthew, it seems as if through such a mass we could never find the promised Life. We wonder at what point of so desolate a Horeb God will fix his tabernacle of fire.

We are bound to consider the value of the fact that Christ throws himself upon the past; he chooses his own tribunal, and it is one to which no Jew at least could object. Looking at the subject generally, this much is clear — that the mystery of the birth is in keeping with the mystery of the prophecy, and it now remains to be seen whether the mystery of the doctrine is in harmony with both. Whatever a fuller examination may disclose, there is before us, even so far, a great breadth of homogeneous mystery, — unique, unbroken, unparalleled. Any discrepancy here would vitiate the whole succession. No lapse of time, no combination of circumstances, can repair an error at this point. A well-known rule in law will hold good here: " Quod initio vitiosum est, tractu temporis convalescere non potest." If Christ is to command our confidence, he must continue to be what his claim to the prophetic past, and the alleged preternatural conditions of his incarnation, *necessitate*. A common man cannot be tolerated after so uncommon a beginning. If he be only a young man of high and most ambitious spirit, he has chosen a most perilous course, a course which must break down somewhere. It cannot be an easy task hypocritically to represent God upon the earth, without now and again letting the mask slip aside. How can the finite steadily carry the Infinite, when the Infinite is at war with him? Christ must be more than a good man, or worse than the worst man. If he be not God, he is the Devil.

CHAPTER II.

THE WRITTEN WORD.

THERE is a document which alleges to be authentic, and which certainly comes before the world as no other book does. The Book claims to have had an origin as mysterious as the birth of Christ, — combining the human and divine. The hand is man's, the voice is God's. While this Christian document is before us, we are not called upon to write a life of Christ, but to interpret a life that is written, or to show cause for rejecting the document. Our relation to the document should be first ascertained. Are we to reserve the right of discrimination in reading the documentary evidence? If so, by what law, or under what conditions, is the discriminative faculty to be regulated? To receive the book just as it stands would be simply an exercise of faith; to adopt an eclectic course, would involve the rendering of reasons for abandoning the immemorial orthodoxy of the Church.

No doubt the Book is often thought of in a narrow and even unreasoning way by its admirers. Certainly, it is so sparing in details, as apparently to leave much of life unprovided for. It does not occupy a tenth part of the ground traversed by Plato, who, in connection with many lofty speculations, discoursed concerning lands and dwellings, hunting and fishing, cemeteries, monuments, and epitaphs, family quarrels and injury to property, rhetoric and geometry, with a thousand other subjects. Compared with this elaborate treatment of nearly all questions, the statements of the Christian writings are exceedingly bald and poor; yet there may be more in those writings than in all the tomes of philosophy. God's first book, the book of nature, apparently leaves much of life unprovided for; yet as men acquire skill to turn over the ponderous pages, they find that every want has been anticipated. Adam would hardly know the world of which he was the first occupant; yet the primal forces and characteristics of nature are just the same as when he kept the garden of Eden. Modern civilization can hardly understand how men could subsist in ancient times, yet the earth abideth forever without appendix or supplement. What was wanting, was the faculty of interpretation. Men saw the water, but could not interpret it into steam; they saw the lightning, but mistook it for an enemy; they saw the sun, but could not fully interpret all he signified by the eloquence of light. The human power of interpretation grows; yet after it has grown, it often forgets both the process and the fact. The volume of nature is precisely to-day as God published it; but the latter readers are more sharp-sighted and inquisitive than the former. Civilization becomes wiser, keener, more ambitious and inclusive, year by year. Men were partly afraid, partly unable, to decipher the writing of nature; they read the illuminated title, and settled down into contentment or indifference; as if when "God finished the heavens and the earth," he also finished all the uses and applications to which future ages would be disposed to put them.

The Christian writings abound in seminal ideas; they are full of beginnings. The outlines are many, but there are no finished pictures. The value of those writings may be best represented by the term *Life*. We know they are inspired, because they are inspiring. The living man is the best confirmation of the living book. This book is not a plumb-line by which to test the perpendicularity of a wall; it is a living spirit, quickening and regulating spirits capable of illimitable development. With infinite appropriateness, therefore, it closes with an apocalypse,—not with a final line, but with prophecies of a future which shall eclipse the splendor of all earlier light. The Old Testament closed with a prophecy; the New Testament culminates in a revelation. The New Testament is only the beginning of books; not a finished and sealed document, according to popular notions of finality, but the beginning of a literature punctuated and paragraphed by tears and laughter, by battle and pestilence, and all the changes of a tumultuous yet progressive civilization. The Apocalypse looks towards the future with ten thousand eager and glowing eyes. What if that apocalypse be fulfilling under our own observation, and Christ be saying to us, " Ye hypocrites, ye can discern the signs of the sky; how is it ye cannot discern the signs of the times "?

God is, so to speak, issuing ever-enlarging editions of the New Testament—so rapidly, indeed, that the world itself can hardly contain the books. Though we no longer know Christ after the flesh, yet we walk with him in the holy sanctuary of the spirit; and from among the golden candlesticks, he throws out all the rays by which we read to-day's story and to-morrow's apocalypse. He is still "the light of the world," and still there is about him all the mystery of light. The light which reveals the landscape, needs itself to be revealed; so paradoxical is nature, like nature's God, that we are dependent for revelation upon what is itself a mystery! If we have ceased to know any of the facts of the Book — its temples, sacrifices, washings, oblations, and miracles — it is because we have come to a deeper sympathy with its spirit. We have now transcended the use of the grammar and the lexicon, except for the most rudimentary and initial purposes. We are not now dependent upon the scribe, but by a divinely regulated instinct we know the hand and the voice of God. Our faith cannot be broken down by a misspelt word or a mistaken date; the heart is enthroned as arbiter, and it knows the " going " of the divine step.

No doubt the Book does contain contradictions more or less real. So does the book of nature. The desert contradicts the garden; the storm contradicts the calm; summer and winter are utterly discordant; one plant grows poison, another is impregnated with healing juices; the savage beast and the creature of gentle blood face each other in the contradictory book of nature. The world is full of contradiction, and an intolerably insipid world it would be but for its anomalies. Every man is his own contradiction. In ten years, a growing man will throw off many tastes, companionships, and habits, which to-day are pleasant to him. There is nothing without an element of contradiction but death, and death itself is the great contradiction of God. Human maxims and policies are continually at strife. Out of contradiction comes education. But what is contradiction? Not lying, necessarily — not even opposition, absolutely; contradiction may simply mean incompleteness, or may arise from ellipsis. Two gases may mutually antagonize, yet may be held altogether by a third. Two statements may be discrepant, until a missing link is supplied. A man may pursue two divergent courses of conduct, yet may hold his integrity without a breach; when smitten on one cheek he may turn the other, and yet he may rebuke an offending brother; he may judge no man, yet he may refuse to cast his pearls before swine, or give that which is holy unto the dogs: this supposed contradictoriness he has learned of Jesus Christ, who, though he had not where to lay his head, promised to those who followed him "a hundredfold more in the present world;" who reproached men for not coming to him, and then told them that no man came unto him except the Father drew him, and afterwards gave them to understand that they would be damned if they did not come unto him; who preached trust concerning to-morrow, and then told men to make unto themselves friends of the mammon of unrighteousness.

All this appears to be most contradictory and perplexing, yet the same kind of contradiction marks the whole life and speech of men. One book may be many books, as the New Testament is literally. Its chapters may be addressed to different men, or to the same men under different circumstances; or cautionary words may be interposed in anticipation of possible abuse. One of the New Testament writers states plainly that there are in the revelation two distinct kinds of spiritual aliment, known respectively as "milk" and "strong meat;" one for babes, the other for men. When babes eat men's food, what wonder if they suffer from doctrinal dyspepsia, and be excluded from the Church as heretics? And when men appropriate the babes' milk, what wonder that the Church should suffer in robustness and power? There is one remarkable saying of Christ's which prepares us for ever-widening revelations of his purpose in relation to man: he said, "I have many things to tell you, but ye cannot bear them now: howbeit when he, the Spirit of Truth, is come, he will lead you into all truth." Among the "many things" would be explanations of hard sayings and complements of unfinished circles. The plan of revelation, too, hinted that man should become more and more independent of the scribe, and more and more reliant upon the Spirit. Writing is a human contrivance, but thinking is a divine operation. The scribe for the child, the Spirit for man. The instructions of a parent or schoolmaster amply illustrate the whole case alike as to method, instrument, and result. At one period, the child is addressed as if he were irresponsible, and at another, as if every deed would be brought under judgment. The schoolmaster first sets before the pupil the most detailed methods of calculation, and insists upon every step being taken; afterwards he shows the pupil how to abbreviate the processes of doing the very same work, and actually ridicules him if the calculation is carried on in the detailed and minute method which at first was affirmed to be right. So a man is educated in proportion as he becomes able to group and summarize details, and by scientific ellipses to pass rapidly towards results. All this is part of a great movement from the letter to the Spirit, from the symbol to the life. This is man's upward course towards God; a deliverance from manual toil, and an entrance upon the joys of a work which never satiates the appetite, and never wearies the faculty. When we are "perfect as our Father in heaven is perfect," we shall escape the tedium of manual processes, and work from the spiritual centre.

According to the processes, so may be the verdicts which men may pass upon one another. The pupil who is only able to do a sum in simple multiplication would not be "able to bear" a revelation respecting the differential calculus; but in proportion as he was able to acquit himself well in multiplication, the teacher would be justified in saying that he was a good scholar, and yet that he knew nothing;—good, as far as he had gone, yet ignorant in view of the vast region which remained to be explored.

When Christ tells men to come unto him, he is addressing them in their alienated condition; when he tells them that they will not come unless the Father draw them, he is but cheering and confirming their Christward desires. The statement is equivalent to this: 'I am so unlike what all men have expected, and I have commenced my work in so unlikely a manner, that no man could possibly come unto such a poor, friendless, homeless man, except my Father draw him; I present no external charms, I can appeal to no sordid motives; if any man, therefore, feels the slightest drawing towards me, he may regard the inclination as divinely inspired, for no man cometh unto such a person as I am, except the Father, which hath sent me, draw him.' In this view, we have the meaning of the expression, "My Father worketh hitherto, and I work." Men are moved by opposites. While there is a falsehood in extremes, there is a moral leverage in them also. The servant is on the road to mastery; the humble man is travelling to the throne; decomposition is a step towards reproduction: so this lowly outcast Christ, by the very depth of his humiliation, lifts society towards the altitude of heaven. He could not have done his work at any of the intermediate points of the social scale; he must go down until there was no man below him — until he was despised and rejected of men; so that by an action on his part from the depth, and a concurrent action on his Father's part from heaven, he could say, "My Father worketh hitherto, and I work; no man cometh unto me except the Father draw him."

But is it not declared, in other parts of the Christian writings, that certain men are foreordained and predestinated to eternal life; that God is likened unto a potter, who may fit one vessel unto honor and another to dishonor; that he hates one man and loves another; that he subdues and hardens whom he will? Is not this contradictory of much that Christ said, and confirmatory of other of his sayings? In the interpretation of all such sayings, the heart is to be trusted before the dictionary. Christ often put the understanding of divine mysteries upon the base of an analogy between fatherly and divine government: "If *ye*, ... how much more your *Father?*" This is a method of interpretation which refers decisions to the natural and universal instincts of man, and such a method is absolutely essential where grammar and lexicon cannot disclose the inner meaning of language. Christ goes back to the interpretation of consciousness where literal interpretation fails. Tried by this higher tribunal of criticism, such meanings as have been attached to the idea of predestination simply *cannot* be correct. The heart repels them; nature shudders with horror when they are suggested. The fatherly instinct of the human race, to which Christ himself appealed, instantly, without flutter or misgiving, says, 'If God calls all men, and yet determines that only a few shall come; if he mocks men by offering gifts which he has rendered them powerless to accept; if he makes some men vessels of dishonor, and then breaks them to pieces because they are not vessels of honor; if he can sit on his judgment-seat, and see men going down to hell because he determined from all eternity that they should not go to heaven; if when he says 'whosoever' he means but a few, — then let all honest and noble men leave him alone in his hateful heaven, and go down to hell in company with poor injured creatures who have deserved better at his hands.' This is the conclusion of that very instinct of parenthood which Christ himself challenged in the interest of the divine government. Nowhere in the sacred writings is God represented as falling below the promptings of that holy instinct, but everywhere as transcending them in love and beneficence; but the interpretation which reprobates any portion of the human race shamefully and cruelly dishonors all that is compassionate and generous, not to say that all is equitable and just, in the common nature of man. Christ's new canon of interpretation renders men independent of technical criticism, and when the instinct upon which it is founded is entirely purified, it will render men independent of all written codes. So far, the parental instinct enables men confidently to affirm, that whatever may be the meaning of predestination, it cannot narrow the affections, or pervert the justice of God.

It has been suggested, by the narrowest and hardest school of theologians, that God may, as a sovereign, damn anybody without being held accountable, or without giving any shadow of reason to his creatures. This, however, is a notion which proceeds upon a mistaken apprehension alike of divine and human nature. There is not only a fallacy, but a falsehood, in the very heart of such a representation. God himself *cannot* so act with *moral* beings. In proportion as any creature is endowed with the moral element, in that proportion is the sovereignty of God limited in relation to that being when debated questions arise between the creature and the Creator. It is by virtue of the moral element that man stands upon a common plane with God. Sovereignty is a matter of power over forces and events which do not come within the sphere of responsibility. The whole tenor of the Christian writings goes to show, that as a sovereign God could not even *save* man; his sovereignty was limited to the method by which salvation should be offered; on all questions of plan, time, and circumstances, God's sovereignty was absolute, but no man could be saved apart from the exercise of his own will; the moment that force entered would be the moment of his degradation as a man. If man could have been saved simply by a volition of the sovereign, then the humiliation and agony of Christ constituted a circumlocution in the divine government which could be accounted for only on the ground of the most wanton cruelty on the part of God. Salvation and reprobation alike lie beyond the limits of sovereignty, except in such points as have just been named. It is not our business to enter upon an interpretation of such passages as are supposed to justify the theory of reprobation; but it is our business in thus canvassing the Christian writings to point out the canon of construction which Christ himself appealed to in illustrating the immeasurable bounty of God towards man. Christ set up the human parent as the best representative of the divine Father, and thereby elevated the parental spirit into an interpreter of divine things.

With such real or apparent contradictions before us, it becomes of the first importance to determine what is to be done with the Christian writings? Are sophisticated and foolhardy men to be turned into them indiscriminately, and left without guidance as to their divisions and applications? Is the Church an authorized and necessary interpreter of the written Word? The determining distinction between a book that is true and a book that is false is, that the true book, with all its ellipses, brokenness, and literal discrepancies, may be trusted anywhere, for the spirit that pervades it will be its strong defence, and it will grow upon the consciousness of men in proportion as they learn more of the brokenness and ellipsis of life itself. The bad book, on the other hand, with all its artistic consistency, will cheat every promise it offers, and fail most where it is needed most. The position which the Christian writings have attained is the best vindication of their claim to be the declarations which God has authorized; not a position of finality, or apprehension as to encroachment, but one of inspiring and self-spreading life, which encompasses all the wants of man.

Words already cited from Christ's own lips show that we are not living under a dispensation of the book, but under the dispensation of the Spirit; and this fact harmonizes with the whole of God's educational method so far as we have discovered it, that method being one of continuous advance from the seen to the unseen, from " beggarly elements " to all-subduing life. Christ gave a very partial revelation of himself in the days of his flesh. A few strong, startling, and revolutionary words, with a chastened and persuasive tone of consolation, sustained by many mighty works, was all that he gave men, with one exception; but that exception was itself the chief hope of the Church, being nothing less than a promise of the Spirit of Truth. That spirit was to be an indwelling presence in the Church, inspiring and guiding the education of the soul, interpreting the facts which the visible Christ had created, and leading into the truths which those facts dimly outlined. Truth is always deeper than fact. Christ had built up, by teaching and suffering, the world's greatest, holiest fact; but the Spirit was promised to reveal the infinite truth which that fact pointed out. The Christian writings without the Christian Spirit would be a dead letter; but the Spirit, by daily interpretation and application of the written Word, enlarges it so as to extend it over the whole ground of life. Though this is the age of the Spirit, it is appropriately termed the Christian era, for the Spirit "takes of the things of Christ" alone; never changes the theme, but continues to unfold "the unsearchable riches." Christ's personal work was rudimentary in a large sense; he struck across the courses of life in a manner which compelled attention; his words often flashed like lightning, and his step startled like thunder at midnight; but his work has all the appearance of a fragment about it. He has many things to say, but forbears; what men knew not in his lifetime, they were to know afterwards; his own works were to be succeeded by greater, because he was going to the Father. There was much abruptness about this. He had roused the Jewish mind without tranquillizing it again. He had started new conceptions, dismissed old prejudices, removed traditional boundaries, troubled the fountain of individual and national life, yet things were left in a chaotic state: —

> " Obstabatque aliis aliud : quia corpore in uno
> Frigida pugnabant calidis, humentia siccis,
> Mollia cum duris, sine pondere habentia pondus."

All this was to be settled, orbed, illuminated; and much time would be necessary before we could continue the poet's description of the metamorphosis, and say, "Hanc Deus, et melior litem Natura diremit." Christ's work, looked at entirely by itself, simply as a three years' ministry, was certainly fragmentary, though perfect so far as it went; yet looked at in relation to the whole width of human history, it was suggestive, not exhaustive; preliminary, not final; vernal, not autumnal. Throughout the whole of his work the Spirit expounded simply the doctrines of Christ, not any doctrines of his own: "He shall not speak of himself; but whatsoever he shall hear, that shall he speak; and he will show you things to come. He shall glorify me, for he shall receive of mine, and shall show it unto you." Here, then, we have the solution of the difficulty as to the interpretation of the written Word; there is a Spirit whose particular function it is to reveal the historic Christ more plainly, and so to keep pace with the enlarging capacity and power of the world. This Spirit operates upon a homogeneous spirit in man himself, and thus a mutual "witness" is established — a witness which in many cases transcends the difficulties suggested by merely verbal criticism.

CHAPTER III.

THE WRITTEN WORD—*continued.*

WE have said that though this is the dispensation of the Spirit, it is yet distinctively the Christian dispensation. This circumstance may throw a sidelight upon one dark saying in the Christian writings, which relates to the unpardonable sin, the sin against the Holy Ghost. Christ taught that a word spoken against the Son of Man would be forgiven, but that a word spoken against the Holy Ghost would not be forgiven; by which he probably meant that in his visible form there was so much that contravened the expectations of the people, that they might, under the mistaken guidance of their carnal feelings, speak against One who had claimed kingly position under a servant's form, but that in the course of events he would appeal not to the eye, but to the consciousness of men; and that when he came by this higher ministry, refusal of his appeal would place man in an unpardonable state. The vital principle would seem to be, that when man denies his own consciousness, or shuts himself up from such influences as would purify and quicken his consciousness, he cuts himself off from God, and becomes a "son of perdition." Speaking against the Holy Ghost is speaking against the higher and final revelation of the Son of Man: in this view

Christ's position in the Godhead is unimpaired; but if a sin against him were *less* than a sin against the Holy Ghost, he could no longer retain divine equality. According to the Christian writings, we know nothing of the Holy Ghost except in connection with Jesus Christ; to speak, therefore, against the Holy Ghost is to speak against Jesus Christ himself, not as he appeared when he took upon him the form of a servant (μορφὴν δούλου), but as he was originally in the form of God (ἐν μορφῇ θεοῦ). As we have already said, truth is larger than fact, so the spiritual is larger than the material, the Holy Spirit greater than any personal manifestation possibly could be. The incarnate Christ was local, the Holy Spirit is universal; the fleshly Christ was a Jew, the Spirit-revealed Christ is the brother of every man; the embodied Truth walked within certain geographical limits, but the spiritual Truth is unlimited in range and inexhaustible in power. The Apostle says that "henceforth we know not Christ after the flesh;" now he is represented by the Holy Ghost, still head over all, though unseen by men.

With this as a start-point, why may not the men of to-day know Christ more thoroughly than did the original disciples and apostles? They know everything else better; why make an exception of the great Life which is giving such revelations of itself as cover all the enlarging breadths of civilization, and fill plenteously, even to overflow, the expanding capacities of manhood? The foremost man in the original apostolate declared of himself that he had "not yet attained," and exhorted others to "grow in the knowledge of our

Lord Jesus Christ." There is no claim of finality in the apostolic epistles. Everywhere the path of progress is not merely pointed out, but the most exciting inducements to persevere are employed in the apostolic appeals. The riches of Christ are declared to be " unsearchable," and the peace of God is said to " pass understanding." All the terms descriptive of Christ, and of the courses of study which may be entered upon concerning him, suggest the impossibility of exhaustion, and by implication suggest the greatness and richness of human nature. Stationariness in Christian study is a sin against the subject, and an injustice to the student. Not that fundamental and spiritual truths can be changed. Newton did not deny that two and two are four when he promulgated the doctrine of gravitation; nor did Coulomb deny the diurnal rotation of the earth when he improved the mariner's compass. We go back to the Book for the primary facts and outshadowings of truth; throwing aside all that was local and temporary, we discover the abiding root of which came the leaves and the fruit which are for the healing and sustenance of the nations.

This term "root" assigns to the Christian writings their true position and value. There is all the difference between the Christianity of the apostolic day, and the developed Christian idea of the present time, that there is between an acorn and an oak. The essential nature is unchanged, but the least of seeds has become the greatest of trees. The Father is glorified when the children "bear much fruit," and much fruit simply means much Christ. When Christ said that he had "finished his work," he spoke as an agriculturist might do when he had sown his entire field with seed, not as the reaper would do when he garnered his sheaves. The seed was small, the harvest is universal; the words were few, and often broken, but they have roused the heart and shaped the course of the world. The tree is gigantic in stature, but it draws all its vitality out of the one root which Christ planted.

It is certain that different men sustain different relations to the first principles of arithmetic, geometry, or any science. The skilled arithmetician does not require continually to refer to tabulated data; he could carry on his calculations successfully, if all written data were destroyed. They are now in him; they are part of his intellectual nature, so that he employs them with the ease which comes of perfect familiarity.* All men, however, are not advanced arithmeticians; they must have something to work at, something on which the eye can rest, for they feel safe in their processes only so far as an appeal is made to the eye. Numbers, however, are dogmatic; they make no accommodations; they ignore all varieties of temperament, faculty, and circumstances, and by so much they differ from the spiritual truths which are the subject of the Christian writings. Still the analogical point is vivid enough for our purpose; some students are yet at the very beginning, wondering at the birth, or startled by the works of Christ; others have got beyond the narrow factual boundary, and are revelling in all spiritual luxuriance. It would be as impertinent in the arithmetician who has not yet mastered the first four rules

---

* *Ecce Homo*, 183, 4.

of his art, to rail against the learned algebraist, as for the tyros in Christian literature to reproach men who have the word of Christ dwelling in them richly, having forgotten or left behind the elementary facts of the Gospel.

Any survey of that portion of human society comprised within the limits of modern civilization which ignored the practical power of the written Word, would not only be partial, but unjust — openly and scandalously wicked, indeed. By influencing society at the vital centre, it touches the remotest angles of the social idea. Its effect upon young life, upon all the multitudinous aspects of human sorrow, upon the development and consolidation of generous sentiment, is written in living characters upon daily life. Even where its dogmatic form is denied, its spiritual results are evident; and some, who find a thousand difficulties in its letter, are penetrated and ennobled by its principles. If a question of comparison between this book and any other were started, Christ's own standard of judgment would best meet the case; looking forward to the false prophets who should seek to undo his work, he said, "By their fruits ye shall know them." Modern civilization should be the field of research on both sides. Which book has done most for liberty, justice, progress? Which book has most persistently branded, defied, and threatened every form of tyranny? Which book has spoken with the truest pathos to the wounded and sorrowing heart? Which book has done most for the poor man? These inquiries may be put in no declamatory spirit, but simply with a view to the discovery of facts. The test is fair. It is marked by a high sense of honesty on the part of Jesus Christ. He adopts no method of overriding human judgment, but, on the contrary, elevates the discriminative faculty of man, and in a manner throws the responsibility of the conclusion upon men's own common sense. This is not the plan of necromancers, soothsayers, and self-elected prophets: Christ appeals to his own works and the works of others, asking the verdict of the world upon their respective claims to truth and veneration. There is no cunning legerdemain, no rebuke of human severity, in the examination, no indulgence bespoken on behalf of the worker: the words and works are before you — judge them, said Christ; and "believe me for the very works' sake."

The important concession that different men may sustain different relations to the Christian writings, may provoke an inquiry, bearing upon some aspects of church-life to-day: What of the consistency of those who, being far advanced, having come into a great liberty of faith, are still teachers in those churches that are yet only in the rudiments, and whose published dogmas give no hope of expansion? The answer to this inquiry cannot be difficult. To the end of the world churches, as promiscuous aggregates, *must* be in the rudiments only, and the teachers of such churches must accommodate themselves to the elementary faith of their hearers. Often the teachers will come to know what Christ meant, when he said, "I have many things to say unto you, but ye cannot bear them now." The wisest teachers are the most reticent men. They reserve all the deeper interpretations, knowing, from a wide observation of human nature, that many who have eyes, see not, and many who have hearts, do not understand. Wise teachers will speak in one set of terms to the great multitude, and in another to the foremost men, when they can go aside and commune secretly. They will often have to hide their meaning under a parable, and give explanations in an undertone. This is what Christ did. He had special interviews with his disciples, in which he spoke of the deeper things of his kingdom; and when one of his followers gave utterance to a testimony respecting his Messiahship, more full and emphatic than had yet been rendered, he pronounced it an immediate disclosure from heaven. Again and again, too, he enjoined silence upon his disciples as to the higher questions which had passed between them, as if revelation was to be regulated by time, and to-morrow's work was not to be dragged into to-day's service. These graduated revelations are compatible with the mystery of his own manifestation before men, and the method by which he educated the disciples. His representatives are right as they follow their master's course. No man is bound to open all his heart to unappreciative spectators. To the esoteric circle he may fully reveal himself, but to the exoteric crowd his demeanor may be reserved. He knows that to some men he must not tell the dream, until he can also tell the interpretation; but that others can help him in the changeful visions and tumultuous upheaving through which the soul passes into the higher ranges and sweeter experiences of truth.

It is to be remarked that Jesus Christ never wrote anything, nor did he instruct his disciples to commit anything to writing. We have broken reports of many of his addresses, and very fragmentary memoranda of his conversations and disputes, but no provision of a literary kind seems to have been made to secure permanence. Anything more fugitive, apparently, than the words and works of Christ, it is impossible to find: no hired scribes report the utterances or chronicle the deeds of this wonderful Man; he founds no library, leaves no chronicles to be hidden in secure places, but works out his twelve hours, and then passes into rest. We come to no sign of permanence, until we receive the promise of the Holy Ghost; he was to quicken the recollection, as well as to disclose further aspects of the truth. The memory was not to be left unaided; a great light was to be held over all the way in which the disciples had walked, so that they might see the minutest detail, and tell or write their story with all the clearness and certitude of personal observation.

The written Word is a repertory of facts, a revelation of doctrines, and a standard of appeal upon all questions to which it bears any relation. The only interpreter of this Word is the Holy Ghost, and he operates through the consciousness of the reader: it is not a Word superimposed upon man, but a word in harmony with all that is divine in human nature, and therefore having power to carry the entire conviction and sympathy of all who read without prejudice. Upon these principles the subsequent inquiry will be conducted.

CHAPTER IV.

THE INAUGURATION.

THE measure of consciousness is the measure of life. The life of intelligent beings is not merely a question of years; lapse of time may not increase vitality; life is to be measured by the sensitiveness and enlightenment of consciousness, so that over-consciousness may be one meaning of precocity or prematurity of manhood. The first public intimation of consciousness of his great position, on the part of Christ, if we except the answer which he made to his mother, is found in immediate connection with his baptism. When John remonstrated with him, saying, "I have need to be baptized of thee, and comest thou to me?" he answered, "Suffer it to be so now." There is here clearly personal consciousness of his identity as the long-announced Man who was to be at once Son and Lord of humankind. At that moment he knew himself. The fire which had been in him from the beginning shot up into a bright flame, which John saw, and which all who were afar off were to see. Up to that time, in all probability, Christ was not fully conscious of his Messiahship. The poor frail flesh which he had inherited from a depraved race could not have borne the presence of full consciousness for thirty years: when it did come, it consumed him in as many months. He had but three years of avowed battle. Such a man could never do his work with indifference. Every moment was a strain upon his life. No man ever gave so much to time, or ever exacted so much in return. To assume full consciousness on the part of Christ during the years of his obscurity seems to separate him too widely from man, by reducing his humanity to a minimum; but to assume that he " grew " in consciousness, as he " grew in favor with God and man," is to bring him into close fellowship with the weakest of his followers. We cannot afford to contract in the least degree the amplitude of Christ's manhood; it is upon that side particularly that he belongs to us; it is as the ladder reaching unto heaven whereby men may ascend. By so much as he was human he was limited, during his obscurity, in consciousness; by so much as he was divine, his full consciousness overbore his humanity. All men who have done any notable work in the world have felt the consciousness of its importance, as a fire in the bones. They could not languidly dream of it, nor contemplate it from a hazy and mellowing distance. They have hasted unto the battle; they have said, " I am straitened until it be accomplished." Such a consciousness makes men die young. It carries the soul into an agony of passion. It drives the blood along the channels with an urgency which greatly distresses nature, and strains the intellectual nerve until the brain sees strange lights, and often trembles for its own safety. Only men of strong natures know what is meant by this lavish expenditure of life — this willingness to taste death for every man.

Common life supplies the example of consciousness in the matter of mutual affection. Wisely and mercifully, this has been made a matter of growth. Human nature would be altogether overdriven did this consciousness set in fully during the period of education and discipline. From the general kindness and simplicity of childhood we advance until the heart begins to individualize its sentiments, to concentrate its energies; by and by there seems to be but one life in all the world, and then begins the consuming passion of perfect love. Human lives grow gradually up to this. To so great a passion they must have come by wisely graduated degrees, or it would have rent and destroyed them. Still, all through there has been a consciousness of love, and in all the simple trust and generosity of young affection there have been hints of a great possibility, which only time and circumstances could develop. And this full love means, if need be, sacrifice, cross, death! All love is ready for the thorns and prepared for the slaughter; only by so much as it is so ready is it worthy of the name of love. It may not be driven so far along the line as these things lie, but these things do lie in the line of pure, self-oblivious affection. Man is never so near the cross as when he is in the highest mood of love. To misanthropy, to all narrow-heartedness and self-worship, the cross must be the sum of all horrors; they stand on different planes, they speak languages mutually unknown; but the cross is the very next thing to love: there is but a step between them!

This may illustrate in some degree the growth of consciousness in Jesus Christ. The three years of his heart-consuming ministry were backed by thirty years of quiet and thoughtful life. In such backing lies the strength of all great workers. Nothing consumes like love; how soon, then, must *he* be consumed who did nothing but love! The brevity of his life must have some meaning. Three years as reckoned by human tables are but a span; there must have been in those three years a fire which burned fiercely, and made them unlike any other three years in all human history.

This view of Christ's consciousness detracts in no degree from Christ's deity; rather it throws into bolder and more peculiar relief the elements which contradistinguished him from all others, while it retains him amongst us as the Man Christ Jesus. The horizon seems gradually but surely to have widened, until he who " came to his own " saw " all men coming to him," and he who was " lifted up " drew all nations to his cross. This might have been, would have been, too much for the youth in his humble home at Nazareth. All was getting in readiness for the dove that was to mark the opening of the new era. There was to be a descent upon him — a special point of concurrence which was to signalize the quickening of perfect consciousness. It is to that concurrent point that we have now to look.

Christ passed, so to speak, through two gates, the one strait, the other straiter, respectively named Baptism and Temptation. The inaugural processes are characterized by the same mystery that has overshadowed us all along. They are congruous with all that we have seen in the foretelling and in the birth.

The duality remains without wrench or flaw. There is an upward, there is also a downward side. There had been, to us suddenly and most inexplicably, a brief dispensation interposed between Christ and his work — a dispensation embodied in one man, and that man as little like Christ as the thunder-storm is like the calm which it precedes. Other dispensations had been long, this was brief; other prophets spake, but saw not; this prophet baptized the very man of whom he prophesied. Never did divine processes seem to hurry upon one another so urgently as about this time, for from the Inauguration to the Ascension but three summers shone! The movement of events never faltered for a moment. Jesus Christ, as he had been the burden of other dispensations, was to be the burden of this. He was to find his name on all other pages, and now it was to be written on this rugged leaf which tells the story of the "voice crying in the wilderness." Men are valuable to us as teachers in proportion as they represent a great compass of history. When the aroma of all lands floats from their robes, and the accents of all languages blend in their speech, they have a right to speak with authority. The world's Saviour must have come through the world's great throng of hearts; he had come through Moses, the minstrels, the prophets, and on His way he now takes up this transient dispensation of the " voice." Thus Christ publicly identified himself with the current of divine purposes as shown in human history. He worked *with* man as well as *for* man, and was thus the contemporary of all ages. Men should study the divine idea of each age, and become intelligent co-workers with God. Christ's example shows that obedience to the divine spirit of the time ever brings fuller disclosures and attestations of the divine blessing. The heavens are opened to every obedient man, and the Spirit of God descends on the last as on the first. John's baptism had gone no farther than repentance, but Christ, standing with the dove resting upon him, showed that there was a baptism unto holiness. By John's baptism men were put into a right relation to the past, but as they followed Christ they were put into a right relation to the future; from the negative condition of repentance they passed to the affirmative attitude of holiness. This is the culmination of human history. We have come through man, servant, prophet, messenger, up to *Son*. The very nomenclature is pregnant with sublime moral significance; we pass from "made" to "begotten," from "upright" to "beloved," from the "us" of the creating Trinity to the "my" of the benignant Father, from the "very good" of the first Adam to the "well-pleased" of the second. "Οὗτός ἐστιν ὁ υἱός μου ὁ ἀγαπητός ἐν ᾧ εὐδόκησα."

John's baptism looked towards repentance: why then should Jesus Christ undergo it? To prove his human nature, his vital connection on his mother's side with the whole human state, and to supersede it by fulfilment. The world could be taught only gradually; it needed "water" before "fire," the bodily lustration before the spiritual fervor. The dispensations have all worked from the outward to the inward, from the body to the soul; but Christ inverted this method, and established the only really spiritual dispensation. Did Christ, then, need to repent? No more than he needed to pray, or to do any religious exercise that men do. In so far as he was human, it became him to adopt the duties of each dispensation.

The place of baptism in the Christian system is one of great simplicity. Men like — indeed require — something objective. They cannot at one bound attain that which is purely spiritual. Ceremonies, and all ordinances, great or small, are only accommodations to human weakness. Men require something to fall back upon. Even a recollection may come up in the soul with all the gracious power of inspiration: the simple fact that we have done something, or that something has been done for us, may save us from despair and incite us to do more. Many a soul that has sunk from God in higher things has been stayed in its sinking by coming against the fact of its baptism in its downward course. It was well, therefore, as an accommodation to human weakness, to conjoin baptism with faith in framing the evangelical commission. If any man wishes to undergo the "baptism unto repentance," it may be a question how far he is at liberty to take a backward step in the dispensations; but to baptize children (who do not need repentance) unto holiness is an act infinitely beautiful in simplicity and infinitely charming in pathos. Baptism provides for the lower and coarser part of human nature. It associates in a very natural way fact with faith, something done with something yet to be done, and thus it is made a help to us. To make anything more important of it would be to abet the theological charlatanry which has kept back many souls from the kingdom of God.

CHAPTER V.

THE INAUGURATION: THE DIABOLIC PHASE.

THERE was another dispensation to pass through — the dispensation of the devil. Human history would not have been what it was but for the diabolic element; it was impossible, consequently, for Jesus Christ to enter upon his work without a very demonstrative antagonism at the very beginning. With infinite propriety does the temptation follow immediately upon the baptism. The devil had been at.work before, in persecution by means of Herod, obliquely, so as to suit the less pronounced periods of the new life; but as soon as the Baptism had brought Christ the seal from heaven, and proclaimed his true relation to God and man, a more formal and critical contest became a necessity. Christ could not have passed to his work with a merely indirect recognition of the devil's existence; the recognition must be full, emphatic, solemn. Any man who proposed to himself the fabrication of the story of the wilderness, entered upon a most perilous task. It must be difficult for human genius to contrive a consistent devil, or to maintain in dialogue the conscious power of God. On the other hand, who could historically write the account of the temptation? No one was present with pen and ink. No one overheard the interlocution. How, then, does it find a place in history? It must have been outlined by Christ himself in conversation with his disciples. Many a time the conversation would turn upon the devil and his kingdom, for the Christian monarchy was set up to put the diabolic monarchy down. When the conversation so turned, nothing would be more natural than that Christ should relate his experience in the wilderness, and found upon it many of his most practical directions. The account is obviously fragmentary, and in one or two points must be read figuratively, not literally. Temptations cannot be written. The process is not conducted with all the precision of a Socratic dialogue. The heart can give but a meagre account of its spiritual conflicts; its wounds cannot be translated; its triumphs are too subtle for words. At the same time all Christian hearts have, according to their capacity and susceptibility, gone through the very course of temptation given in the New Testament narrative. All such hearts have been tempted to make bread in an illegitimate and forbidden manner; have been tempted to risk their lives and their destinies presumptuously; and also tempted to offer the homage of the soul as the price of secular aggrandizement. Upon such points as these the whole world has become a wilderness of temptation or a wilderness of discipline. To-day the great strife of the world is proceeding upon these very issues, — Bread, Desperation, Sovereignty. Man has been victimized by the sophism that it is necessary for him to *live*, and therefore necessary that he should make bread, either legitimately or dishonestly; but Christ alone broke through this sophism by showing from what the true life of man is derived, that there is something deeper than the sensations of the body, which cannot be a guest at men's tables, but must feed on the very truth of God. Man has been also tempted to risks that are unlawful, especially on the pretence that he was but acting up to his faith; forgetting that there is a limit to human liberty, and that a narrow boundary separates trust and presumption. Man has further been tempted to bid for great dominion, and in some cases under the glare of the delusion he has bent his knee before the deceiver. So man himself has passed through the series of temptations recorded in connection with the name of Christ, and can understand what is meant by Christ having been "tempted in all points like unto his brethren," showing that Christ took up the very temptations which had been plaguing the world for thousands of years, and did not introduce a new and unfamiliar class of temptations which had never troubled the life of the world, and which, even when overcome, left the common temptations of society untouched. This view does two things: first, it shows the barrenness and utter poverty of the devil's resources; stripped of all that is accidental, merely decorative or diplomatic, they really consist of one thing, viz: the exaggeration and idolatry of self; and second, this view brings Jesus Christ into very close and tender sympathy with every tempted man. They stand on the same line; they bear the same tremendous shocks; they war with the same weapons. Did Christ, then, merely suffer in the wilderness as any other man has done? Suffering is a question of nature. The educated man suffers more than the uneducated man: the poet probably suffers more than the mathematician; the commanding officer suffers more in a defeat than the common soldier. The more life, the more suffering; the billows of sorrow being in proportion to the volume of our manhood. Now Jesus Christ was not merely *a* man, he was *Man;* and by the very compass of his manhood he suffered more than any mortal can endure. The storm may pass as fiercely over the shallow lake as over the Atlantic, but by its very volume the latter is more terribly shaken. No other man had come with Christ's ideas; in no other man was the element of self so entirely abnegated; no other man had offered such opposition to diabolic rule: all these circumstances combine to render Christ's temptation unique, yet not one of them puts Christ so far away as to prevent us finding in his temptation unfailing solace and strength.

The temptation of the Beloved Son is important as an historic fact, but infinitely more important as a doctrine giving hope to men who are tempted by the devil to some degree of the same enormities. Could Christ have been overthrown? Most certainly; otherwise his temptation has no message to man, except one of despair. Whatever is less than infinite, is temptible and peccable; Christ's humanity was less than infinite, therefore his humanity might have been overthrown. Sympathy can proceed only from community of situation. To say that Christ could not have been successfully tempted, and that the result of his temptation should comfort men, is equal to saying that, because no man can blow out the sun, therefore no man can blow out a taper. The record of the temptation is an act of cruelty, if it have no bearing on human strife; but an analysis of the temptation shows that the methods of assault are fundamentally the same, and that every answer is available for every tempted man.

When, however, it is affirmed that Christ could have been successfully tempted, the words require to be carefully considered. The possibility relates, of course, entirely to the human side of his nature. So far as the weakness of the flesh was concerned, Christ was open to all the results of diabolic seduction; but there was in him that spirit of perfect trust in God, which rendered the fiercest assaults of the enemy simply futile. He did not come upon the tempter as Eve did; she was necessarily inexperienced — she could not foresee the result of disobedience; Christ had the history of the world as a living illustration of the course of diabolic policy immediately before him, so that he could give the lie to every diabolic suggestion.

A common illustration will simplify the idea that the spirit of perfect trust which was in Christ, taken in connection with the results of sin which abounded everywhere, rendered temptation utterly futile. Take the most respected man of a given neighborhood — a man whose honor and integrity are known to be above suspicion, and it may be affirmed of that man, that it is impossible to persuade him to defraud his neighbor of a penny. The idea of his doing so would be regarded by those who knew him best as an imputation not to be tolerated for a moment. But why? The man is only human, like other men, why then this indignation at the idea of fraud? Simply because the spirit of honesty within him is too strong to succumb to such a temptation. But increase the force of the temptation; raise it from a paltry penny to ten thousand guineas, and multiply the ten by ten, and add the assurance that no human being can ever be cognizant of the fraudulent deed, and if that amount will not reach to his full moral stature, add to it according to his integrity; and thus a tremendous rival force may be set up, with which the man may find it difficult or impossible to contend. In the case of Christ, the devil pursued this climacteric course, rising from the mere satisfaction of hunger to the rule of all kingdoms. Still the Messianic spirit towered far beyond the pretentious offer. The deceiver could not attain the overshadowing height; other men had been measurable and conquerable, but this man was of gigantic stature, and his shield was impenetrable. While, then, looking strictly to the human side of Christ, it may be affirmed that he was exposed to all the risks of temptation, it may be affirmed with equal truth, looking at his spirit, that it was impossible that Christ could fall. There is a great truth in each representation, and the combination of the two can alone give us the reality of the case. One fact will show that the temptation of Christ was designed to be a source of strength to every tempted man: all the temptations are such as might have been addressed to a merely human being — not one of them was adapted to a being believed to be divine. With a Socinian creed, the devil adopted a Socinian policy. He assailed the man; he aimed no weapon at the God. He regarded him, indeed, as a man of great name and bold pretension, but a man still. The first temptation has an air of benevolence about it, — "Thou art hungry: make bread!" The second is marked by a spirit of inquiry as to the reality of creeds, — "It is written: prove the truth of the writing!" The third is an appeal to the senses, — "All these will I give thee!" Through this course we ourselves have been taken, and it would be a poor consolation to know that there was no point of sympathy between Christ and our souls.

In further elucidation of Christ's spirit, showing that it represented not only innocence but holiness, not a negative but an affirmative condition of soul, one remarkable circumstance should be noted. Eve and Christ returned precisely the same answer to Satanic suggestion. Eve referred to the word of God, so did Christ; Eve answered, "God hath said," Christ answered, "It is written;" yet Eve fell, and Christ stood. The strength, therefore, was not in the mere answer as containing a piece of information. Life is greater than intelligence; sympathy is profounder than obedience. The world's first woman was necessarily inexperienced; she had no historic footprints to go by; she knew her instructions, but they were set on no background of guilt and sorrow. The world's second Man was rich in history; he had no formal instructions, but brought with him the spirit of all caution and strength. The divine word is potential only as it represents the full consent of man's mind, soul, heart, and will. Eve gave her answer simply without doubt; Christ gave his with perfect faith.

The temptation was a movement towards humanity on the part of Christ. Men had lost sight of him for something like thirty years, with one exception. He was near them at his birth, with all the promise and hopefulness of morning twilight; and again he approached society when he was twelve years old; but now that he is in the wilderness, he seems nearer to human hearts than before. From the baptism he went up, as it were, towards God as the "Beloved Son," but from the temptation, he comes earthward as the Son of man. The Jordan lies on the heavenly, the wilderness on the earthly side of Christ. There is a "river," but there is no wilderness in heaven.

The particular manner of the inauguration, so far as its demonstrativeness is concerned, seems to have been required by the protracted seclusion of Jesus Christ. It is not a little perplexing that one whose birth had been attended by such marked, such unparalleled circumstances, could have been allowed by his contemporaries to subside into obscurity for a considerable succession of years. In some respects it seems impossible. Judging by the passionate urgency which marks every great movement of to-day, we should think that Nazareth would have been watched day and night; that all the learning and religion of the land would have adjourned thither, and impatiently demanded a decision respecting the destiny of the Child. Instead of this, the most marvellous birth of the ages is allowed to fall into partial, if not into total oblivion. The demonstration attending the birth makes this subsidence the more remarkable. The song of angels, the homage of wise men, the sensation in Jerusalem, all increase the wonder. It is to be borne in mind, however, that by many the sword of Herod was supposed to have taken away the Child of the Star and the Song. When that Child reappeared at the age of twelve years, he did so without any of those demonstrations which had accompanied the birth, simply exciting attention by his unusual sagacity. It was a long way, too, in those days from Bethlehem to Nazareth; and in that contemned Galilean town, the ear of corn could die before reappearing in its multiplied form. Strange, tumultuous years they must have been for the mother, though. Her heart must have been darkly overshadowed by that mysterious Son of hers, and must have sunk under the great burden of its own reflections, had not "the power of the Highest" been her continual defence and rest.

This long seclusion seemed to require an inauguration corresponding, in some degree, with the annunciation. Instead of the Star we see the Dove; instead of the Song, we hear the Voice from heaven; and instead of the flight into Egypt, we have the withdrawal into the wilderness. At this point, we get another glance at the unity of the double mystery of Christ. He took the dispensations as he found them; he underwent circumcision, and gave to the Lord a pair of turtle-doves and two young pigeons; long years afterwards, he found God's purpose set forth in a particular baptism, and openly identified himself with it; then he was taken into the wilderness, to be tempted of the devil. Why hesitate to say so plainly, and believe so literally? A man who had not been tempted would have been of no use to men. He would have been a stranger to their mental history; only able to talk *at*, but never *to* their spirit: all his words, refined and lustrous, would never have penetrated into the deep rips and wounds of human nature. There is no need to gloss the bare and startling announcement that Christ was led up of the Spirit into the wilderness, to be tempted of the devil. It is better to put the fact thus boldly before men. The weary, aching heart cannot feed on metaphors, or the cunning sleights of rhetoric; give it a Christ tempted, yet victorious, and the fact that one man has overcome the devil will sustain its own endeavors in the same daily conflict.

The scene in the wilderness illustrates the risks of solitude. The self-diabolizing spirit of man always reveals itself to the lonely contemplatist, either in moments of vacancy, or under the stress of spiritual crises. Eve was tempted when she was alone; the suicide succumbs when he is pushed into the last degree of loneliness; the darkest clouds of the conspirator becloud the mind when he has most deeply cut the social bond: when man is alone, he loses the check of comparison with others; he miscalculates his force, and deems too little of the antagonisms which that force may excite. All these are among the risks of solitude. The solitary man either degenerates into a misanthrope, and the tool of the diabolizing spirit, or he enriches and strengthens his life by reverent and subduing contemplation. Wherever we can descry the course of the diabolic spirit, we are left in no doubt as to the value which he sets upon the individual heart. He teaches a new doctrine in numbers. We calculate majorities by units; he teaches that the unit itself may be the majority; he counts by *much*, not *many*, his majorities being measured not by numbers, but by force. The minority may be the majority. Cæsar is more than all Cæsar's legions. When Eve was overthrown, a world was conquered. The persons whom the devil has elected to high offices in his government, have been strongly individual in character and faculty; from Eve to Judas, the succession has been marked by the coolest subtlety or the intensest passion. As the devil won a world when he won Eve, he knew that he would have won it twice, and forever kept it, if he had subdued her Son.

But the risks of solitude, it should be added, are in proportion to its value. Man cannot reach his full stature in the market-place, or in association with the excited throng. The wilderness must form the counterpart of the thoroughfare, — great breadths of contemplation alternating with great breadths of service. This was Christ's example, illustrated most vividly at one exciting point in his history: the disciples of John went and told Jesus that their master had been murdered by Herod; the intelligence seems to have shocked his spirit with a terrible disappointment; sickened and saddened by this tale of blood, "he departed thence by ship into a desert place apart," as if to avenge the murder upon the diabolic instigator, or to weep great drops of blood; yet we are told in the very next verse, that "Jesus went forth and saw a great multitude, and was moved with compassion towards them, and healed their sick." These were the hemispheres of his life, — secrecy and publicity; praying in the desert, and healing in the city; weeping alone, and working in the presence of many witnesses. The desert was to Christ a holy place, after the initial battle; the sight of the old footmarks inspired his depressed heart; the echoes of the victorious quotations became as voices of promise. In the first instance, he was led up of the Spirit to be tempted; often afterwards he was led up of the Spirit into the same wilderness to be comforted. So all through human life: recollection becomes inspiration, and Memory speaks to the soul like a prophet of the Lord.

The answers which Christ returned to the tempter illustrate the intensely spiritual nature of the temptation, and show how man is dependent upon an objective revelation in seasons of trial. Not one answer was returned from within; the soul looked out of itself for defence, yet gave the answers with the firm emphasis of perfect trust, as if their doctrine carried the entire conviction of the speaker. Man cannot do things simply because they are "written." The action comes from the harmony which is established between what is felt, and what is "written;" consciousness and revelation must be at one, and then the citation of written authority is not a sign of personal weakness, but a token of vital fellowship with God. If merely to say "it is written" were enough, then no man would fall; the point of failure is where the written Word and the life of the soul are not entirely at one. Men are not kept by revelation, but by the acceptance of the heart of that which is revealed. Yet objective revelation is of the highest consequence in human life. It stays the soul in special conflicts, and as men may feel stronger and safer in company than in loneliness, so the heart feels braver by the very presence of a written Word. A subjective revelation might have been the only revelation given, and might have been enough under primary conditions; but by so much as man fell from those conditions, he required a book as well as a conscience. Nor does Christ's example militate against this position, for throughout he combated the diabolic spirit as a *man;* nowhere did he launch the lightnings of his proper divinity in reply, but ever made the simple answer of a man who had read the revelation of God. Other courses were open to Christ. He could have recalled the tempter's own memories of heaven, the ancient sentence, the terrible deposition; the indwelling God might have shone through the human eyes, and abashed the Tempter by the light from which he had been expelled; yet all this side of defence is untouched, and the tempted man shelters himself behind the rampart of the written Word. Every assault is encountered upon the human side: to have met the Tempter otherwise, would have been to deflect from the only course possible to man, and to have divested the wilderness period of the Incarnation of all the features which endear it to probationary manhood.

CHAPTER VI.

THE MIGHTY WORKS.

THE baptized and tempted Son was now prepared for his mission. There is a very striking and suggestive consistency between the preparation and the work. So much power had been held in restraint for so long a time, that it was not to be wondered at that on its liberation "mighty deeds should show forth themselves in him." One of his biographers, as if overpowered by the number and splendor of his miracles, instead of introducing detailed statements of supernatural cures, groups in one impressive mass the beneficent works of many days; and the grouping is the more remarkable as coming at the very beginning rather than at the end of the narrative. If the miraculous mission had been opened leisurely, with a cure here, and a storm quieted there, the narrator would probably have given detailed accounts on his first pages, and as the miracles increased, he would have summarized towards the conclusion. Instead of this leisurely introduction of the miraculous element, we are startled very early with this announcement: "They brought unto him all sick people that were taken with divers diseases and torments, and those which were possessed with devils, and those which were lunatic, and those that had the palsy; and he healed them." All was as easy as bringing ice into the presence of the summer sun, that it might be melted. The unity of the mystery is again evident. Even in this marvellous statement there is nothing out of harmony with what has preceded. Is there anything to be wondered at, with sceptical wonder, that the Man who conquered the devil in the wilderness, should conquer the devil's works in human nature? The greater involves the less. All true conquest must be fundamental, and to be fundamental it must be moral. To the man who has conquered himself, all other conquests must be easy. Only a man's bad elements stand between him and the greatest achievements. If the prince of this world finds nothing in a man, that man is free of the checks and impediments which limit abnormal human nature.

Miracles can be difficult of credence only according to the low spiritual altitude from which they are viewed. As wonder is a sign of ignorance, so unbelief is a sign of incompleteness. The unlettered man is amazed at language which to the learned man is perfectly simple, just because the learned man has conquered himself by bringing his powers under adequate discipline, whereas the untaught man is ruled by his own ignorance. The novice, in anything, is necessarily impressed with the difficulty of a great work, whereas the adept has overcome all the disturbing sensations which inevitably accompany inexperience. The novice invariably first sees the difficulty; he is conscious of a disparity between the forces at his command, and the result to be attained, and soon augments difficulty into impossibility. The man of diminutive faith, a man in whom the self-element is uppermost, is astounded at the miracles of Jesus Christ; while the man of large faith, in whom the self-element is subordinated, accepts them with composure. Christ himself taught the doctrine both negatively and positively, and with incessant urgency, that faith was the nexus binding the natural to the supernatural. In proportion as any man has faith, is he led away from himself; and this brings us to the point just stated, that self-conquest makes all other conquests easy. Christ said that faith even so small as a grain of mustard-seed was more than a match for mountains. Why not? Power is mental rather than physical. It would be a poor thing to be a man, if he could not make himself master of the dust on which he lives. But the highest mastery is moral, and if the moral element is wrong, his dominion is of course abridged or upset. Wickedness is weakness. As the intellectual man inhabits a wider region than the man who is ignorant, so the good man has a power compared with which the bad man's rulership is a pitiful travesty of influence. The bad man has the power of destruction, the good man of restoration. Any beast can do *mischief*. But more on this point presently.

There is nothing in the nature of things to prevent miracles being wrought to-day as well as they were ever wrought. The Yogis among the Hindus believed that they could acquire perfect mastery over elementary matter. They sought to effect a vital union between the spirit that was in the body, and the spirit that was in nature, and having effected that mystic union, the Yogi was master of the situation, traversing space, raising the dead, rendering himself invisible, and going up to Siva, the spirit and essence of all creation. There is a good deal more in this philosophic dreaming than our modern notions may be prepared to allow. It was not the mere power of the hand which the Yogi sought, but the wider and grander empire of the spirit. What the Yogi sought to effect was a union between spirit and spirit; and this was precisely what Christ sought to effect when he demanded faith as the condition of miraculous healing. Where this union was complete, the working of miracles was as natural and easy as breathing. They were miracles only to the observers, not to the workers, for the workers stood on a moral elevation high above them, and saw their exact relation to God and man. It is not extraordinary that the faith which is not strong enough to work miracles should not be strong enough to believe that miracles can be wrought, though it may be narrow enough to brand him as a fanatic who affirms their possibility. Man cannot advance to the miracle except through the faith. There can be no doubt that the faith of the world has gone down; and in part this may be accounted for by the intellectual transition through which we are being driven by revived and ambitious science. We have come upon an era which has hardly time to pause and add results; information is arriving so quickly, the messengers throng upon each other so tumultuously, that most of men have taken upon themselves the duties of recorders; and if sometimes they are a little heedless of the punctuation, and by mistaking a comma for a full stop they do now and again speak too soon, the impatience or the precipitancy is not difficult of explanation. In fact, it is a hint that men are longing for the end. The great, suffering, human world feels that its day must be approaching sunset. It has been a long, troubled, changeful day, and men are now sighing for release and rest. The shaking and damaging of faith is a hint of a crisis, and the old words, sad as a sigh from the heart, come up with great force — "When the Son of man cometh shall he find faith on the earth?" There is a touching plaintiveness in the inquiry; he seems to have anticipated but a poor reception for himself. Perhaps, however, as in the days of his flesh, the unfaith of those who ought to have been nearest will be counterbalanced by the trust of men now supposed to be afar off.

It is a mistake to imagine that faith has anything to fear from science. Wherever science stops, faith must begin. Science has in many things altered the standpoint, or extended the domain of faith, but has never rendered faith unnecessary. It has enlarged the faith of childhood into the faith of manhood, but every hint of light which it has discovered has pointed out a great gloom beyond. It was intended that *Credo* should be succeeded by *Scio;* yet knowledge is valuable, not only for what is in itself, but as showing how much there yet remains to be known, and by so much as it does this it actually increases the sphere of faith.

One of the most persuasive features of the Christian miracles is that they were associated with a true human compassion on the part of Jesus Christ. They were not displays of mere power. They made a heavy drain upon his sympathy and love. When he saw blind, deaf, insane, tormented men, he had compassion on them. His emotional nature was profoundly stirred. Christ's was not dry power — huge, unsympathetic strength. As in all great characters there was much womanliness in Christ. The tear was never far to fetch. With one human parent only, it seems as if the full force of his mother's tender nature was reproduced in him. When Omnipotence weeps, we should consider the meaning which lies behind the tears. It has been pointed out that the Olympian gods contrived to keep themselves free from the pains and cares of the mortals whom they ruled. For them it was enough to govern — it was too much to suffer. In bitter accents did Achilles reproach the gods, as he attempted to comfort the hoary Priam.

ὣς γὰρ ἐπεκλώσαντο θεοὶ δειλοῖσι βροτοῖσι
ζώειν ἀχνυμένοις· αὐτοὶ δέ τ' ἀκηδέες εἰσίν.

But Christ's life was not "griefless;" his word of power was spoken with a tenderness which the world will remember forever. It is not difficult to see the consonance of the mystery here. The man who came to be a Saviour, and to found a monarchy upon himself, should be possessed of the finest and most accessible sensibilities, for monarchs can be monarchs only so long as they hold the hearts of men. Monarchy, in its highest application, is really a double-sided term, meaning not only rulership, but rulership by consent. Men cannot be permanently held by mere power; they will fear it, admire it, and then throw it off. Everything tires but love. Prophecies fail, tongues cease, love alone is immortal. The monarchy of Christ was founded upon the heart, upon love, and therefore with a consistency which is too profound to be accidental he had *compassion* upon all who trustfully invoked his power. He wanted the healed man afterwards. The client was to become the ally. Gratitude was to become loyalty, and on this deep base the world-wide kingdom was to be established.

Another feature of the mighty works, coincident with the compassion which they expressed, is their *unselfishness*. The worker is everywhere not powerful only, but good. Once indeed he gave an intimation, incidentally, of what would happen if he were to let loose his power in all its terribleness; the damning word fell upon a fruitless tree, and to the very roots it withered away. What if the same annihilating word had fallen upon useless men? It was well no doubt to leave one such memorial of mere power, that society might see how short a distance lay between life and death. It has been pointed out by a recent writer, as a curious circumstance, that men should hazard so much open, contemptuous, and even violent opposition to a man who carried such resources of power. They did not stand in awe of him, but contradicted him to his face, and took up stones to stone him. This does seem contradictory to the general expectation which such circumstances naturally excite. Looked at from this distance of time, and under the conditions of our ordinary life, it is impossible to believe that men should be so insane as to take up stones against a man who had just shown that he could open the eyes of the blind, cleanse the virus from the blood of the leper, and reanimate the dead. They had not heard of his doing so, but had actually seen him. If they believed their own senses they could have no doubt about the fact of Christ's unexampled power, yet they took up stones to stone him; it was worse than attempting to stone the lightning, — madder than throwing dust in the face of a storm! Yet they did it. The explanation of this circumstance lies deeper, probably, than has been recently suggested. In one view of the case, the action of taking up stones to stone such a man was on the part of the Jews not only natural, but, considering their traditions and circumstances, rather admirable than otherwise. They were Old Testament men, and all Old Testament men believed in stones. They would in a moment answer an idea with a stone, and cleave down erratic thinkers with the edge of the sword. But the action of the Jews was admirable rather than otherwise, on the ground that they showed how religious conviction lay deeper than all fear of mere power. The Jews were religious men; they had sacred historic documents to refer to, with many traditional legends; the man before them laid claims to dignities which they could not harmonize with interpretations of the oracles; and though he seemed to be able to do as he willed with the universe, yet in the very face of his stupendous and never-baffled power they took up stones to stone him. Their action was really a grand tribute to the force of religion in the heart of men. Their theism was arrayed against this Christism, and with little of physical power they opposed a man whom they believed to be a blasphemous and mendacious talker.

This probably goes nearer to the reality of the case than some recent theories, though they too are not without value. It is quite true that Christ had always used his power beneficently; " not to destroy men's lives, but to save them," was written on all he did; the fear which his works were calculated to excite was not alarm, but religious awe; his power was constructive, not destructive. This view was much strengthened by Christ's own method of meeting those who took up stones to stone him, for in his turn he showed the power of deep religious conviction on human life. He did not lay them at his feet as dead men, nor did he even send upon them temporary blindness, or any kind of physical distress. What he *could* have done! When they stooped to take up stones he might have fastened them in their stooping attitude, and left them as warnings to the whole progeny of scoffers. Instead of this he reasons with them, cites the good works he has done, and asks them to point out the particular one for which they stone him. He calls them to calm consideration. He shows no fear of the stoning, does not even care to condemn it — probably he was touched by their zeal for God; that was something to begin with and to work upon, and he could not witness it without feeling more and more the depth of human nature and the importance of its restoration. They believed in one side of his own nature, had they but known it! "Ye believe in God, believe also in me," — only an " also" between God and Christ! The boldness of his scheme, too, considered in a purely human view, is the more apparent by his first appearing among a people who knew and revered the true

God. He did not try to impose upon an idolatrous or ignorant people, but began under the very light of the Shekinah, among the people whose prophets had heard the voice of the Eternal. He operated upon the oldest and ripest theism of the world. This was dangerous work for a fanatic. He must be not an impostor, but a madman, who challenges heaven and earth in the interest of a lie. Having to encounter a theism so advanced, because so true and simple, Christ could well understand how the Jews would be indignant at any dishonor put upon God; and this indignation, which at first sight was a great hinderance, was the natural expression of a fact which would one day be turned to the best account. They seemed to feel themselves safe from his power while they rested upon the God of their fathers, and so made a claim upon the practical resources of the pre-Christian theology which would not shrink from comparison with the boldest confidence which men can repose in Christ's own promises. Fearing God, they were lifted above all other fear. The ancient songs of trust were repeating themselves in their souls — "God is our refuge and strength;" "The Lord is my light and my salvation: whom shall I fear?" On the other hand, Christ also showed the power of the divine element in man. He was alone, or if not literally alone, his companionships were such as to constitute a bitter satire upon his claims to be considered Messiah, Redeemer, King. His companions made him look ridiculous in the eyes of the ruling classes. Yet with so little visible background, he talked and worked with the consciousness of a man who could not be put down, and could not even be stoned. As he could not Christianize men by miracles, so he could not be deposed from the Messiahship by stones. On both sides, mere power was shown to be useless as a moral agent. The battle must be fought with different weapons. Spiritual results must be attained by spiritual processes. Still the mighty works, bearing, as they did, a constructive aspect, were auxiliary to the main end. They certainly called attention to the worker, and as certainly they made a powerful appeal to the persons who were benefited by them. One of those persons, for example, made a trenchant and powerful defence of Christ before the Pharisees. Like a common-sense man, he took his stand upon the simple facts of the case; despising all the cajolery of the baffled and incredulous critics, he said, with the charming and unanswerable frankness of an honest and thankful man, "Whether he be a sinner or no, I know not; one thing I know, that whereas I was blind, now I see." Christ had thus, by his miraculous power, made a marked advance upon the man's nature, — he had established "one thing" in his convictions, and thus prepared the way for further conquest. Accordingly we find this to be the case, for the man afterwards "worshipped him." The mighty Worker was admitted through the body to the soul. We have only to take this instance as a specimen, and to multiply it by the number of the mighty works, to obtain a comparative view of the value of constructive miracles in the propagation of Christian faith. Not only upon the clients themselves, but upon thoughtful observers, the miracles produced very helpful impressions, as may be seen from the confession of a ruler of the Jews, who candidly said, "Rabbi, we know that thou art a teacher come from God, for no man can do these miracles that thou doest, except God be with him." This was the conclusion of a reasoner, who did not examine effects in the light of religious prejudices, but who considered them in relation to adequate causes. He had seen displays of human power, and he knew the general range of human ability, but these particular miracles of the despised Rabbi went far beyond all that he had seen, far beyond all he had imagined, and compelled the conclusion, willing or not willing, that this man was at least a co-worker with God, carrying keys of power, such as he had never seen on the girdle of the strongest man.

Then, too, as already hinted, the miracles bore a special relation to the devil himself. The miracles were polygonal; one side looked towards suffering men, another towards observers, a third towards doubters, a fourth towards the devil, and so on. Christ's struggle with the tempter was only begun in the wilderness; it was continued to the very end of his earthly course. No devil, would have meant no Christ. Peter put the case concisely and strikingly, when he talked to Cornelius: speaking of Jesus Christ, he said, "He went about doing good, and healing all that were oppressed of the devil." The works of the enemy were on every hand; they must be thrown into contrast by the works of the Son. They must be distinctly charged upon the enemy, and the responsibility must be publicly and immovably fixed upon him. No doubt must be left on men's minds as to the source of all evil and suffering. The two workers were thus brought, as it were, face to face before society, and each was openly identified with a particular course. On the one hand there was destruction, on the other restoration. Men thus had an opportunity of seeing that Christ's opposition to the devil was the controversial aspect of his love for man; an opportunity which owed much to the miraculous works which immediately appealed to the physical senses and the common instinct of the observers. The opportunity would not have been marked by the same commanding breadth, if Christ had confined himself entirely to teaching; the cure of the body being more easily appreciable as an introductory step, than a direct attempt at the illumination of the mind. Every miracle was a challenge to a comparison of powers. Every healed man was Christ's living protest against death. The mere fact of the miracle was but a syllable in Christ's magnificent doctrine of *life*. Christ's mission may be summed up in the word Life; the devil's, in the word Death; so that every recovered limb, every opened eye, every purified leper, was a confirmation of his statement, "I have come, that they might have life."

The limitation of miraculous power was twofold. There was, first, the limitation which came from the unreceptive condition of the people; and there was the limitation necessitated by the difference between the outward and the inward, the material and the moral. At one place Christ could not do many mighty works because of the unbelief of the people; the utmost he could do was to lay his hands upon a few sick folks and heal them. The electric current was incomplete. The inhabitants were self-involved;

no tendril of the heart was putting itself forth in search of protection; all the fibres were knotted in impenetrable selfishness: Christ himself had no power there. He must have faith as a starting-point, otherwise no miracles in harmony with his moral purpose could be wrought. Miracles of mere power he could have performed anywhere, but such miracles were not included in his plan of life. His omnipotence was the agent of his mercy, and consequently it was the province of mercy to determine where the services of omnipotence should be offered, and where mercy was rejected omnipotence was held in abeyance. On one occasion, indeed, Christ's power operated in a direction that was merely destructive. A legion of devils besought him to let them enter into a herd of swine (a terrible illustration of the intolerableness of life in hell), and on obtaining permission the whole herd, to the number of two thousand, ran into the sea and was destroyed. Much has been said against the people who besought Christ to leave their coasts on finding their swine destroyed; they have been charged with sordidness, selfishness, and low ideas of the value of human amelioration: though we may steal a cheap reputation for magnanimity at the expense of those unfortunate people, yet they were right after all in desiring such a man as they took Christ to be to depart from their midst. Their request was the expression of a great principle in the human constitution, implanted there by the Creator. Men cannot be benefited by mere power, but they are necessarily reduced to a meaner manhood by the presence of a power that is destructive. The history of despotism proves this. To have in the city or nation a power that is incontrollably destructive is to live in perpetual fear, and fear can never train a noble and generous manhood. People never beg thunder and lightning to continue amongst them, but they often wish that summer would never go away. The Jews, therefore, who lost their swine, showed what would have been the result if Christ had given full scope to his power of destruction; men would have been overshadowed by a great apprehension, and in the darkness of such a horror would have dwindled into a pitiable dwarfishness. Besides, as said before, there is nothing so common and so vulgar as destructive power. The meanest insect can destroy the loveliest flower: the coarsest lips can utter defamatory and injurious words. All destructiveness, individual, social, national, lies in the same direction, and the beginning and end of that direction is the devil. The constructiveness of the Christian miracles is a most emphatic confirmation of Christ's claim to be the Saviour of the world. They are consonant with the natal song — "good will to men;" — they are opposed to the unchanging diabolic policy under which the world has endured so much, and they prepare men to accept the promise of a higher salvation than that of the body.

We have said that there is nothing in the nature of things to prevent miracles being wrought to-day. This is true abstractly, yet miracles are practically superseded by the dominion of the Spirit. The working of miracles in a purely spiritual dispensation would be an anachronism. Miracles were quite in accordance with the personal superintendence of the visible Christ, but now that Christ is no more known after the flesh the whole system of objective demonstration has gone up with him. What, then, is in harmony with the rulership of the Spirit? Not miracles, certainly, but science probably. Intellect is now summoned to a new and critical position. Creation has apparently exhausted its period of reticence, and seems now, using figurative language, to be prepared for a frank communication of its secrets; — or better, man has been educated so far by Christian agencies as now to be master of the right method of holding intercourse with the laws which have been the problem and even the dread of many ages. Humanity has been carried forward by the mystery which began in Christ — forward from the material to the spiritual, from the miraculous to the moral. Thus reason, which has been so long reviled, is no longer necessarily the corrupt and misleading agent that it was, but an honorable, because divinely-appointed guide. This is the inevitable result of a spiritual dispensation. The visible Christ made appeals to the natural senses; the Spirit does the inward and vital work of *conviction*. The Holy Spirit, as becomes his nature, stands in the line of the intellectual faculties, elevating them, purifying and strengthening them, and giving them new power of investigation and appliance. Distinctively, then, this is the dispensation of the Spirit, the age of mind, the era of reason. It does not follow, though, that Reason has completed her education; and by so much as Reason is incomplete it must be carefully distinguished from Understanding. The danger which some persons apprehend from what is termed Rationalism arises from a confusion of terms. Reason is an instrument, Understanding is a result. In proportion as reason is educated, a prudent hesitation marks all its processes. Philosophy is more tolerant than ignorance. He who knows most of the strength of the human mind, knows most of its weakness. Truth has nothing to fear from rationalism, but from irrationalism. The era of reason is preliminary to the age of understanding. The greatest reasoner in the apostolic church always kept this in view: he said, "I know in part;" "I see through a glass darkly;" afterwards, under the inspiration of a splendid hope, he added, "but then shall I *know*." The world never could have been reared by understanding, only by promise; this is in keeping with the whole constitution of things. The child of the philosopher is not permitted to begin where his father ended, but is driven back to start with the child of the unlettered peasant, as if his father had not made one attainment in learning. In this way society in all its breadth is carried through the same experiences, and educated to a common sympathy. Promise, then, not knowledge, has been the great stimulant of human education; and as for understanding, *that* lies far beyond this initial sphere. Early in the world's history it was shown that knowledge was out of place, except under such conditions as required the presence of hope to inspire and impel mankind. The knowing man, consequently, was sent out of the sphere which he had desecrated, and a flaming sword was made to show that knowledge might be bought too dearly.

The Holy Spirit presides over the intellectual development of man, leading him, as Christ promised, into all truth — the truth of the body, the truth of nature, as well as the truth of religion specially so called. The miraculous is now set back in distant history as one phase of divine revelation, which may yet teach us much of power combined with mercy; but the spiritual sheds its penetrating lustre over the future, charming men into deeper investigation than was possible to the ages which have been trained by symbol, and enigma, and miracle. What function Christ assigned to the Holy Spirit will, however, be considered more in detail in another chapter.

CHAPTER VII.

THE CALLING OF MEN.

HITHERTO the Beloved Son has been alone. In his Baptism and Temptation no man stood with him; but shortly after, he began to move more conspicuously in society, and to clear for himself a space in the world. Christ's call upon men to join him is, perhaps, more astonishing than many of the miracles which he wrought. First words are generally key-words. They commit the speaker to a policy, and when spoken to minds which have been excited by great expectations are probably never forgotten. Looking at Christ's moral work in the light of his miracles, one cannot but wonder why such a man did not prosecute his work single-handed. What need had he for fellowship? how could men be associated with him without feeling most oppressively the impassable chasm which lay between him and themselves?

Christ used the imperative mood freely at the beginning of his ministry; " Repent," " Follow," were among his earliest public words. In the wilderness he had gradually risen to an imperative tone — from a great principle which underlay all life to a written revelation, and then to a moral indignation which could not tolerate the presence of the enemy — " Get thee hence, Satan." This seems to have been the process through which he passed to the highest courage: it was not at first that he commanded Satan to begone, it was not until attack had followed attack that the tone of personal supremacy penetrated the heart of the tempter. On leaving the wilderness he brings with him this noble courage, and opens his ministry by calling upon men to repent and to follow him. Had he left the wilderness other than as a conqueror, his tone would at least have been hesitant; but having dealt the first shattering blow upon the diabolic head, he follows it up by publicly drawing a line of separation between one class of men and another. The subtle consistency between the tone of the victor and the tone of the evangelist should not be lost sight of in estimating the value of the Christian argument. The quality of the voice is the same in both cases; the same firm emphasis; the same direct appeal. The postponement of the call, too, until the close of the temptation, is a fact of supreme importance. What confidence could an untried man have in himself? The man who has no faith in himself is weak; the man who has a false faith in himself is deceptive; the man whose faith is founded upon the fact of a great conquest is strong and honest in proportion to that faith. The devil had never been ordered out of the way so peremptorily before, and the utterance of such an order, straining as it must have done all the forces of the soul, was succeeded by a period of great prostration. Angels came and ministered strength, and then followed just what has followed in all human experience — a consciousness of tried power, a calm but fervent determination to put the hard-gained influence to further uses. He who had successfully ordered off the devil must now do other work. The great battle must be succeeded by a great construction.

Christ, claiming to be King and Ruler of men, began his society with two obscure laborers. The narrative gives no warrant for concluding that the men had heard any private and special exposition of his views, doctrines, or plans. In common with all Jews, they might have had expectations and desires in reference to a king, but there is no authority for saying that they had had any preliminary intercourse with Jesus Christ. The call met a deep craving of the heart, and at once they joined Christ the Man, without knowing anything of Christ the Doctrine. The heart wanted a heart: life demanded life. The world had lived long enough upon written promises; the cold parchment was becoming colder day by day. There was an aching at the heart of society — a great trouble — an exciting wonder. The call had a peculiar charm about it in so far as it demanded attachment to a visible person. Not a Creed but a Life bade them "follow." The men who were called were not likely to know much about doctrine. Who could at the beginning? Life can be reared only by life. It is so in the family, and must be so in the church. The last thing that earnest inquirers care about is a written, formal, dogmatic creed. Such a creed, in fact, is simply a sign that there has been overbearing dictation on one hand, or hypocrisy on another. A written creed is in the nature of things only an inconvenient convenience. The heart can never write all that it believes. What wonder then if, when a living and

THE CALLING OF MEN. 87

glowing love comes to read the tabulated doctrines of the church, it should complain, hesitate, or rebel? It has often been asserted that Christ did not set down in sequential order what is known in these modern days as a system of divinity. The assertion is not only true as a matter of fact, but true as an evidence of his Godhead. The divine, the immeasurable, the eternal, cannot be formulated. Life cannot be systematized. Architecture may, so may astronomy, botany, and all other arts and sciences. But life is not a science: the soul is not an art. Immediately that the scientific line is crossed, the power of systematizing, if not lost, is so crippled and deranged as to be but a poor accommodation. Language itself, as partaking of the nature of a system, is often felt to be an inconvenience, useful for expressing what is uppermost, but nearly powerless in the articulation of what is deepest in the soul. Wisely, therefore, Christ wrote nothing, for written language is more difficult of interpretation than spoken language. The eye, the tone, the smile, help words that are spoken; which is but another way of saying that life is the only true interpreter. The moment that the grammar and the lexicon are called in, strife begins, and logomachy deposes wisdom. A tone would do more than all syntax to give the meaning of some doctrines. The spoken word is life; the written word is statuary. To have come, therefore, with a written creed in quest of signatures would have been a vain errand. The world has differed more over the interpretation of its own writing than over anything else — so much so that the interpretation of writing has become a profession, in which the directest contradictions are constantly maintained at the cost of vindictive or credulous clients. Parliamentary debates may be ambiguous, but Parliamentary Acts are incomprehensible.

Probably the greatest stumbling-block to the extension of Christ's influence is scholastic or formulated theology. The world is now waiting for a voice crying in the wilderness that men are to be saved not by theology but by Christ. The Church must go back to Christ's own living and mighty way of talking to craving and aching hearts. Men must behold the Lamb, not the controversies which have raged about him. Throughout his ministry the exaltation of himself was the most conspicuous feature: "follow me," — "come unto me," — "he that believeth on me," — "he that loveth father or mother more than me is not worthy of me," — this is the personal strain from beginning to end, and it is the only strain adapted to the capture and redemption of the world. It is often possible to understand a man when it is difficult to understand his creed. The author may be less a problem than his book. Christ calls men to himself without first setting forth a list of points to be accepted; men go to the doctrine through the man, not to the man through the doctrine. We dare not ask Christ what he believes, or what we ourselves may have to believe at some future time; we have to believe in the Revealer, and then we shall have no difficulty about the revelation. In the first instance we go to the Man Christ Jesus, and sit at his feet, waiting, wondering, and loving much. We are touched by his love, subdued by his tenderness, before we are enriched with his doctrine.

THE CALLING OF MEN. 89

The call of the Church often differs from the call of Christ in being a call to theology. In some places in modern Christendom it will be found that the Lord's table is surrounded by theologians, persons who have passed successfully through more or less of a theological examination; and that many feel themselves excluded from the memorial service because though they love Christ and could die for him, yet they cannot pronounce the doctrinal shibboleth. What does a newly-quickened heart, coming up out of the waters of penitence, and just about to move into the wilderness of temptation, know about the Trinity in Unity, the federal headship of Adam, the philosophy of sacrifice, or the metaphysics of theology? Probably nothing. Yet such ignorance is not incompatible with young life. Does the infant know the mystery of love when it is clasped in the parental breast? Do parents insist that their children shall study agriculture before they eat of the fruits of the earth? When a man declares that he loves Jesus Christ, he has a right to eat of the bread and drink of the cup which the Lord appointed. Love first, knowledge afterwards: with love to begin with, all else will come quietly, "without observation," yet with unspeakable joy. The heart will build up a belief as it wants it, and wear it gracefully because it is its own. Sling or mail, no matter, provided the man be a warrior cool and resolute. The faith which Christ seeks is probably not to be found in any one sect; part of it is in all, and when it is collated and arranged, it will be the best representative of national churchism. Uniformity of theological creed is a simple impossibility, and as undesirable as it is impossible. The object is the same, yet the views are different; the foundation is the rock, yet each man may adopt his own architectural style; the parents may be the same, yet in stature, form, faculty, disposition, the children may be entirely different. The sun brings all manner of flowers out of the earth, varying endlessly in hue and fragrance; what if the light above the brightness of the sun bring a still more varied summer out of the winter-bound heart of man?

This view does not diminish the influence of belief. It merely points out that the man comes before the creed, and that there is a difference of the gravest importance between trust in the living Christ and the acceptance of a few theological statements about him. In the former case there is a full surrender of love, in the latter a mere intellectual assent, unaccompanied by moral enthusiasm. The one is necessarily associated with passion and demonstration, the other may consist with the lowest indifference.

The manner of the Call was quite consonant with the mystery of all that is summed up in the word Christ. Its abruptness cannot be overlooked. The ages had been undergoing a long and exciting preparation, and by the very strain of eager watching and listening had been educated to the finest sensibility. Otherwise how can the promptness and unstudied grace of the fishermen's response be accounted for? There was no personal intercourse, so far as the narrative goes, no collusion, no pre-arrangement; yet at a word the lowly men abandon their vocation, and assume a new attitude towards society. At once the Abrahamic call is suggested: * here is the same abruptness, the same urgency, the same mystery of the end. Men of quick ear have heard the same tone in the second call as was heard in the first, and have come to know better what was meant by the bewildering statement, "Before Abraham was, I am." But these men were not Abrahams. Though we make their acquaintance somewhat abruptly, we do them no injustice in saying that we do not see in them the breadth and general vitality of manhood which were so prominent in the father of the faithful. When we first meet Simon and Andrew, they are but names to us; we have had no preparatory hint of the quality of the men, and cannot therefore but hesitate before coupling them in the same commendation with Abraham. A man with an historic reputation is not to be dwarfed into the stature of men whose world hardly extended beyond the boats in which they spent their unknown lives. We think we hear an earlier call than that of Abraham; this seems to be a call of something beautiful out of something rude; and whether or not it does not accord with "Let us make man," is a question which ought not to be left unconsidered. The material was low and rough; if out of such dust man could be rebuilt, the rebuilder must surely be God. Another word on this presently.

In all revolutionary movements there have been men who have heard nothing but "Follow," and have gone bravely forward to what was mystery at first, but what became familiar and venerated truth at last. Such men cannot be accounted for. The

* *Ecce Homo*, p. 40.

common rules have no application to them. They are the enigmas of history. We have seen them go, and deemed them mad, but in the end have been compelled to withdraw the charge from them, and fasten it on ourselves. They " saw a hand we did not see, and heard a voice we did not hear." The prospect before such men has generally been unalluring, often most disheartening; cloud and storm darkening and streaming from the sky, bitter wind striking them in the breast, and treacherous bogs lying between them and the promised land. Still they heard the "Follow" which was inaudible to duller ears, and went forward at the cost of their whole reputation for sagacity. What had Simon and Andrew to "follow"? Looked at from the common point of view, their decision was simple fanaticism. The man who had invited them was nameless and powerless, according to conventional notions of fame and influence, yet they went with as prompt and complete a surrender as if a king had offered them the riches of a kingdom. It is true that the men were called to a higher vocation; they were to be not fishers only, but "fishers of men;" yet even this promised elevation does not compass the mystery of the obedience, for multitudes declined Christ's invitations, and unnumbered millions to-day hear his voice, and yet practically treat his promises as they would treat so many lies. The result of Christ's first call cannot but be interesting to all students of his life. What if Simon and Andrew had treated his appeal with contempt? What if James and John had laughed in his face? What if he who conquered the devil had been overmatched by men? The experiment was most perilous for an impostor, was impossible to a mere man, and could have been undertaken by God only. An impostor would have begun more warily; a mere man would have begun at another point; only God would have begun where Christ began. These little circumstances are great revelations.

The persons, then, who were called are not such as might have been expected; yet on examination it will be found that they were the only persons who could have been called, in harmony with the whole mystery of Jesus Christ. The method of calling men which Christ adopted is worth studying, if only to see how statesmanlike, how philosophical, yet, on the face of it, how absurd it was. He announces his purpose in one concise sentence: "I came not to call the righteous, but sinners to repentance." This brings us to a wider meaning of the term "call" than we have in the word "follow;" yet take the declaration as an authoritative exposition of Christ's visit among men, and examine it as a method of stating an object, and we shall see how profound is the conception of human want which it expresses. This is quite a new voice on the earth. It had been understood up to this time that "sinners" had to be "consumed," "destroyed," "ashamed;" "confounded," "desolate;" their teeth were to be "broken," and their soul was to be "slain." Every man was apparently under the impression that he praised God in proportion as he cursed the sinner. The evangelical prophecies are no exceptions to this rule, for they were, of course, one with the spirit of him whom they announced. The rule relates to the general spirit of the world, to the tone of government, even government as administered by righteous men. Jesus Christ propounds the startling doctrine that he had come from heaven for the express purpose of calling bad men to him. Could any doctrine, abstractly considered, be more horrifying? We have become accustomed to its repetition, until we think nothing of it; but put the shadow upon the dial back eighteen hundred years, and say, how should we like to put ourselves side by side in the public streets with a man who had openly announced that his sole business on earth was to hold intercourse with bad hearts? The worse the man, the deeper the interest Christ took in him. Polite society was shocked, and "righteous" society horror-stricken: still he held on his way, and still he graciously answered (so graciously that one wonders that every heart on hearing it does not instantly admit him as its Lord), "I came not to call the righteous, but sinners to repentance." It was a hard errand to come upon, and only the Son of God could have undertaken it. What eye that was merely human could see the grandeur which was concealed under the ruins of humanity?

Christ began at the lowest point in society. The kingdom which he came to establish was to be an everlasting kingdom; and everlasting kingdoms must have adequate foundations. Christ recognized the essential distinction between *men* and *man*, and this fact gave him a reach and power over his work which otherwise would have been unattainable. The worst men make the best. A little nature could not accommodate a legion of devils — one man held more than could be held by two thousand swine. By so much as a man is diabolized may he be deified. It was, therefore, a great tribute paid to the worth of human nature when Christ spent his life in gathering and rebuilding its very ruins. He "came not to call the righteous, but sinners to repentance."

No statesman can afford to omit the common people from his calculation. They are the very root and core of society. Kings are only the blossomings of the national tree. The roof is more dependent upon the foundation than the foundation upon the roof. Nearly all, if not quite all, the movements which have changed the thinking, and determined the new courses of the world, have been upward, not downward. The great revolutionists have generally been cradled in mangers, and gone through rough discipline in early life. Civilization is debtor to lowly cradles; and unknown mothers hold a heavy account against the world. This is God's plan of uniting all classes of the family of man.

Christ worked in harmony with the spirit of this plan. People that were rejected on every side became his servants, and brethren, and friends. Even bad women (often so near being the best!) were drawn towards him, as if they could get from him "the piece that was lost." Some of the most touching scenes in his life relate to such women. One of those scenes, if nothing else remained, is enough to bind the world's heart to him forever. The occasion was one which brought out the characteristics of the interlocutors very sharply. A Pharisee had asked

Christ to break bread with him, and "a woman in the city, which was a sinner, when she knew that Jesus sat at meat in the Pharisee's house, brought an alabaster box of ointment"—probably all she had in the world—"and stood at his feet behind him, weeping, and began to wash his feet with tears, and did wipe them with the hairs of her head, and kissed his feet, and anointed them with the ointment,"—so near being an angel was this poor sinning sister! Never was modesty so modest,—stood at his *feet*,—stood *behind* him,—stood behind him *weeping*: only God can interpret the full meaning of such tears. The cold-eyed Pharisee saw nothing in her but a "sinner;" Christ saw a *woman*, flesh and blood of his own mother, and his great gentle heart was shaken with unutterable pity. The Pharisee saw his opportunity; like all little natures, he knew more of logic than of philanthropy, and instantly he set up this argument: "This man, if he were a prophet, would have known who and what manner of woman this is that toucheth him, for she is a sinner." Men are often the victims of their own logic,—always, indeed, when logic leads away from love. The eye that saw the "woman" under the "sinner," saw the sneering sceptic under the observing but silent host. That eye read the Pharisee through and through. "Simon," said Jesus, "I have somewhat to say unto thee. There was a certain creditor which had two debtors; the one owed five hundred pence, the other fifty, and when they had nothing to pay, he frankly forgave them both: tell me, therefore, which of them will love him most?" Simon liked a case of this kind; it was not above his intellectual stature, though he little knew its moral compass. "I suppose," he answered, "that he to whom he forgave most." The answer was right; the appeal was overwhelming. "Simon, seest thou this woman? I entered into thine house, thou gavest me no water for my feet, but she hath washed my feet with tears, and wiped them with the hairs of her head; thou gavest me no kiss, but this woman, since the time I came in, hath not ceased to kiss my feet; my head with oil thou didst not anoint, but this woman hath anointed my feet with ointment. Wherefore, I say unto thee, her sins, which are many, are forgiven, for she loved much; but to whom little is forgiven, the same loveth little." The man that spake these words ought to be dear to the world's heart forever! The calm tone, the beaming eye, the inimitable pathos, all brought to bear upon the stony Pharisee, with his paltry notions of propriety! It is truly better to fall into the hands of God, than into the hands of men. A case like this does more to confirm the Godhead of Jesus Christ, than can be done by a sanhedrim of theologians, armed with the genius and the lore of ages. We have in it all the God we need. The Being that saw the woman in the sinner, and the sinner in the woman, that penetrated the dishonorable thoughts of the haughty self-idolater, and pronounced the contrite woman forgiven, comes before the world with claims which God only could sustain. In the presence of such an incident, all verbal criticism becomes contemptible; the stormed and grateful heart exclaims, Ecce homo! Ecce Deus!

Multiply this simple story by the number of "sinners" in the world; let every one of those sinners love as much as this poor woman loved, and then say if ever king reigned over such an empire as that in which Christ would be enthroned? The bond of union is essentially personal. The love of each heart is lavished upon him. All low motives are expelled by a pure, intense, ever-deepening love. In this way, too, we see light streaming upon an overshadowing and most appalling mystery, viz., the comparative relation of sin to the happiness of the universe, when the divine purpose is completed. The principle laid down by Christ is that they who have had much forgiven, love much, and that there is joy in the presence of the angels of God over one sinner that repenteth, *more* than over ninety and nine just persons that need no repentance. Who can measure that "*more*"? Sin is thus made to have its compensations. The twice-born man shall be a double joy in his Father's house. Sin shall not be all *loss*. Even for sin's sake, heaven shall be filled with a sweeter and gladder hallelujah.

By going to the lowest stratum of human nature Christ gave a new idea of the value of man. He built a kingdom out of the refuse of society. To compare small things with great, it has been pointed out by Lord Macaulay that in an English cathedral there is an exquisite stained window which was made by an apprentice out of the pieces of glass which had been rejected by his master, and it was so far superior to every other in the church that, according to tradition, the envious artist killed himself with vexation. All the builders of society had rejected the "sinners," and made the painted window of the "righteous." A new builder came; his plan was original, startling, revolutionary; his eye was upon the contemned material; he made the first last and the last first, and the stone which the builders rejected he made the head stone of the corner. He always specially cared for the rejected stone. Men had always cared for the great, the beautiful, the righteous; it was left to Christ to care for sinners. When Eumæus was reproached with having invited a beggar to the palace of Ulysses, he did not care formally to deny the charge, but met it with scorn, as if the very absurdity of the idea was its best refutation — πτωχὸν δ' οὐκ ἄν τις καλέοι, τρίξοντα ἓ αὐτόν; this inquiry showing that he did not rank himself with fools. Even the gods were attracted by beauty, as in the case of Ganymede —

"Fairest of mortals; him the gods on score of beauty crowned."

The general tone of history was such as to give Christ's method an appearance of the most grotesque absurdity; he began where no other worker began; precedent, the terror of secondary men, was against him; and his contemporaries either pitied or despised, saying with much bitter meaning in their tone, "This man receiveth sinners and eateth with them." The unity of the mystery is here apparent. He himself, on the one side, began at the highest, and on the other, at the lowest, yet the Child of the manger came to be King of the world. Society is moved by its extremes. Christ showed the value of the extreme that from immemorial time had been despised.

It is remarkable that Christ is never said to have called a woman to follow him as he called the disciples; and quite as remarkable that, so far as the evidence goes, no woman ever spoke a word against him, while many women were last at the cross, and earliest at the sepulchre. It seems as though he had assumed that the womanly side of human nature would not require any calling; that the heart of woman would instinctively welcome him as the solution of all difficulties, the sum of all charms, the sovereign of frail and needy creatures who have immense capacity of suffering, but little satisfaction in the results of mere logic. Christ was emphatically, uniquely, *the seed of the woman*. What woman could reject her own son? Does not every woman look with intensely hopeful love upon the son of her womb? He will be her comfort, her song, her saviour; she no longer lives but in him and for him; through him she interprets the future, and for his sake takes a kinder view of all mankind. Christ was born to every woman. Men required to be called, women only to be attracted. Women had but to see him in order to claim him as the fairest among ten thousand, and altogether lovely; to recognize him as the tenderest and wisest friend of womanhood. They needed no call. The dew waits for no voice to call it to the sun. Few women ever go to Christ through the medium of mere doctrine. They live beyond the cold propositional region. The dew finds its way up to the sun without knowing anything of the laws of motion or the mysteries of light, and womanly hearts go up to Christ often knowing little of objective theology, yet wise because inspired and guided by the love which is the elect interpreter of God. God is love, and by her superior capacity of love woman is so much nearer God than man can ever be. It is hardly to be wondered at that millions of Christians even now feel that heaven itself requires the distinctive presence of the womanly element, and express the feeling by addressing Mary as the mother of God. If Protestantism were less technical and more human, it would hesitate before condemning the feeling which dictates this startling appellation. The fact may be that God is more human than traditional doctrinism has yet dared to conceive. We think of humanity too exclusively by the flesh. It is to be remembered that the body is the lesser portion of man, and that we speak rightly of the human *mind* as well as the human body. It is on the mind side that we approach God, through the mind side that we communicate with God, and on the mind side that we resemble God. In this sense God is more human, or man more divine, than has yet been authenticated by the councils of Christendom. God is not declared to be power, but he is declared to be love; whoever, therefore, can love most is most like God. It is not to the point to argue that men excel women in pure intellectual force; even allowing as a conceit what we cannot concede as a fact, it amounts to nothing in this case. A lion is stronger, an eagle swifter, than man, yet it is not to be inferred that they are nearer God than man is; but God is love, and nearness to him in soul-quality is a question of love. Nor is it to the point that women have fallen into great depths of sin; the greater the depth the greater the nature. If God himself could sin, all other sinners would be forgotten in the darkness of the stupendous apostasy.

Christ's tender recognition of little children was part of his call. Little children are included in the kingdom of heaven; and in this particular, Christ's idea of the Church, which must be the true idea, is totally different from current ecclesiastical notions. It is now taught that children have to be converted; but Christ taught that men were to become converted, and to be like little children — a direct inversion of narrow theological churchmanship. It is declared that children are born corrupt, but where is Christ's authority for saying so? Christ said, " Of such is the kingdom of heaven." Whatever was of the nature of that kingdom must go to Christ. As the founder of a permanent monarchy, Christ knew the value of young life. When the blood is fresh the enthusiasm is fervid; and what is a monarch if he be not supported by the passionate love of the national heart? *Passive* allegiance is a pompous circumlocution which signifies death.

CHAPTER VIII.

CHRIST REJECTING MEN.

WHEN Christ said he came not to call the righteous, but sinners to repentance, there must have been a strong ironical tone in his pronunciation of the word "righteous." Most truly we cannot infer from his reported words who the righteous were, if there were such. Not the Pharisees certainly, as was most impressively shown upon one memorable occasion. A Pharisee had invited Christ to dinner, and when the guests were ranged in order Christ openly said, "Now do ye Pharisees make clean the outside of the cup and the platter, but your inward part is full of ravening and wickedness; ye fools, did not he that made that which is without, make that which is within also?" This sentence excludes the Pharisees from the category of "the righteous." And the Scribes were associated with them, for on the same occasion, addressing them jointly, he said — "Woe unto you, Scribes and Pharisees, hypocrites! for ye are as graves which appear not, and the men that walk over them are not aware of them." This denunciation, which in modern days and Western lands would be deemed an unpardonable abuse of hospitality, could not fail to make a deep impression upon the minds of the guests; this was clear from a singular incident. One of the lawyers brought the matter to an issue: "Master," said he, "thus speaking thou reproachest us also." The answer was probably much clearer and fuller than the lawyer expected; the spirit of judgment asserted itself in the boldest manner in Jesus Christ: "Woe unto you also, ye lawyers! for ye lade men with burdens grievous to be borne, and ye yourselves touch not the burdens with one of your fingers. Woe unto you! for ye build the sepulchres of the prophets, and your fathers killed them. . . . Woe unto you, lawyers! for ye have taken away the key of knowledge: ye entered not in yourselves, and them that were entering in ye hindered." This exasperating talk produced a most singular effect upon the guests. Probably they had never come so decidedly in contact with this new spirit of judgment before, and as they were all together at the time they felt the stimulus of association, and being stung by the rebukes of an uncourteous stranger, "they began to urge him vehemently, and to provoke him to speak of many things: laying wait for him, and seeking to catch something out of his mouth, that they might accuse him." There is a good deal underlying all this. They might think that they had caught Christ at a disadvantage. Was he inflamed with wine? How could he who came to call men to himself encounter some of the leading classes of society with language so repulsive? They could not comprehend this new spirit of judgment which had come to hold its assize among men, and in their ignorance they sought to drive judgment into indiscrimination, and thus deprive it of the moral element. They found nothing on the side of his love, so the hungry wolves ran round to the side of his anger, and waited savagely for prey.

Where, then, were the "righteous"? The fact is, that a man was truly, not notionally or reputedly, righteous just in proportion as he felt himself to be a sinner. There is many a paradox in Christ's teaching, and this is one of the number. He set forth this doctrine most graphically by telling of two men who went up to the same temple, at the same hour, for the same purpose. One was a conceited self-idolater, appraising himself very highly, the other was a self-abased and earnest suppliant, who could find no better term for himself than " sinner," — no other term so deeply probed his consciousness or expressed the tone and spirit of his life. The sequel showed that in God's view the "righteous" man was the "sinner," and the "sinner" the "righteous" man. Such sinners were the only men who could really hear Christ; the other were so impenetrably fortressed in their own conceit that no call could be loud enough to be audible above the thunder of their self-applause. Their sin was self-involution and self-satisfaction. They were their own Alpha and Omega. There was no way of moving them but by calling other men away from them. They must be isolated until they felt their position, and raised the signal of distress. Christianity thus became indirectly a most powerful appeal to the very men whom it had apparently left in all the paltry splendor of an artificial righteousness. By calling other men from them and leaving them utterly alone, their very selfishness became intolerable, and through the mere stress of circumstances they were driven to inquiry and consideration. Extremes are their own cure.

On another occasion Christ took an effectual method of showing who the righteous were. A number of hollow-hearted men, who mistook an interest in criminal statistics for philanthropy, as all hollow-hearted men are prone to do, brought an unhappy woman before him to be judged. They had witnessed many displays of the new spirit of judgment in various directions, but here was a case which would test the moral quality of that spirit. With infinite delicacy he said, "Let him that is without sin cast the first stone." This was not only a new spirit of judgment, but a new spirit of administration. The guardians of virtue were henceforth to be virtuous. Judgment was henceforth not to be learned from a statute-book, but from the inspired heart. Penalty was to be an outburst of moral indignation. Without repealing the Mosaic law, or interfering with criminal prosecutions, he threw the inquirers upon a principle which carried its own justification. The answer fell upon them like the fires of judgment, and man by man they slunk from the place, until the sinner and the Saviour were left alone. The difference between the woman and the prosecutors was that her sin was known and theirs was hidden, but the new spirit of judgment showed that concealment was henceforth an impossibility. The Saviour gave the "sinner" another chance of life; he called her to himself by kindling a new hope in her despairing heart. A new hope is equivalent to a new birth.

The "sinners" alone, we have said, could hear the

call of Christ. This is true in civilization as well as in religion. Whoever has a new idea to propose will find no disposition to listen to it on the part of those who are satisfied with the old ideas or taken up with their own notions. He must seek prepared men, and deliver his call to them. They are conscious of a want; they are dissatisfied with the past; they look yearn-
* ingly and wonderingly towards the future. Christ came with the cry of repentance; a cry which by its very nature divided society and developed strong feeling on both sides. The cry "Repent" was a call to change the very springs of life. It implied — indeed it expressed — a heavy charge against society. It simply meant — You are wrong — wrong in heart, wrong in life — and you must change if you would enter the kingdom which is at hand. Such a call of necessity set men thinking as they had never thought before. It put men on the defensive. It did not give them an opportunity of saying guilty or not guilty, but assumed the guilt and demanded penitence. Instantly the "righteous" set themselves against it. They massed themselves as an army, and obstinately contested the revolutionary idea. Hardly any other cry could have produced such an effect upon them; it was intended to work self-conviction, but failing in this it necessarily consolidated the moral conservatism of the unbelievers. It was to be expected that a great division would follow the cry, and that henceforth a marked line would show the space occupied by those "which trusted in themselves that they were righteous and despised others." The call of Christ was the instrument of election, pointing out those upon whom

it could produce the intended effect. All calls to other life, good or bad, have in them of necessity an effective principle, simply because they separate and classify men. Christ acted in this matter precisely as sensible men act under similar conditions; they turn from those who do not want them, and work with those who appreciate their purpose. The nature of the call determines the nature of the society that will be summoned by it. Christ uttered a call which plainly said that men needed to change their course, and it was natural that such men alone should draw around him, that they might learn all that he meant with reference to their future. To any man conscious of want, or sin, or ignorance, the call to repentance is the very call most suited to him. Instead of throwing him into despair it gives him hope; it shows that an opportunity is still left, and that one man at least is willing to point out how that opportunity may be turned to advantage. The call of Jesus Christ means that no man need sit shivering upon the ruin he has wrought, but that he may arise and rebuild and enter into rest.

Imagine the effect of a contrary cry. Instead of "Repent," say "Be satisfied." Sides would then have changed. The men who were consciously wrong, or who had dreamed of a brighter day, could not have accepted the words as expressing a right direction, but the righteous would have pronounced the speaker an "excellent Daniel." The call to repent brought to the speaker exactly what he wanted, — the most susceptible, self-distrustful, and unsophisticated men of the time. When any of the so-called "righteous" did hear his words, and were disposed to inquire the terms of fellowship with him, Christ was invariably severe in stating the conditions. He did not by any means give them a cordial welcome. By any ordinary reformer they would have been considered invaluable acquisitions; having education, money, influence, and all those advantages which usually give a new idea a bold and commanding aspect. By Jesus Christ they were regarded in no such light. He knew that they were but so many flattering varieties of a man's *self*, and by so much as *self* was uppermost was a man unfit for the kingdom of heaven. Consequently he was so cautious as to be almost stern, so exacting as to be almost oppressive. So, at least, it must have appeared to the righteous, as they saw the "gate" narrowing as they approached it, and heard his voice in its most incisive tone saying, " Strait is the gate, and narrow is the way." So strait was the gate that no man, could take any appendices with him; all decorative matter was to be left outside; only the man, without background or surrounding, could be admitted. One conspicuous example will occur to all who have read the life. A very "righteous" young man came to him with an eager inquiry: the young man made out that he was nothing less than an embodiment of the Decalogue, — he had gathered the very elements of his life on the rough and quaking slopes of Sinai. Surely Christ could not resist this modern edition of the Ten Commandments. They were written on tables of stone, but here was a table of flesh. Christ was actually more severe with this young man — required more of him than he required of the publican, the adulteress, and the thief. Why not? Tall men can reach higher than short men. Others brought nothing but sin, this man brought the Decalogue without (as he imagined) a wrinkle or a stain. What wonder, then, seeing that strait is, the gate and narrow is the way, that Christ should answer, " Go and sell all that thou hast, and give it unto the poor, and follow me"? The man had grown prosperous, with all his commandment-keeping, and now he required to be pulled sharply up on the side of his wealth to see whether the commandments or the money had the greater hold upon him. There was no other method of meeting the case. The fortress of self must be stormed. Every prop must be struck down, every link broken, or he must remain outside the strait gate. The young man knew not that the gates to all great kingdoms are strait, and that the ways are narrow; he had thought much of the kingdom, but nothing of the way. This instance certainly shows that Christ did not care to give merely numerical strength to his cause. With him, as with all true calculators, the question was not one of numbers but of hearts. One heart under the inspiration of love was of immeasurably greater value than any number governed by the shifting policy of the hour. The *I am*, not the *I have*, was Christ's standard of valuation. How, then, could any man who had " great possessions " reconcile himself to settlement in Christ's society? The thing was impossible. The outside was greater than the inside, so a catastrophe was inevitable. Manifestly the young man could not move through riches to

Christ, though many a man has moved through Christ to riches. There is nothing in Christ to prevent a man having " a hundredfold more in the present life," but much in the present life to hinder a man having Christ. To-day this fact is illustrated on an extended scale; most of the rich men who are now in Christ's society came to him when they were poor. It is difficult, from so narrow an observation as one individual is able to make, to pronounce definitely upon the subject, but the peril of censoriousness may be escaped by merely putting a question, — How many men having great possessions pass the strait gate set before the kingdom of heaven? Does the spiritual or the material exercise the keener influence upon such men? Is the expression " How hardly shall they that have riches enter into the kingdom of heaven!" with or without application to the men of to-day? There is nothing in the constitution of the Christian kingdom to prevent a man becoming rich, but there is much in wealth to keep a man from thinking seriously about the Christian kingdom. It alters a man's whole relation to wealth, taking away the idea of mastery, and substituting the idea of stewardship, displacing the notion of carnal security by the spirit of Christ-like bounty. This kingdom necessarily casts out all other masteries, declaring to all men as they seek admission, " Ye cannot serve God and mammon." In Christ's day, too, expensive organizations within the church were unknown. Christ wanted no advances made on behalf of his " cause;" he had no long accounts to be audited, no begging-books to distribute, no high-priced pews to let; as long as there was a Father in heaven nourishing the lily and keeping the bird upon its wing, why should he fear about storehouse or barn? He viewed all human necessity in the light of God's immediate Fatherly goodness, so that every want became as a holy place where the Father met the dependent child. Money, as a regulative power in Christ's society, was not known. Christ had no institutionalism to support. In his day men gave themselves, not a guinea, when an appeal was made. Love had not then found out that it could buy itself off for an annual subscription; it was mad enough to toil and suffer in the very heat of the day. Only spiritual insolvents think of compounding with God for a guinea when they owe him their whole life. When Echepólus bought himself off from the war by giving Agamemnon a mare, probably Agamemnon made a good bargain, for a mare might be more useful at Troy than a rich and heartless poltroon; but proxies should not be allowed in the spiritual war. In the "brave days" of the first disciples, things did not shape themselves as they do now.

> "Then none was for a party,
> Then all were for the state,
> Then the great man helped the poor,
> And the poor man loved the great.
> Then lands were fairly portioned,
> Then spoils were fairly sold:
> The Christians were like brothers,
> In the brave days of old."

In giving the young man this view of money, Christ sent him away "very sorrowful." This was not without peril to the new government. The young man, in trying to reconcile himself to himself, would have a narrow escape from underrating the zeal of those who had fallen in with such apparently extravagant notions; and as no man in a low moral condition finds it easy to forgive one who has shown him that he is not so good as he supposed himself to be, the young man might seek to exalt Moses at the expense of Christ. It was necessary that Christ should accept all such risks. He could not build with wood, hay, and stubble, as he was erecting a kingdom which was to be tried with fire. Thus a universal call came to have special bearings, according to special circumstances, and out of this fact rejected men began to weave the grossest doctrinal slanders respecting the partiality of Jesus Christ— slanders from which his name is still suffering.

This was natural. Rejected men felt themselves called upon to set up a theory of rejection, and the last thing which that theory would admit would be error on the part of the individual himself. Take the case of the young rich man: as he retired from Christ he could hardly escape the tortures of the most penetrating and solemn reflection. "I have been practically rejected," he might say; "what can be the reason? From my youth my conduct has been irreproachable; I have kept the law, and to-day I can defy public criticism; yet this man refuses me admission into his society except upon extreme and indeed impracticable conditions: he must be mad or insincere; the fault is with him, not with me." The man's mind was started on a course of speculation, and all the probabilities are that his speculation could take no very favorable turn in regard to Christ. He would have his own way of representing the case to his friends and companions, so that, while Christ was calling men to himself in one direction, the young man would be at the head of a counter-movement in another. His representations would acquire strength from his well-known morality, and from the fact that he had personally sought admission into Christ's kingdom. In this way the Christian idea has been impeded by misunderstanding and unworthy men.

Christ had different methods of calling men — always, however, making the gate straiter and straiter as he was approached by the "righteous." To the young man just spoken of he made the gate very strait on the side of property; to a certain lawyer he made it strait on the side of the two great commandments; and when Nicodemus came to him, he made it almost impassably strait by saying, "Except a man be born again, he cannot see the kingdom of God." He seems to have given three different answers to the same question, while in reality he was but varying the answer according to the circumstances of the inquirer. Take the case of Nicodemus: to have said to him, "Go sell all that thou hast and give to the poor," would not have met the mood of the Rabbi's soul. Probably he could have accepted this condition of entrance without reducing the amount of *self* which was in him; his property might be small, or he might hold it with a careless hand, so that its surrender would not have made any drain upon his self-importance. So also to have said to the rich young man, "Ye must be born again," would have bewildered a youth who knew little or nothing of such deep expressions; he must be moved from the side of his property. The master in Israel must be met in his own sphere, and talked to in his own language; the worldling must be met in the midst of his estates, and talked to in the language of the market-place. The conclusion will be the same in both cases. Nicodemus, when born again, will be willing to sell all that he has, and the young man, when he has sold all his property, will be born again. This circumstance shows the necessity of discrimination in preaching the Gospel. Christ addressed men in different ways; the Church has a few stereotyped directions for all. How many of the Evangelical preachers in England dare tell a rich young man that he must sell and distribute all his property as the condition of his entrance into eternal life? The man who did so would be marked as a legalist, though he would be a most Christ-like preacher. There are some who aspire to be more orthodox than Christ himself; who, by insisting upon one set of technicalities, throw many inquirers into despair, and clothe many a plain truth with mystery.

Take the matter of being "born again:" Christ did not use such words to the common multitude, but specially to "a master in Israel." He never used them again, so far as we can learn from the narrative; yet, because he used them in such an exceptional case, thousands of preachers perplex promiscuous congregations with them every Sunday. To a master in Israel they were precisely adapted, yet it does not follow that a direction given to a learned man in a private interview is to be proclaimed to the common multitude. Nicodemus was accustomed to metaphysical inquiry; his faculties were trained to analysis; and though he might start at this profoundly spiritual answer, given by a man whom he had distinctively known as a mighty worker, yet he could meditate upon it as in harmony with the genius and bent of his whole intellectual life. That life it immediately assailed — not the man's character, but the man's mental habitudes and moral purposes. His inner life must start from a new point; so radical a change must he undergo, that no figure can so expressively denote it as a new *birth*.

This reference to regeneration opens the question of original sin. Many inquirers find it difficult to believe themselves innately bad, simply because they have been told that such a belief is required of them. No man taught the doctrine of original sin, commonly so called, so impressively as Jesus Christ, and yet he never mentioned it! His whole scheme was founded upon the assumption that men were wrong. Every call to a new point, every frown upon sin, every encouragement of well-doing, meant that society needed regeneration. Men may come upon the doctrine of original depravity in one of two different ways; for example, they may come upon it as a dogma in theology. The first thing that some theologians do is to abuse human nature, to describe it as being covered with wounds and bruises and putrefying sores, and as deserving nothing but eternal burning. Human nature resists this as a slander: it says, " No; I have good impulses, upward desires, generous emotions towards my fellow-creatures; I resent your theological calumnies." So much for the first method of approaching the doctrine. The second is totally unlike it. A man, for example, heartily accepts Jesus Christ, studies him with most passionate devotion, and grows daily more like him in all purity, gentleness, and self-oblivion. From this altitude he looks back upon his former self; he compares the human nature with which he started, with the human nature he has attained, and involuntarily, by the sheer necessity of the contrast, he says, "I was born in sin and shapen in iniquity." This conclusion he comes to, not by dogmatic teaching, but by dogmatic experience; what he never could have understood as an opinion he realizes as a fact.

Suppose a tree to be conscious, and let it illustrate what is meant by growing into a right understanding of this hard doctrine. Tell the tree in April that it is bare and ungainly in appearance; very barren and naked altogether. The tree says, "Nay: I am rooted in the earth; my branches are strong; I live in the light; I drink the dew; and I am beautiful; the winds rock me, and many a bird twitters on my boughs." This is its April creed. Go to the same tree after it has had a summer's experience; it has felt the quickening penetration of the solar fire, quenched its thirst in summer showers, felt the sap circulating through its veins; the leaves have come out on branch and twig, the blossoms have blushed and bloomed through long days of light; fruit has been formed, and mellowed into maturity. Now hear the tree! "I am not what I was in April; my very identity seems to be changed; when men called me bare and rugged I did not believe them a few months ago; now I see what they meant — their verdict was sound: I thought the April light very beautiful, but it is nothing to the blazing splendor of the later months; I liked the twitter of the spring birds, but it is poor compared with the song of those that came in June: I feel as if I had been born again." The parable is broad enough to cover this bewildering, and at times horrifying, doctrine of hereditary depravity. Men cannot be in April what they will be in September. Each year says to growing hearts, "I have many things to say unto you, but ye cannot bear them now." In old age men may accept the rejected doctrines of their youth. Experience brings us round many a rugged hill, and gives us better views of condemned, because misunderstood, opinions. The point to be observed by all teachers of Jesus Christ's doctrine is, that it is unnecessary to force recondite theological dogmas upon those who approach the kingdom of heaven. Let them enter the kingdom on the sole ground of their love to the King, and their subsequent life may be devoted to doctrinal study. Jesus Christ was constantly correcting the errors of his immediate followers, yet they were his followers, notwithstanding their errors. Where love is ardent, knowledge will be attained by experience.

We have thus seen Christ calling men and Christ rejecting men. This discrimination gives a hint of the quality of the society which he aims to establish. Can he *keep* those whom he has *called?*

CHAPTER IX.

THE CHURCH.

FOR what purpose did Christ call men? Were they to be his body-guard during his presence upon earth, and to be disbanded after his ascension? or were they to be confederated into a perpetual memorial of his earthly mission? This brings us to an analysis of the ecclesiastical idea.

The men who obeyed the call were classified under a special and most sacred designation. They were first known as "My disciples;" long afterwards "believers," "saints," "Christians" became synonymous and interchangeable terms, the whole of them being frequently expressed by one word, — *church*. This was a confederation of hearts, founded on a purely moral basis, subsisting continually upon a deep love for the Christ who had called them to his fellowship. The root idea of the church is that of a particular relation of man to man, originated by a common relation to Jesus Christ. When men are ardently attached to their native country, they are related to one another as compatriots, though they may differ upon every question in political science. It is the same in the church; attachment to Jesus Christ is everything; the widest differences upon theology may exist, but no doctrinal heresy can break up the vital and eternal union of souls which is brought about by an all-absorbing love for Jesus Christ.

It may appear that faith is an almost insignificant condition of membership in Christ's kingdom. Not so, however, when the matter is carefully considered. The word "belief" is not simple, but compound, — a term most inclusive and exacting. Popularly understood, "belief" is supposed to denote an act of the mind in relation to statements which may be laid before it: as, for example, a man believes that Milton wrote "Paradise Lost," that Columbus discovered America, or that a ship will leave Britain for Africa upon a given day. But such a belief may amount to nothing more than that the man does not *disbelieve* these statements; or if it mean that he has examined the evidence for himself, yet not one of the statements may touch his deepest nature. It would give him no concern to know that Milton wrote the "Iliad," and that Homer wrote "Paradise Lost," or that the ship in question is not going to Africa, but to Asia. The man cannot be said to "believe," in any deep and true sense of that term. Belief means more than any act of the mere understanding can ever mean. Religion is not so much an appeal to the intellectual as to the moral nature; this is true of *all* religions, but preeminently characteristic of Christianity. The intellectual is to be affected through the moral; the mind is not to lie dormant, it is to be brought into the most active service; but the law is, "Thou shalt *love* the Lord thy God with all thy ... *mind.*" *Loving* with the *mind* is the idea; the very intellect is to be turned into an organ of affection, logic itself to be a-glow with moral fire; it is not, Thou shalt *believe* with thy mind, but, Thou shalt *love* with thy mind: "with the heart man believeth unto righteousness." Belief thus becomes more than an assent to a set of notions. It carries with it the whole man, dominating over his entire course; in fact, it is more even than this — it is *life* itself. Whatever a man lives for is his faith. Without faith it is impossible to please God. What then? Is this extraordinary? It is one of the veriest commonplaces in life! Without faith it is as impossible to please man as to please God. Give any man to understand that he has lost the faith of his compeers, and he will realize the most complete humiliation and impoverishment. In this vital sense the belief of man is challenged by Jesus Christ: out of it is to come the whole purpose and strength of life. Christ is to absorb affection, and his will is to be, not the arbitrary, but the heart-elected Master everywhere. A man may believe that a house has been robbed, but his belief is altogether a deeper reality when he is given to understand that the house which has been robbed is his own. That which was merely a piece of information lodged in the mind becomes a compelling and ruling power in the life. So a man may say of Jesus Christ, "I believe he lived, died, and rose again," and may yet know nothing of the ruling force of these events in his heart. The facts have not become truths to him; they are outside realities, not internal and undisputed sovereignties. When he lives by them, he believes them; when he believes them, he lives by them; when belief and life are synonymous terms, the man is a member of the church of Christ — his name is written in heaven. He may hold the most extraordinary conclusions in speculative theology, but he cannot be unchurched by metaphysics. Where the love is right, the notion is of small consequence. A man may keep his whole self and accept all technicalities in theology, but a man cannot love without giving up himself. He must either "sell all he has and give it to the poor," or he must be "born again" into a new spirit in which there shall be no self, and then he is in the kingdom of Christ.

This shows the inclusiveness of the church. The sect can hold but a few, the church may comprehend all. Christ established no sect; he founded a church. To be a Christian, it is not necessary to be a theologian; nor is it necessary to choose a sectarian appellation; nothing is necessary but perfect love of the "Beloved Son." It is with Christianity as with patriotism, to recur to an illustration: love of country is independent of love of party; a patriot might die for his sovereign without knowing the subtle degrees of loyalty which are indicated by party nomenclature. Entrance into the church is a transaction between Jesus Christ and the individual heart; whoever has given his love to God's Son *is* a member of the church: whether, for the sake of convenience, or for purposes of evangelization, he may join a sect, it is for him to consider, but most assuredly he is in Christ's church, by the indefeasible and all-comprehending right of love. The immortality of love is the immortality of the church. The small mud huts of bigotry will be submerged by the mighty cataclysm of human progress, but the church founded upon a rock will remain above the floods. Love is the security of the church.

Horror at what is called heresy may be accounted for on natural grounds. It is natural to venerate the ancient; it is natural, too, for the timid to dread what is speculative or experimental. Men hesitate before cutting down a bridge which bears the footprints of many generations, though a better bridge may be erected. Man cannot easily shake off the associations of time, nor is it desirable that he should. The known has certain advantages over the unknown. In business, in politics, in medicine, in government, and most of the concerns of common life, the same regard for the past prevails. Changes, it is thought, always involve more or less of risk; and though results may be right, processes may be hazardous and difficult. But by the noble boldness of many recent inquirers, even change itself is enriched with hallowed and inspiring associations. The heretics in civilization, not to speak of theology, have done most for the world. Timid men cringed, and selfish men denounced, when the heretics struck openly at the old methods of doing things. They dreaded changes as men might dread floods which carry destruction everywhere: —

> "Expatiata ruunt per apertos flumina campos;
> Cumque satis arbusta simul, pecudesque, virosque,
> Tectaque, cumque suis rapiunt penetralia sacris."

Such swollen rivers as Ovid describes have been greatly dreaded in the church, as if no promise lay around that church as a perpetual defence. Poor buttresses can be made of paper; but who can storm the fortresses of love? It is forgotten, besides, how great a guarantee of security has been provided by Christ in the condition requiring discipleship to be attested by the most practical service. Jesus Christ and his disciples were not a band of contemplative philosophers preambulating in the cold grandeur of isolation from all the rough world, in some charmed Lyceum; they threaded their enlightening and healing way through the thronging multitudes; and daily were the disciples shown that love and work were the hemispheres of the Christian life. Love was not a mere sentiment, a self-considering and self-satisfying passion, but the spring of an inclusive and intensely practical philanthropy. Christ drilled his disciples in a reverent and generous regard for the human body. He told them to divide their small stock of provisions in the desert place with the five thousand strangers, and when he sketched the proceedings of the great judicial day he sent men to heaven or to hell according as they had been philanthropic or misanthropic towards himself as atomized by the least of his brethren. He asked no man what he believed, but told every man how much he had done to mitigate the sufferings of good men, or what opportunities of such mitigation had been neglected. Philanthropy was made the test of love towards God, for who can love God without loving his brother also? This is a valuable, and not less so because incidental, illustration of the inseparableness of the two great commandments of the law, — Love God and love thy neighbor. The love of man comes from love of God, and in the judgment love of God will be tried by love of man. The apostle John, who is generally supposed to have been incomparably amiable, said plainly, that if any man says he loves God, and yet hates his brother, he is a *liar;* and no liar shall enter the church: he may creep into the sect, but shall have his portion in the lake which burneth with fire and brimstone. The true church-member can never become a heretic in any bad sense of the term: his love towards God and his love towards man keep him perfectly balanced; he has no time to go astray, as well as no will. The priest and the Levite will probably be excommunicated, but the philanthropist is too busy with wounded and dying humanity to be in any danger from theological riddles and metaphysical enigmas. From his continually widening observation of human nature, he may be induced to ignore some of the faded nostrums of traditional quackery, but his heart will be sound and his faith strong. Seeing far into man, he will see far into God, and by loving his brother he will love his Maker more. Christ seldom made inquiry into the *opinions* of his disciples, but he never failed to keep them up to a large-hearted *practice.* When he did inquire into their opinions, it was always to know how they stood in relation to himself; and just in proportion as the disciples saw God in him, did he corroborate their judgment by pronouncing it a divine revelation. The education of the philanthropic element in his church-members was Christ's main concern. We do not know that he ever so much as named Adam and Eve, or that he drew any subtle distinctions, or laid down any precise definitions in reference to supralapsarianism or prevenient grace; but we do know that he drew up such a list of guests as probably never assembled at any board before his time; that he commended the poor, the halt, the maimed, the blind, to the special care of his members; that, with the most practical sarcasm, he measured the rich man by his clothes and his dinner ("clothed in purple and fine linen, and fared sumptuously every day"), and sent the angels to carry the beggar to Abraham's bosom. Christ's philanthropy never failed, it never yellowed, or drooped as if winter were approaching. He was the divive teacher of philanthropy; by which is meant not official intermeddling about poor-rates, prison-ventilation, and workhouse discipline, but simple, hearty, brotherly love of man as man, in all zones and all ages. As such a teacher, Christ taught the doctrine of the Fall more fully than if he had discussed it in daily discourses upon the garden of Eden. He never said, Lift a man up, without recognizing the Fall; he never expatiated upon "the lost" without going back to early events; he said nothing about the Adamic apostasy, but spent every moment of his life in seeking to reclaim apostates. This was the wisdom which cometh down from above.

Two settled and unchangeable principles thus come up as including the idea of the church — love to Christ and love to man. Whoever has experienced this love is in Christ's kingdom a living member; he hath eternal life. This dual love is another illustration of the dual life of Christ. As that life was divine and human, the life of his members is divine and human also; it is not only purity of heart which sees God, but it is mercy which pities men — not only poverty of spirit which claims the kingdom of heaven, but meekness which inherits the earth — not only the mourning which is followed by rest in the soul, but peacemaking which reconciles opposing hearts; it is dual as Christ was dual — weak enough to be bruised on the cross, strong enough to throw off the bondage of the grave.

That men who know the power of this love should seek each other's fellowship is not merely natural, but necessary. A common faith and a common philanthropy bring them into visible union; mark them off from all other men, giving them a lustre which makes them the light of the world, a pungency which makes them as the salt of the earth, an elevation best represented by "a city set on a hill." Their visible union causes them to be known as "the church," in an inferior sense to that already named, and those whom they have left are known as "the world." Speaking of his disciples in one of his prayers, Christ specially marks this distinction: "They are not of the world, even as I am not of the world;" — in it, yet above it — in the form of servants, yet in the spirit of mastery. In early days the disciples were known to one another by endearing terms which our materialistic civilization can hardly use without a significant hesitation; they were "saints," "brethren," "servants of Jesus Christ," "beloved in the Lord;" they were called a "royal priesthood," a "peculiar people," "temples of the Holy Ghost." What wonder, then, if visible union should be a necessity? On lower conditions men enter into organization; artists unite; merchants "do congregate;" philosophers shut out the common people; bankers have their guilds; lawyers their inns; and *savans* their esoteric circles. Why should men with a common faith and a common philanthropy remain apart? When we have been in a foreign country, unable to speak the language, ignorant of all the customs, and have incidentally heard a fellow-traveller speak in our own tongue, has not the surprised and thankful heart almost compelled us to claim acquaintance on the common ground of nationality, or identity of speech? Some such feeling as this must have been largely experienced by the first adherents of Christ; an accent might discover them, an allusion might bring them into mutual embrace. If such unusual conditions do not now elicit such warm demonstration, is it to our credit if the deep emotion of genuine brotherly affection has subsided?

The church thus resting upon a basis so easily comprehensible, it may be interesting to inquire why all who are avowedly ruled by the same faith and philanthropy do not meet as one church, without distinction or difference of any kind whatever? As the conditions and credentials of membership are so simple, why should there be anything sectarian amongst Christian men? This inquiry throws us back, not upon Christ, but upon human nature: in human nature there are endless varieties of temperament, capacity, culture, susceptibility, and relationship. Besides this, two things are to be taken into consideration: first, that upon the two fundamental principles the church can never be divided, for by the denial of either it loses status, it ceases to be a church; and second, that since Christ's day we have had the Epistles, which discuss some theological points and enter into various details, on the interpretation of which readers may fairly differ. Men are not saved by interpretations of apostolic epistles. They have the common organs of criticism at hand, and are responsible for their right use. A number of men may gather around each verse in each epistle, and found as many sects as there are verses, and yet the church may be an unbroken whole. The grandeur of Christ's work is seen in that it descends below all possibility of difference or breach. The differences occasioning denominationalism are but as the variously formed members of the body, while the church is as united and vital as the heart.

No doubt the Epistles have considerably divided men upon various points; still the church is so much richer by the possession of these letters, so full of mixed experience and so fervent with the passion of an absorbing love. It is certainly better to have them than to be without them, though they do furnish a wide ground of controversy. It is impossible but that Peter and Paul, James and John, should write many things as coming immediately from the lips of the Lord, and that, according to their various constitutions of mind, they should present doctrines in more or less of a characteristic manner. If the writers had different methods, how can the readers fail to receive different impressions? The only teacher who can expect to preside over a united school is Euclid, but even Euclid would soon find that, if there were two methods of drawing a straight line, his school would be broken up into parties. A question may be said to be truly great in proportion as it admits of multitudinous variations of opinion and expression, yet binds men by a mastery at once irresistible and beneficent. They differ about it, yet they love it; they fight with one another about it, and yet unite against any man who would injure it. Little questions cannot permanently divide mankind; great questions will always divide men, yet always unite them at some point. Men would hardly fight about the best method of going up a ladder, but a hundred battles have been fought on the best method of training a child. So all through life: the deeper the question, the deeper the opposition; men who would only laugh at a magician might crucify a Christ.

On the whole it may be doubted whether differences, properly argued, are not of advantage to religious progress. Now and again somewhat violent attempts are made to bring about visible unity in the Christian denominations, but they do more harm than good by calling attention to differences which are not vital, and giving what ought to be held quite secondary a factitious importance. All strained efforts after denominational unity are by their very nature bad. Unity must come, not through schemes, but through vitality, and it would be well if the most zealous charity would cease from its favorite pastime of setting traps for the capture of denominationalists. What is denominationalism but an inconvenient convenience? Rise or fall, it does not affect the church as we have ventured now to define it. It meets the temporary peculiarities of human nature; and if it be reproduced in a higher form as principalities, thrones, and denominations in the world to come, that will not alter its relation to the sublime embodiment of triumphant Sorrow sitting in the midst of the throne. As men reside in different houses and are yet inhabitants of the same city, so Christians may worship under different denominational politics and forms, and yet love the same Saviour. It would be as reasonable to reduce all soldiers to the same stature in order to present a commanding front of patriotism, as to bring all denominations under one polity to exemplify Christian unity. The world is educated by opposition, and it is more than doubtful whether such a world as it is could be educated in any other way. Men may be "provoked" even "to love and good works."

Union will be best attested by charity — not charity in any low sense, but charity as a phase of justice; not the charity that condescends, but the charity which concedes on equal terms. Wherever infallibility is claimed, the possibility of union is a blank; where liberty is conceded, union is already a fact. Christ is in all denominations where he is loved. The Romanist feels that he needs the crucifix, the penance, the Virgin Mother, the intermediate fire: let him have them; he will be saved, not by the alloy, but by the fine gold. The Protestant offers a less ornate worship: let him do so; he will be heard, not for his sternness, but for his sincerity. The Trinitarian firmly holds the doctrine of the triune Godhead, and the reverent Unitarian (not the scoffing Socinian) feels that if he has finished with *Ecce Homo* instead of with *Ecce Deus*, he will ultimately be led by gentle chiding to exclaim, " My Lord and my God!" Men are saved by the crucified Christ, not by the superscription which Pilate wrote.

We have endeavored broadly to mark the difference between the church and a sect. By an undue (may we not say criminal?) protrusion of the sectarian phase of religious life, a most erroneous idea respecting the church has been encouraged. If a man has not accepted a sect, it is often contended that he has not entered the church. It has been said, the act of joining the church has been regarded as a transaction between man and man, whereas is it not entirely a transaction between the spirit and Jesus Christ? Take an illustration: in some places the approach to the table of communion, or the Lord's Supper, is considered as the sign of church-membership; but before that table can be approached, the intending communicant must undergo some kind of official examination as to his theological views. Where is Christ's authority for this? Does not such an inquiry proceed upon the principle that the Lord's Supper is an administration rather than a communion — something to be dispensed by a superior hand rather than taken with a trembling joy by the man himself? In *such* a service who could be elevated to the dignity of an administrator? For mere convenience the emblems may be carried round by the teacher or his assistants; but this is an arrangement required by order, not a superiority conferred by God. Around the cross all men are equal; around the table, which represents the cross, all men must be equal too. But this equality cannot co-exist with the idea of dispensation. Men cannot meet in any official capacity whatsoever at the Lord's table; there they may assemble only as persons for whom the body was broken and the blood shed. The clergyman is not a clergyman, the officer is not an officer, when seated at the board of communion; the communicants are there as sinners who have accepted salvation through Jesus Christ. But is not examination needed? Yes, but it must be self-examination. Paul's words are explicit: "Let a man examine himself, and so let him eat of that bread and drink of that cup." It is feared that an open table might be taken advantage of by designing persons. The answer to this is evident: no plan will keep out designing persons; they can accommodate themselves to any process; if unworthy persons do approach the table, they eat and drink to their own condemnation, not to the condemnation of other people. This is in striking accord with all that we have seen in the life of Christ, who continually threw men back upon their own consciousness, and compelled them to judge their own actions; it is, too, in perfect harmony with the liberty which he came to inaugurate and establish among men, purifying each man's judicial faculty and giving him the highest advantages with a view to self-rectification.

If men choose to build places of worship and to lay down special regulations and conditions of attendance or membership, they may be at liberty to do so; but no man can ever be at liberty to alter the terms upon which salvation is offered to the world. He who attempts to do so is guilty of the worst form of blasphemy. The sect which has perverted a communion into a dispensation has interfered with the incommunicable prerogative of Christ. No man can dispense the light, or the wind, or the rain, or any of the primary forces or gifts of God; no more can any man dispense, except in the way of mere order, the body and blood of God's Son. In the widest sense, Christ *gives* himself; of such a gift there cannot be a secondary giver — hence communion alone can save the dignity and value of the gift.

The place of the Lord's Supper in the church is a subject on which diversity of opinion prevails. At first sight the idea of eating and drinking together suggests the socialism of fellowship in Christ, and pleasing sentiments of equality before God, both of which are perfectly true, and yet other and more may be meant by this communion. It is pleasant to think that in such common things as bread and wine Christ found emblems of himself; pleasant also to think of a whole community coming together from time to time to ratify their bonds. But is not all this beside the mark? With regard to the idea of hospitality, Paul sharply reproved the Corinthians for their practice at the table. "What," said he, "have ye not houses to eat and to drink in? . . . . If any man hunger, let him eat at home." The social idea, it would appear, however pleasant in itself, was not the idea contemplated in the establishment of the Communion. Men could not be social around the broken body of any man, specially of any man whom they had accepted as their Lord. However sacredly some persons may regard a club dinner,* it ought to be borne in mind that bread and wine are not mere viands for refreshment, but the emblems of Christ's body and blood. Only cannibals could dine, in any sense of a club dinner, off a crucified man. There must, then, we think, be something more, something deeper, too, than the idea of friendliness or fellowship.

* See *Ecce Homo*, p. 187.

Christ's own explanation ought to be final: "Take, eat," said he, "this is my body, broken for you;" "This cup is the new testament in my blood." The author just referred to says, "A common meal is the most natural and universal way of expressing, maintaining, and, as it were, ratifying relations of friendship." * This is true in itself, but the very idea of a "meal" is foreign to the spirit of this communion. As established by Christ, the Supper did not refer to "relations of friendship," but exclusively to himself. Is it not so? The terms of the service, as cited by the New Testament writers, certainly imply it: "*This do in remembrance of me;*" and again, "This do ye, as oft as ye drink it, *in remembrance of me.*" What is there about "friendship" here? That "friendship" would be purified and elevated by such an act is undoubted, but what was the primary idea of the Supper? That idea is described as combining recollection and anticipation. Not only is it written, "This do in remembrance of me," but also, "As often as ye eat this bread and drink this cup, ye do show the Lord's death till he come." And why retain the memory of that event? Because it was "*for you:*" "This is my body, which is given for you," — "This cup is the new testament in my blood, which is shed for you." The personal interest of the communicant in the sacrifice of Christ is the reason for preserving the memory of "the Lord's death." The author of *Ecce Homo* says, "It is precisely this intense personal devotion, this habitual feeding on the character of Christ, so that the essential nature of the master

* See *Ecce Homo*, p. 187.

seems to pass into and become the essential nature of the servant — loyalty carried to the point of self-annihilation — that is expressed by the words 'eating the flesh and drinking the blood of Christ'" (p. 176). We think there is some confusion of idea here. Men could have "fed on the character of Christ" without having a sacrament, so to speak, imposed on them; but they could not "show forth" the Lord's death without a sacrament, the very idea of "showing forth" requiring visibility and symbolism. "Feeding on the character of Christ" is purely a mental act, but a club dinner is more. And, again, if eating the flesh and drinking the blood of Christ expresses "intense personal devotion," where is the idea of "ratifying the relations of friendship"? It can only come in secondarily, not primarily, as it did in the first part of the argument.

The Lord's Supper is a memorial. It does not necessarily imply the joint act of a number of persons. A single man may show forth his "Lord's death." The club idea is not in the nature of the service at all. Men stand in a personal, not in an associated relation to that death, and the communion must be personal, not one with another, but each with the Lord. The club idea is more pertinent to the church coming together to feed on the divine Word as it may be read and expounded publicly. In the Old and New Testament men are often represented as eating and drinking the word of God, and as speaking to one another about the bounty and goodness of the feast. Job said, "I have esteemed the words of his mouth more than my necessary food." The Psalmist said, "How sweet are thy words unto my taste! Yea, sweeter than honey to my mouth;" and Jesus himself said, "My meat is to do the will of him that sent me, and to finish his work." Men are invited to "eat and drink abundantly," and to let their "soul delight itself in fatness," and God is proclaimed as making "unto all people a feast of fat things, a feast of wines on the lees, of fat things full of marrow, of wines on the lees well refined." There is much in this imagery to favor the idea of a club dinner, and to give a meaning to the expression, "feeding on the character of Christ." If it be suggested that each man should partake of the Lord's Supper privately, the suggestion would involve the cessation of all public service; men can pray alone, sing alone, read alone; but Christ called men to himself, constituted those who came into a church, and that church is to-day his representative and the treasurer of his testimony.

With regard to the expression "eat my flesh and drink my blood," it should be noted that it was not used in connection with the Supper. It forms part of an appeal to the general multitude which pursued Christ after the distribution of the loaves and fishes. He knew that the people sought him because they "did eat of the loaves and were filled," and thereupon he discoursed concerning himself as "the living bread which came down from heaven." His method of putting the case was likely to create strife among the literalists who heard him; and as the Jews "strove among themselves, saying, How can this man give us his flesh to eat?" Jesus answered, "Except ye eat the flesh of the Son of Man and drink his blood, ye have no life in you : whoso eateth my flesh and drinketh my blood dwelleth in me, and I in him." The circumstances clearly show that the expression did not relate to the Supper, but was part of what we should now regard as a sermon or a religious address. In this sense there is no incongruity in rendering it as equivalent to "feeding on the character of Christ." The hearers had eaten of the natural bread, and as usual Christ conducted them to a spiritual interpretation of natural circumstances, and so put himself before them as the living bread — a strong figurative representation of his person and work. It is as though he had said, — You have eaten of the bread that perisheth; as that bread nourishes the body, there is another bread which nourishes the mind; as the body could not exist without the former, so the mind must die without the latter; I myself am the living bread, the mind must feed upon me as specially provided for its quickening. In so addressing the people, Christ elevated a fact into a figure; he took the circumstance of the hour and hung upon it lessons of eternity; he did not import the figure as an original conception, but found it in the passing event. To press the allegory further would be unjust, and would bring other allegories under an interpretation which would be absurd. Also to associate the expression with the Supper is to put it out of place, and to force upon the Supper violent and untenable meanings. That points of analogy may be discovered is clear enough, but what two things are there in the world which do not bear some resemblance and relation to one another?

The argument which we have sought to establish is,

that Christ founded his church upon a common faith and a common philanthropy; that the church is one and indivisible; that the sect is not to be confounded with the church; that the church is immortal, though the sect is temporary; that entrance into the church is purely a transaction between Christ and the individual; that within the church there is a sacrament called the Lord's Supper, a sacrament which is not a dispensation, but a communion; a sacrament which may be approached without official examination, but not without severe self-inquest; that the Supper is a memorial and a hope, — not a club dinner, even in its most refined and legitimate sense, but a special communion between the communicant and his Lord.

CHAPTER X.

THE CHURCH LEFT IN THE WORLD.

NOW that men have been called and united, it may be time to inquire into the laws by which they are to be personally and relatively governed. Life is continually presenting new aspects; and a widening civilization is perpetually throwing up questions which challenge the consideration of men who profess to go beyond "the world" for their doctrine and policy. Side by side with the Christian organization called the church, many a powerful rivalry has been growing up, so that a persistent competition has been brought to bear upon the interests, real or supposed, of the whole community. We have seen that Christ regarded his disciples as "not of the world," yet to-day "the world" is setting up a claim for the suffrages of the disciples. The line of separation is supposed by some observers to have faded much. Is it so in reality? It may be worth while to inquire how Jesus Christ, simply regarded as a bold and far-sighted propagandist, proposed to keep vast masses of men in permanent union — in other words, to consider how men can be in the world, yet not of it; can live in it, and yet be above it; can be united with one another, yet separate from sinners. No *imperium in. imperio* is so great a mystery as the church in the world. Christ surely proposed a hard thing to his disciples when he required them to remain in the world and yet to continue not only to be superior to its contaminations, but to make daily encroachments upon its dominion until its authority was completely upset. In one of his prayers Christ said, "I pray not that thou shouldest take them out of the world, but that thou shouldest keep them from evil." Here is the difficulty.

In attempting the negative work of keeping men from evil, it is customary to set down in systematic order minute regulations and directions respecting things which are to be avoided. Christ did not adopt this plan. Rather by allusion than by detailed statement, he indicated certain forbidden territory, and then betook himself to the affirmative side of his plan. He did not hope to keep men from evil by lecturing about it, by elaborating a penal system, or by any appeal to the lower instincts of human nature. His simple plan was to counteract death by life. Thus, instead of telling a man not to despond, he inspired him with a new hope; instead of telling a man to do no murder, he gave him such notions of the sanctity of human life as took away the very tendency to anger. This was his fundamental plan. "Thou shalt *not*" was adapted to a ruder age of the world; "Thou shalt" was now to take its place. The ineffectiveness of merely negative instruction is shown every day. Take the case of the gambler: tell him that gambling will bring him to ruin or inflict ruin on others; insist upon it that gambling is a perilous and mischievous practice, and not improbably the gambler will assent to the doctrine: but will he abandon the habit? Go further: imprison the gambler; take from him all gambling instruments, and condemn him to live in penniless poverty all the rest of his days: does he cease to be a gambler? Only in the lowest sense; he is still a gambler in spirit; the evil is untouched. What does Christ propose in such a case? He not only casts out the devil, but he puts in the Holy Spirit. He gives the gambler something better to do, and proves his entire success by leaving the man in the world, yet keeping him from the evil. It would be a poor thing to take the man out of the world; if he required to be so taken, that very fact would prove that he was not perfectly healed by Christ. The most conclusive testimony which is afforded of the divine force of truth is that men continue in the world, though inhaling the atmosphere of heaven. Satan is put under their feet. They are still in the region of war, but protected by impenetrable armor.

The fact that life must have occupation, shows the inutility of merely negative teaching. Life cannot remain quiescent; it has appropriative and distributive functions, and must operate accordingly. If it be not pursuing good, it must be doing mischief. How does Christ propose to engage those functions?

We may simplify the course of inquiry by confining it to the subject of amusements. The mirthful side of human nature must be provided for. The sects have shut up the theatre, the race-course, and the dancing-saloon; they have forbidden game after game; the Ten Commandments they have displaced by a hundred of their own, each commencing with "Thou shalt *not*." Nothing was easier, and nothing was more useless. A man loves the drama passionately; he sees only the ideal side of it; the true interpretation of a great poem is to him the most refined of luxuries; he is entranced by the genius of art. The sects say to him, You must give up the drama, and he receives the intimation with great surprise, probably too with some disgust. The intimation may be given to him by a man who hardly knows the meaning of the word drama, who has no soul for poetry, no eye for art — a man who would throw jewels away because the casket had been spotted with mud. Are the feelings of the dramatist not easily conceivable, and do they not under such circumstances call for sympathy? Christ never told his disciples not to go to the theatre, the race-course, or the revel; from end to end of his teaching no such prohibition can be found. What then did Christ do? He said, "Make the tree good, and the fruit will be good;" don't trim the leaves, vitalize the root; don't attach, but develop. He opened, as we have seen, a wide field of philanthropic service, healing the sick, feeding the hungry, clothing the naked, preaching liberty to the captive; he filled men with his own spirit, and then left them to go whithersoever it would conduct them. Christ did not teach from the outward to the inward, but from the inward to the outward. It is better to give a man a good principle than a good practice; it is better to be good than merely to behave well; the one is character, the other is convenience. Christ's plan of meeting the wants of all sides of human life was stated in one sentence — "*I have given them thy word.*" He had put a spirit and a standard within them. The law was henceforth not an outside letter, but an internal voice. The holy Word gave place to the Holy Spirit. It was as if a new sense had been added to the Christian nature — a sense of immediate and accurate moral touch which instantly discovered the quality of every doctrine or act. This is given to every man who is in Christ; who has eaten his flesh and drunk his blood, and so become essentially one with him.

As to questions in casuistry which come up again and again in practical life, one of the ablest reasoners in the early church has laid down principles of universal and unerring application. Christ determined the fundamental point, and Paul followed with special illustrations. It may be well to spend a moment with Paul, that we may see what his interpretation of Christ's idea was. There had been a discussion in one of the Christian communities respecting eating, which was not unlikely to create a serious division. The great apostolic casuist, who had in him a volume of humanity second only to the Son of Man, and who could consequently see most sides of a controverted subject, argued the cause with characteristic acumen and cogency. "Let not him that eateth," said he, " despise him that eateth not; and let not him which eateth not judge him that eateth : for God hath received him." He insisted upon strict individuality of judgment and conscience in the case, and became indignant with all censoriousness of criticism : "Who art thou that judgest another man's servant? To his own master he standeth or falleth. Yea, he shall be holden up, for God is able to make him stand." The spirit of mastery must be put down in the Christian fellowship ; there is one Master, and all judgment on the part of the servants is so much detraction from his supremacy in the church. On matters of detail, then, there is no common law in the Christian brotherhood; no amusement is prescribed, no amusement is forbidden; a man may drink wine, or a man may abstain from wine; a man may eat meat, or he may subsist on herbs; a man may esteem one day above another, or he may esteem every day alike. Let the indwelling Spirit determine. "Why dost thou judge thy brother? or why dost thou set at nought thy brother? for we shall all stand before the judgment seat of Christ." The church is not confederated upon questions of casuistry; it is founded on a common faith and a common philanthropy. It may be inquired — Since the Spirit is the same, ought not the results to be the same? Certainly not. The results come through the idiosyncrasies of each man's constitution. No two men are alike, though all men are made by God. One man is naturally contemplative, another active; one melancholy, another mirthful; one enterprising, another conservative. Christianity does not change the basis of a man's individuality, but gives him a new spirit by which that individuality may be properly trained. As to amusements or recreations, most of which are supposed to lean towards the devil, their election is an individual question. It is for Christians to say how far they can go into the world of recreation. There is a solemnity which is more sinful than laughter; there is a laughter more acceptable to God than solemnity. Some men never laughed, — cannot laugh, but they have a ready talent for condemning laughter in others; what is wanting in mirth is made up in censoriousness. They have but a small endowment of life to answer for, and cannot, consequently, comprehend the many-sided men who, while open to all the influences of mirth, have their holy hours of deep and probably agonizing devotion.

So much for the personal side of the question; but we are to consider the law which is to govern not individual men only, but men who are organized into a church. How is individuality to stand in relation to community? While each man may be a law unto himself, each man is not a church unto himself. We may continue to argue the case, by still keeping to the simple illustration of an amusement. Differences of opinion do obtain as to amusements, but it should be borne in mind that the church, as such, is never asked to adopt any method of amusement or recreation; it is exclusively a personal matter, and can only relate to the corporate body on the ground of influence or example. The reputation of the whole may be compromised by the action of a part. Paul lays down this doctrine: "I know, and am persuaded by the Lord Jesus, that there is nothing unclean of itself; but to him that esteemeth anything to be unclean, to him it is unclean." The important point of this statement is, that it is given on Christ's own authority; and it certainly is of the utmost consequence to have it laid down by Jesus Christ himself that "there is nothing unclean of itself." But the question forced upon men by their association is, how far private tastes are to be controlled by the public opinion of the body? Are they to be controlled at all? Paul says that some are "weak in the faith," from which it may be inferred that some are strong: how then? Are the weak to consider the strong, or the strong to consider the weak? If family life may afford a suggestion, nothing can be clearer than that the strong are to consider the weak; the mother lives for the infant, not the infant for the mother. The case is put in the clearest light by Paul: "Let us not therefore judge one another any more; but judge this rather, that no man put a stumbling-block or an occasion to fall in his brother's way." This is the very spirit of Christian philanthropy, the considerations of self being subordinated to consideration of others. "What!" some one may exclaim, "am I to surrender my pleasures, because there are persons called weak brethren in the world? The pleasures are to me perfectly legitimate, and I think it unreasonable that any man should be offended by them." A strong case, indeed, when viewed from any point but that of Christian philanthropy. It is just here, however, that the stress comes upon that philanthropy, and tests it. The philanthropy is not a mere sentiment, but a controlling power, having no *self*, and knowing nothing but man in the image of God. In proportion as a man gives up the very smallest enjoyment for the sake of his brother man, he comes to know what is meant by sacrifice, by self-sacrifice, and gets at least a distant glimpse of the Philanthropist who "pleased not himself." Why the shock at such a proposition as is above suggested? The very principle is carried out in family life. The parent denies himself many enjoyments for the sake of his child: is not the church a family? When the parent says, "I shall not do this, because my child may get from it a wrong impression of life; the thing itself would be right enough to me, but he cannot yet comprehend my reasons for doing it: therefore, purely for his sake, I shall abstain;" he will see new and overpowering meanings in such expressions as — " Christ pleased not himself;" " Christ loved us, and gave himself for us;" " For their sakes, I sanctify myself;" " He took upon him the form of a servant." These expressions cannot be opened by the lexicographer; they are known only to the practical philanthropist. The heart receives the interpretation, while the head can but wonder. A man has been heard to say, that never until he saw his own little child in pain, did he know what was meant by the words, " Like as a father pitieth his children, so the Lord pitieth them that fear him." His own nature became the interpreter of God's. Through an analogous process we come to understand somewhat of the mystery of Christ's sacrifice. As a written doctrine, it is little more than an external beauty, thought to be too sacred for imitation or reproduction in any degree; but when once the spirit of sacrifice has been developed, it brings with it a sweetness beyond all other sweetness, and a consciousness of spiritual dominion, kindred to being " exalted to be a Prince and a Saviour." The range of self-sacrifice is more extensive than is commonly supposed. The child who sits silently in a sick room lest a dying parent should be disturbed, is within that range; so is the mother who gives up her days and nights to her sickening infant; so is the man who divides his last loaf with his hungering neighbor; and so is the noble creature who denies himself a luxury, lest a weak brother should stumble. All this is included in Christ's idea of sacrifice; with this difference, however, that while the parent sacrifices for his child, and the neighbor for a man of kindred heart, Christ died for his enemies. This disclosed the greatness of his nature. He saw in man what no other eye could see. He did for his enemies what few men would do for their friends, so that from his lips as from no other could come the command, "Love your enemies."

In this way Christ broke in upon the organized selfishness of the world, and "troubled" society with his unearthly doctrine of self-abnegation. And in this way he proposed to keep up eternally the distinction between the church and the world, and so to preserve his disciples from evil, while they continued more or less in the very midst of their old associations. The spirit of sacrifice is the best defence against evil; not the spirit of criticism, not the sharpness of wit, not the resources of experience, but the spirit of self-suppression as it was manifested by Jesus Christ in the Temptation. Every temptation was an appeal to *self;* every answer showed how self could be held in perfect subjection. This was the root of his power; it came to fruition on the Cross.

Reverting to the church, we find a distinct law laid down by Paul for the regulation of associated life: "Ye have been called unto liberty; only use not liberty for an occasion to the flesh, but by love serve one another." We have still the same principle of philanthropy called into exercise. It is perfectly true that a man has liberty, but it is also true that liberty is to be the servant of love. Liberty is consistent with self, but love is not; therefore love is the final law. The possessor of mere liberty (assuming that to be possible) may take counsel with himself as to enjoyment; may write a detailed programme, and repel dictation; but the man whose liberty is controlled by love will ask how this or that will affect the persons who observe his conduct, or come under his influence. He will instantly explode the sophism that men should come up to him rather than that he should go down to them; like his Master, he will take upon him the form of a servant, that he may deliver those who are in a low estate.

To those who have come into liberty, but have not yet attained perfect love, it may be well to recall the purpose of discipline. Every man should be king over himself. Christ insists upon the supremacy of the whole over the part, when he commands the cutting off or plucking out of an offending member of the body. To be able to look at a pleasure, yet to keep it at arm's length for the sake of a brother, is the highest attainment of discipline. The disciplined man enjoys the spoils of a large conquest; in conquering himself he has conquered his principal foe. He can look at the forbidden tree, acknowledge that it is pleasant to the eyes, and, probably, a tree "to be desired to make one wise," and yet tell the damning serpent that there is no folly so great as the wisdom which comes through violating love. The fear is that the disciplinarian may become ungenial in judgment. The man who has cut off his right hand may be tempted to think that other men should cut off their right hands; and the man with one eye may think it hard that other people should have two. Christ foresaw this, and constantly turned men back upon themselves to consider what was wanted by their own peculiar constitution, and he gave them the benefit of his own prayers, as in the case of Simon Peter, for whom he specially prayed that his faith might not fail. One of the main purposes of discipline will be frustrated if it fail to give men a firmer control over their critical faculty when they institute a comparison between themselves and others. Censure is inconsistent with philanthropy, and philanthropy is the last result of a perfect discipline.

The disciplined man will not keep men from evil by shouting moral maxims at them, as the modern church has been doing for a long series of years. The great disciplinarian, who knew both how to abound and how to be abased, who kept his body under, and checked himself at every point, lest, after having preached to others, he should become a castaway, adopted the only successful method of maintaining a permanent hold upon men — a literal transcript of Christ's method, — " Though I be free from all men, yet have I made myself servant unto all, that I might gain the more. And unto the Jews I became as a Jew, that I might gain the Jews; to them that are under the law, as under the law, that I might gain them that are under the law; to them that are without law, as without law (being not without law to God, but under the law to Christ), that I might gain them that are without law. To the weak became I as weak, that I might gain the weak: I am made all things to all men." This is the fruit of discipline. Paul looked at things from every man's own particular stand-point. To each man he said, "I shall come round to your point of view, put myself in your circumstances, establish a common sympathy, and so work my way back to Jesus Christ." This gave him a marvellous advantage. When a man goes *down* to teach, he takes with him considerable overplusage of power; but when he goes *up* to teach, he goes in the wrong direction, and strains himself greatly to the disgust of those who are above him. The only true way of getting up is by going down; the way to gain life is to lose it. "Thou fool, that which thou sowest is not quickened except it die."

The church (now understanding by that term the organized sects) is not willing to "lose its life" that it may "gain" others; hence it is the weakest, and, humanly speaking, the most despicable institution which men are now tolerating. It is afraid of amusement; it is afraid of heresy; it is afraid of contamination; it is afraid of sinners; it is afraid of the devil. All this must come from a low condition of vitality. It shuts itself up within thick walls, sings its hymns, hears its periodical platitudes, and then skulks into the common streets, as if afraid lest the multitude should know what it had been doing. Nothing can be more un-Christlike that is not positively devilish. The worst feature of this cowardly fear is that it is often expressed in a bad spirit, venom being mistaken for strength. The sin is not so much in the thing said, as in the way of saying it. It is forgotten, too, by the sect-church, that there are other sins than those which reel in the streets or swing on the gallows. The man who makes a long prayer, and then oppresses the hireling, is as an unclean beast in the sanctuary; so is the man who would not part with a leaf from his catechism, yet makes his home a very hell by a fiendish temper; so is the man who spends his life in scenting the heresies of doctrine, and yet cultivates the blacker heresies of life. Such a course brings Christ into disrepute. He is crucified by those who bear his name. Christ's work must be done in Christ's spirit, and in Christ's way. He went among men turning the water into wine, and celebrating the prodigal's return with music and dancing. The sect-church has imagined that it must stand aloof from bad men lest it should receive contamination. This is a melancholy confession of weakness, bringing the most undeserved and humiliating discredit upon the power of the Holy Ghost in the human soul. It is as if the salt should stand aloof from the flesh lest it should be corrupted; or as if the light should stand aloof from the darkness lest it should be obscured. Christ never shut himself up from the wicked, and yet never seemed to be so far from them as when in their very midst. Other men's refinement became vulgarity when contrasted with his gentleness; their wisdom became folly under the lustre of his revelations; and Solomon's grandeur faded beside the lily which Christ pointed out. When bad men meet alone they lose the advantage of moral contrast, and measuring themselves by themselves they commit the falsehood of exaggeration. Christ saved men from this in his own day, and would save them from it now, but for the narrowness of sects. The coarsest man feels a measure of restraint in the presence of a gentle, pure woman; what might not the evil sections of society feel in the presence of the embodied holiness of the Infinite God? "No man lighteth a candle to put it under a bushel, but he setteth it on a candlestick, that it may give light to all that are in the house." There is a good deal in the setting, as well as in the candle; a few inches on this side or that may make all the difference between usefulness and uselessness.

Thus we have incompletely sketched the position of the church in the world, and shown how the church is to be protected from the evils by which it is surrounded. Evil is to be extinguished, not by mere verbal denunciation, but by the spirit of goodness, the Holy Spirit. Darkness will not be removed by anathema, but by light. Individual liberty is to be regulated by common philanthropy. The church is to be kept from selfishness by sacrifice. This is Christ's method, as illustrated in particular cases by his great interpreter the apostle Paul. Christ gave his followers power to go everywhere, and to take up even deadly things without being hurt. He had no fear of their being corrupted, but gave them energy to save others from corruption; his own Word dwelling in them richly. He sent them as sheep among wolves, with wisdom and gentleness as their defence. They were to pursue evil persons in every direction, and to "torment" them "before the time," by the presence of an august yet genial purity. They were safe, because their Lord was with them. Their power was moral, — not the power of purse, or scrip, or sword, or many coats, which exercise so illegitimate an influence in the world. Not what was *on*, but what was *in*, was their strength. We look for the same self-repression to-day, the same moral majesty, producing the same startling contrast. Where is it? Hidden, no doubt, in some degree under the folds of an elaborate civilization, but still, we doubt not, in existence; not all in this sect or in that, but partly; widely scattered, yet not beyond the call of the Voice which brought order out of chaos. We cannot take so discouraging a view of human society as to believe that Christ's influence is diminishing. If it is less demonstrative, it may not be less vital. His church has not slipped out of the world into a secret and nameless grave, though its original compactness and accessibility are not what they were. The very inquiry which men are now pressing with unexampled urgency, is a good sign; when the anxiety is extreme, the satisfaction will not be long delayed. There may be a law of subsidence or rest in the progression of the Christian society. The tide may be advancing, notwithstanding the refluent wave. There is, too, an *intensive* as well as an *extensive* operation of life; so that what is wanting in demonstrativeness may be made up in penetration. Anyhow, Christ's vitality cannot be lost in the world; the seed of the second Adam shall be as the sand upon the sea-shore, innumerable.

CHAPTER XI.

CHRIST ADJUSTING HUMAN RELATIONS.

CHRIST prayed that his disciples might be kept from evil, but he had also a work to accomplish on a larger scale; not only had he to keep the disciples who were called by himself personally, but to extend their numbers; and we propose now to consider how he intended to do this, grouping our suggestions under the general title given above. To say that Christ found human relations disorganized, would be to put human history into the tritest form of expression; yet that inclusive fact lies at the bottom of his mission and plan among men. The man who was made "upright," found out many "inventions," but among them all was not that of regaining the equilibrium which he had lost. If man had not destroyed his nature, he had disarranged his proportions. A very subtle thing is the equipoise. An extra handful of dust on the side of a planet might endanger the universe.

At the risk of violating a strictly logical progression (though not more so than Christ himself apparently did), it may be useful to look at once at the work which Christ accomplished in adjusting the relations between man and man; which will give us, from another point, Christ's view of human nature, and place something concrete and immediately appreciable before us. It is of primary importance to remark that Christ never depreciated manhood in any of its forms or conditions, but, on the contrary, continually spoke of man with reverence and affection; not of the Jew as a Jew, or the Roman as a Roman, but strictly of man as man; thus incidentally illustrating the meaning and force of his own appellation, the Son of Man. In one of his most touching parables, he rebuked Jewish exclusiveness with great dignity, yet in a manner which must have been most galling to the haughty men who heard him. It was the priest who passed by, and the Levite; but it was a contemned Samaritan who stopped and proved himself a practical philanthropist. Would any other Jew but Christ have so introduced a Samaritan? And would Christ himself, if he had not been more than a Jew? On another occasion, he declared that the faith of a heathen woman was greater than he had ever seen in Israel; and as he cast his eye over the nations of the earth, taking in his comprehensive survey " regions Cæsar never knew," he boldly told the supposed favorites of heaven that men should come from the east and from the west, from the north and from the south, and sit down in the kingdom of heaven. When his contemporaries called themselves the children of Abraham, John struck the boast off their vaunting lips, by telling them that God was able to raise up out of the very stones children to Abraham. In the same manner, Christ showed that manhood was not a geographical term, having one meaning on this coast and another on that, but that it was overflowing with moral significance, and stood in very intimate relation to God.

One of his longest discourses was delivered upon the subject of the relations between man and man, and man and his kingdom. The old and vexed question of gradation came up among the disciples, and was referred to the Master for decision. The disciples would soon have rent the new kingdom by this question of position, had their leader not quenched their carnal aspirations, and showed them that they were all equally wrong in their notions. Rulership has always been one of the hardest problems which society has had to solve, and to-day it lies at the root of all war. How can there be a kingdom without rulership? The disciples naturally pondered the inquiry, and entertained some exciting speculations on the point. When the matter so agitated them that they could no longer keep it to themselves, they abruptly laid it before Christ; whereupon he delivered a copious and impressive address on human nature. He called a little child unto him and set him in the midst, and said — You trouble yourselves a good deal about greatness in my kingdom; now let me tell you that except ye be converted — that is to say, radically changed in your self-estimation — and become as simple, trustful, and unconscious of your own importance as this little child, you shall not so much as even enter into that kingdom, much less have any distinguished position in it: great, swollen, self-idolizing men cannot be admitted; the gate is strait; only child-like men may pass through. — Nothing could be more foreign to the spirit of carnal ambition than such an answer.

It did not leave the subject open for discussion. No craft could wriggle out of so positive a doctrine. But the text was not exhausted. The little child was still there, and Christ continued in the most sweet and captivating manner to discourse respecting the great value which he attached to manhood. In effect he said — Human nature is not to be measured by what is accidental, but by what is essential; you must value man as man, even though he be as low in the scale as it is possible for any human creature to be. The image of God, though much defaced, is upon the lowest man; if you despise him you despise me, for the Son of Man is come to seek that which is lost; he will have to go a long way down for it, but it must be found. If you undervalue man, you undervalue my mission and reproach the wisdom of God; but if you value man as man, apart from all that is accidentally repulsive, and receive him in my name, you receive me; and whoso receiveth me receiveth not me, but him that sent me. We all go together, God, Christ, and lowest man; take one and you take all, reject one and you reject all. Take heed that ye despise not one of these little ones, for I say unto that in heaven their angels do always behold the face of my Father which is in heaven. Do not look high, as though men were to be judged by their stature; so important, so sublime, is humanity, apart altogether from culture and development, that whoso shall offend one of these little ones that believe in me, it were better for him that a millstone were hanged about his neck, and that he were drowned in the depths of the sea.

Such talk about human nature was new. Up to

this time men had hardly advanced farther than to a civil regard for those who belonged to their own particular nation. But Christ set man above the nation, the gold above the inscription which had been stamped upon it. This one circumstance is a commanding plea in support of the divine origin of the Christian religion, and is in exquisite accord with the whole mystery called Christ, so far as we have been able to trace it. To reject Christ is, speaking merely in view of his humanity, to reject the most consistent and powerful vindicator of the dignity and value of human nature that ever challenged the attention of the world. If we cannot at once join him in some of the higher ranges of his discourse, we may at least sit down at this point, and learn his view of the capability and worth of our own nature. It is, then, to be distinctly recognized as a primary fact in Christ's teaching that Christ will not allow any man, how sunken soever he be, to be despised. No word of contempt can be permitted; not even a thought that tends in the direction of scorn: "Whosoever shall say, Thou fool, shall be in danger of hell fire." Not only were men to love those who loved them, but to love their enemies, bless those that cursed them, and pray for those that despitefully used them; and this they were to do for a most remarkable and suggestive reason, "That ye may be the children of your Father, who maketh his sun to rise on the evil and on the good, and sendeth rain upon the just and unjust." When men made a feast they were to call the poor, the maimed, the lame, the blind, and they would be blessed in so doing, for the guests could not recompense them, but they should be recompensed at the resurrection of the just. The words are now so familiar, and have, indeed, produced so great an effect upon modern society, that it is difficult to estimate their influence upon the men to whom they were addressed, or the moral courage which was required to utter them in the presence of the most exclusive social system in all civilization. The poor were not to be talked about as a farmer would talk about bog land, but to be treated as sharers with the greatest of a common human nature; and the divine element that was in them was not only to save them from contempt, but to bring them into brotherhood with the foremost men. But brotherhood in its true sense cannot come from the outside. There is a vital difference between patronage and brotherhood. Nothing is easier than for a man to conceal his pride under the forms of humility; actually never to stand so high in his own estimation as when seen in the public highway arm in arm with rags and wretchedness. He then says, "Look at me! this is humility; I am not ashamed to be seen thus." It requires less moral courage to pick a beggar out of the ditch than to be seen on friendly terms with an honest man who earns weekly wages. In the one case the very extremity is its own defence; in the other there is room for several undesirable inferences on the part of genteel observers. To-day the sect-church has conceived an extraordinary liking for institutions which touch the lowest strata of society; the nobility of the land refreshes itself by teaching the ragged and homeless Arabs of England — a very beautiful and even heavenly thing when done with a pure motive, yet covering a most seductive temptation to confound patronage with brotherhood. It is possible to like the rags more than the human nature — possible for the rich man to give Lazarus a coat, and yet to grind the face of his own servants; and by so much as this is possible, society should drill itself in the difficult doctrine that God hath made of one blood, and will call to one judgment, all nations of men. Society is very careful of its extremities, — its purple and its rags, but midway is there not a great cemetery filled with living hearts, whose only hope is death? Is it, then, really human nature or human circumstances on which benevolence is operating? Society has to be saved from mistaking patronage for philanthropy, and can only be so saved by a deep study of the life of Jesus Christ.

Such a civilization as that of the nineteenth century brings society very much under the influence of the richest culture and refinement. The spirit of the age is æsthetic. Even utility now goes abroad gilded and brocaded most elaborately. The humblest industry has been taught to aspire to a position in the temple of the arts; and nation challenges nation to a comparison of handiwork. Under such circumstances there is a special temptation to worship faculty, skill, or genius, — the attributes rather than the nature of man. We now ask for certificates of merit, and make manhood prove itself by competitive examinations. And now that certificates, medals, and titles are so plentiful, it is a bare chance if the uncertificated man escape contempt. Men are industriously trained to criticise the external; they are learned in all artificialism; inexorably exacting in matters of dress, posture, and pronunciation.

What, then, can the unconventional man do? What if he still be "lost"? Then the ministry of Christ becomes his hope, for *he* never forgets the "lost" man, but goes after him till he is found. Refinement brings its own perils. When refinement boasts of itself, it becomes vulgarity. True refinement is a question of the heart, not an attainment of the schools; under the roughest exterior the most tender sensibilities may throb, and under the finest there may be dross and dust. After all, then, the question is fundamental: man, not circumstances; man as God made him, not as he has made himself.

A true conception of the value of human nature lies at the very foundation of Christ's earthly mission. The term salvation is important only so far as human nature is important. The Cross is the only adequate interpretation of man. Would Christ, from all that we have seen of him in this rapid examination only, have died for a trifle? Gather a multitude of the worst characters that can be found, and let the heart say how much of its blood it would shed for their elevation. Not a drop, probably. It cannot see far enough. It sees the worst, not the best. Only God can value man; he knows how he made him; what music there is yet in the untouched chords of the human soul; he knows how terrible would be his own loneliness if the child of his heart were lost. But some men are vulgar: true, yet they are men still, but must be refined. All the gifts of man are to have a downward influence as well as an upward tendency. Refinement is to refine others. Culture is to be an inspiration, not a terror to those who are still rude. The criminal is to see in the judge what he himself might have been, and what even yet he may become. The chaste woman is to be the hope, not the dread, of her fallen sister. Education is not to enclose itself in an unapproachable hermitage, but to move among the rude humanities with a subduing and inspiring grace. This is the very spirit of Jesus Christ. He said, "It is more blessed to give than to receive," and that the chief of his disciples was to be servant of all. Merely, then, as a matter of argument, it must be allowed that Jesus Christ, immeasurably beyond any other teacher, recognized the greatness of human nature. How did he come by this unparalleled estimate? Certainly he had no inducement to flatter it in return for his personal reception on the earth. Sometimes pleasant circumstances force weak observers into an exaggeration of praise; but in spite of the harshest reception Christ affirmed that God so loved the world that he gave his only-begotten Son for its salvation. His verdict is thus the more important by reason of the conditions under which it was given. Had he been asked to give an opinion of human nature before he assumed it, his opinion might, on easily understood grounds, have been favorable; but after he has lain in the manger, been exposed to hunger and thirst and cold, been smitten on the face and condemned as a felon, when he has been laughed at as a fanatic or shunned as a madman, he speaks of human nature with the fond tenderness and lofty reverence of one who was preparing to die for it. Something more than human must explain this humanness. Every other man falls short of it: how came a Galilean peasant to have it all? It is an affront to common sense to say that it is an imaginary sketch; but even if it be, what then? The problem is not solved; for as only a poet can write a poem, so only a Christ could have conceived a Christ.

The first thing, then, that is before us is Christ's adjustment of man's relation to man, giving us deeper insight into humanity, inspiring mutual love, and strengthening the common trust of society. There is no phase of his adjustment of man which, though less commanding, is yet one of great interest — than is his way of setting them towards *nature*. Christ walked much in the open country with his disciples, and gave them a new method of reading the landscape and all natural objects. He turned nature into a great book of illustration; he showed that every bush was aflame with consuming fire and vocal with the utterances of God. He made all nature preach the doctrine of trust in the divine Fatherhood. He spoke of the lilies as pledges of God's care, and pointed to the fowls as an illustration of God's watchfulness over all life. He bade his disciples consider these things, and lay them to heart as defences against distrust or apprehension. Who knows how much life there is in a lily? Who can measure the distance between God and a flower of the field? What connection there is between the lily and the man we have not yet been sufficiently educated to discern, but Christ's lesson is pointless if there is not a line common to all kinds of life, running through and binding all. It would be useless to " consider the lilies " if they and the considerers had no point in common, though in the present state of our faculties it may be inappreciable; as well might the beggar say that he would "consider" the door-plates of the city because the hands that burnished them might feed him. The explanation is that the universe is a series, and that he who cares for the least will care for the greatest; that simplicity and beauty and fragrance and every form of life are all of God, and that the Creator of all is also the servant of all. Christ thus showed not only the refining and stimulating power of nature, but the perfect unity of the Divine government, by teaching that the God of the flowers is the God of the human race, and that He who cared for the ephemeral leaf could not forget the immortal man. This lesson is invaluable not only for its immediate practical comfort, but as warranting the application of inductive reasoning to the Divine nature as well as to Divine processes of education and government. In syntax the grammarians have put *as* and *so* in relation, but Christ teaches us to put them together in the deepest questions of experimental religion and speculative theology, and thus climb our way up to the very seat of the Eternal. He brings men very near to God when, in a parallel which would be blasphemous if it were not true, he says; "If *ye* . . . how much more your *Father?*" — the plane is one, though the intermediate points are immeasurably distant. Christ says — Begin with the lily and reason upward to the absolute, and then descend and teach lessons of loving and reverent trust in God to anxious men, who are foolishly carrying all the weight of to-morrow on shoulders already pressed by the burden of to-day. But can the conscious learn from the unconscious?

Can the man learn anything from the lily? Enough, to know that the lily and the man eat at the same table, and quench their thirst at a common fountain. We have no answer to enigmas respecting the consciousness of nature; but as Christ set men down by the lily to consider it, they may justly feel that there is a mystery in life of the lowest kinds which compels the conclusion, solemn yet gladsome, that the whole earth is sacred with the presence of God — the very gate of heaven.

The third relation which Christ came to adjust (the first, indeed, in order of importance) was the relation of man to God; and in the consideration of this point we shall ascertain something of what may be distinctively termed Christ's theology — Christ's view and representation of God. Christ revealed God, not by direct religious teaching alone, but by the whole tenor of his course among men. It might have been supposed, had the matter been submitted to conjecture, that in the first instance Christ would have delivered elaborate discourses concerning the Godhead, and, by frank statements about heaven and his own preincarnate position therein, have met and satisfied the natural curiosity of his hearers. It does not appear that Christ adopted the most likely means to accomplish his work; on the contrary, he seems to have done everything to excite suspicion and prejudice, to have tantalized expectation, and mocked the efforts of natural reasoning. We have now to deal with his method of revealing God, and putting man in a right relation to him; and we venture to say that however far conjecture may be disappointed in that method, it will be allowed that no teacher ever represented God in so pleasing and attractive a manner. There is depth enough of solemnity, too. No hearer can feel a disposition towards levity while listening to Christ's expositions of God's nature. God, according to those expositions, is not only unseen, but invisible; no man hath seen him, only the Son; no man but the Son can reveal him: here is majesty, — here a feeling of awe steals over the listener. Assuming the truth of these statements, one conclusion cannot be escaped, viz., that all previous relations and all subsequent doctrines respecting the Godhead must be judged by Christ's words, and accepted only so far as they are consonant with them. No greater claim could be asserted by any teacher than to be the *only* revealer of God. This point should be dwelt upon with most careful reflection. When a man separates himself from all other men, and even confines God himself to one instrument of revelation, he assumes a position dangerous by its very extremity, unless the claim be upheld by irrefragable and universally appreciable proofs.

From Christ's teaching respecting God we learn, in so many words, that God is a Spirit, and that God is a Father, — really the only two things that men require to know about him, all else being involved in those designations. In teaching these doctrines, Christ said that spirit must be met by spirit, and therefore men must be born again; and, secondly, that fatherhood on the part of God must be met by sonship on the part of man, and therefore that he had himself come amongst men as God's Son. These high revelations could not be understood at once, and therefore he approached them from distant points, always, however, keeping his eye steadily upon them. Healing the body was an alphabetic way of saying, "Ye must be born again;" ministering to human want was the same way of saying, "God is your Father." He began at the lowest accessible point, and pursued his way to the ultimate truths. An illustration of this happy method of graduating philanthropic service is given in one of the most dramatic and exciting chapters in the New Testament. In that chapter the hero says, "Whether he be a sinner or no I know not; one thing I know, whereas I was blind, now I see." This "one thing" was the rock from which the man could not be displaced, and he was determined to stand there until he should be called higher. Here is Christ's plan of always being behind a man with a fact, and in front of him with a doctrine. The church is exposed to the peril of taking the doctrine into its care and leaving the fact,—a plan of service as ill adapted to the temper and condition of society now as it was in the days of Christ. Men must be met at the points where remedial ideas are most needed and will be best understood. The blind man needs something more than "the concord of sweet sounds;" in his case effort must be directed to the eye, not to the ear. The man who is perishing of hunger needs bread most, not doctrine or prayer. The soul that is possessed with a devil must first be dispossessed, then taught divine doctrines. Instrumentalities must be adapted to circumstances. This was certainly Christ's plan of movement—not in a sudden and startling manner, bewildering the understanding with a recondite dogma, but quietly joining man at the most accessible point, and charming him into deeper companionship, until he who began as a needy client remained as a consecrated disciple. Christ's skill in adaptation is illustrated sharply by the answer which he returned to John's inquiry: "The blind receive their sight, and the lame walk; the lepers are cleansed, and the deaf hear," — that is to say, every man found in Christ "the piece which was lost:" the deaf were not sharpened in vision, they received their hearing; the blind were not quickened in hearing, they received their sight; the leper was not heightened in stature, he was cleansed of his leprosy. By so working, it was indeed sometimes difficult to see the exact relation of the physical deed to the spiritual purpose of Christ's mission — viz., to reveal the Father. We are tempted to become impatient with Christ as he devotes so much attention to details: it seems almost a waste of time for a man who came to save a world to be lingering over a special case of disease. Could the blind man not have had his soul saved without first having his eyes open? If not, what becomes of the blind men of to-day? We think that we could have hastened Christ's movements, especially in the physical department of his service. Why not speak one healing word for all, so that throughout the land every sick-bed might have been vacated at the same hour? What a magnificent introduction to spiritual labor this would have been! How quickly he could thus have come to his main point — the revelation of God! Yet he lingers over individual cases with a calmness which baffles us, considering how much work lies before him. But is it not the same with him whom we know as Creator? Does he not dally most vexatiously in physical processes? How long a time he takes to mould an ear of corn! And what a waste of power it appears, that the earth should bring forth but one harvest in the year! In his physical service Christ was strikingly like what we know of the Creator. The meaning of this slowness may come to us in the higher spheres. In the mean time, impatience is an infallible sign of weakness.

On the matter of setting man in a right relation to God something further will be said in another chapter: it is introduced here as completing the statement that Christ undertook the adjustment of human relations; and while it is thus before us it may be well to repeat that there is nothing revolting in Christ's representation of God, but everything that is pleasing and satisfying to the tenderest instincts of human nature. God is the Spirit; God is the Father; God is revealed by the Son, and there is no way but through the Son to the Father; God loved the world, and proved his love by the gift of his Son. This is Christ's theology. In Christ's God there is nothing to terrify the heart that yearns for him. He has no thirst for revenge, no bloody decree to execute. He is so tender that a heart-wish will move him; so generous, that he will withhold nothing from them that are reconciled to him. His anger with the wicked is only the recoil of his love of the good. This being so, Christ says — Come to him; be as he is; you misunderstand him if you think evil of him;

I know him better than any other being can ever know him, and I declare unto you that his power and wisdom are equalled by his love. A great speech to make to the human world! How sincere it was we may see when we come to study the Cross of Christ.

CHAPTER XII.

CHRIST THE CONTEMPORARY OF ALL AGES.

HAS the civilization of the nineteenth century rendered Christianity obsolete, or has Jesus Christ made any provision for the development of humanity? Was Christ's merely a day's work done in the usual order of things, or had he a reach over the ages, controlling and moulding them to the very end of the world? Is the New Testament to be shelved with "The Republic" or "The Nicomachean Ethics;" or is it the life of the world that now is, with its ever-varying phases and attitudes, its storms of war, and its revolutions of thought? We may be able to gather an answer from Christ's own words.

Christ repeatedly spoke of his own "hereafter," and of the "hereafter" of the church. His criticisms and instructions were by no means confined to the past and the present; they were full of anticipation, overflowing the hour in which they were spoken and making for themselves a channel through all time. There were terms in his speech which denoted great purposes as to time, persons, and moral victories, — such as "unto the end of the world," "forever," "every creature," "all nations," "east, west, north, and south." It seems to be necessary, therefore, to preserve the logical consistency of Christ's method, that as it was "expedient" for the disciples that he should "go away," that some provision should be made for the expected development of human nature and the requirements of the attendant expansion and refinement of general civilization. The world would certainly become larger, could Christ occupy the extended space? The harvest would be great, was there root-room enough in Christ's heart? Christ entirely reversed what we should have considered the proper order of things, and thus gave another check to anything like presumptuous criticism of his method of redeeming and educating the world. The common plan would probably have assumed some such shape as this — Christ must abide personally among men until the redemptive purpose be fully accomplished, not only on his part, but also on the part of the world; it will be best for him to make short work, and to break up the present economy as soon as he has made clear what is meant by his having been given to save men; or, if he continue the present rude structure of society, his disciples will necessarily have many questions to ask and many difficulties to overcome, and he must be continually at hand, so that the reference may be instant and decisive: when the last man is safe in heaven, and every possible spoil has been recovered from the enemy, then let Christ himself abandon the earth, and take the headship of the glorified church. Instead of this, which looks so feasible and tempting on paper, Christ was actually the first to leave the scene of trial, and his disciples were consequently deprived of the inspiration and comfort of a visible Christ. The poor, simple men had been called to a most trying prominence, and the man who called them took the earliest opportunity of leaving them alone in the world! Under such circumstances, how could the future be other than gloomy and portentous? The disciples were committed to an idea; they bore a name which had a bad repute among all the ecclesiastical leaders and persons of social consequence; they were to carry the cross as their characteristic badge, and to be hated of all men for their Master's sake; as sheep among wolves, they were to make their perilous way. Knowing all this, Christ left them. Would he abandon a half-built tower? Did he leave because his resources were exhausted, or because he could better move the ages from the altitude of the heavens?

We may pause a moment to say, that men can be trained to strength only by being thrown on their own resources in certain determining crises. The parent acts upon this doctrine when he sends his son to a distant school, that he may be thrown into contact with rivals and strengthened by daily contest with eager competitors. There is an educational element in opposition, in suffering, and in provocation, and it is for very love of his child that the parent withdraws the comforts of home and places him in circumstances which will test his nerve and rouse his soul. The lad carries with him all the mingled comfort and pain of home associations, upon which his heart will draw when the stress of events is heavy upon him; in their very absence his parents will be present to him with intenser reality than ever, and the hiding of their face will bring with it a deeper disclosure of their heart.

In some such way, only with infinite expansions of meaning, shall we come to know what was meant by that blank dismay which the disciples must have felt when their Master said he intended to leave them.

It is to be noted that in all Christ's teaching there are manifold references to the future. Many a statement was like a sealed letter, not to be broken but by time. The life which Christ sketched was often an ideal life — beginning in a grain of mustard-seed, ending in a great tree. Again and again he hints at what shall be, and from the dim "hereafter" draws motives for immediate direction. Does not the parent help his child over to-day by talking of to-morrow? It is not upon a near future that Christ dwells, but upon the most distant ranges of terrestrial experience, as a father often tells his son what he shall have when he is a man. With much detail Christ outlined the final assize which he would hold upon "all nations," and from the very evening of the world drew considerations for the government of its morning hours. He thus established a practical relation between the events of all time, uniting human history by stretching the cable of a common Judgment from shore to shore. This was enough, meanwhile. He could not, considering the moral infancy of the disciples, describe every line of latitude and longitude, though each was present to his own mind, but he fixed their eye upon a distant and most conspicuous object, nothing less than himself enthroned in his glory and encircled by his angels, and bade them strike their course over the unknown but not ungoverned waters, so that they might eventually reach it. The men who had been with Christ three years, and heard from his own lips a description of the Judgment day, could not go far wrong in any question that might arise in their experience. The spirit of philanthropy was to be the spirit of judgment. It is very remarkable that Christ should have enabled men to bring the remotest fact of time to bear upon the concerns of the passing moment. We can now make every day a day of Judgment; we know the questions which will come up; we know the standard of appeal; we can anticipate our individual colloquy with the Judge; we can hear his voice; we can "go away into everlasting punishment," or into life eternal. This was a most practical provision which Christ made for the development of humanity: by giving us a Judgment day, he enabled us to try our deeds by the very fire of the final conflagration. All nations were to come to the same judgment, and all were to be tried by one Spirit. It is then, to say the least of it, remarkable, considering how many questions Christ left unanswered, that he should have set before men the transactions of the final hour of human history. This he would not have done had he not contemplated an educational effect.

As yet, however, we have but two points, the very beginning and the very end — Christ's personal ministry and Christ's personal judgment: is there nothing between? Probably the strongest men might be able to traverse the distance between those points, but the strongest men are few in number; what is to become of the hosts who are to be watched and kept like children? — men of unsteady purpose, and perverted faculty of self-judgment? Christ foresaw the difficulty, and provided for it. He had given a personal ministry and sketched the great judgment; but how could he cover the whole line of human history between? This inquiry he answered in a sentence: "When he the Spirit of Truth is come, whom I will send unto you from the Father, he will guide you unto all truth." It may be convenient to say in detail what that Spirit is, so far as we can gather from the Christian writings: he is then (1) the Spirit of truth; (2) the Spirit of comfort; (3) the Spirit of liberty; (4) the Spirit of love; (5) the Spirit of holiness, because the Spirit of God. Now, assuming that these statements are true, it is easy to see how Christ has provided for the multiplying wants of an expanding civilization. This Spirit fills, overflows man's capacity, and meets, with all God-like exuberance, every possible necessity of human nature. So to speak, he surrounds man as well as dwells in him, and according to the outward circumstance as well as the inward condition his ministry is regulated. Thus in the order of revelation we have had first that which is natural, afterwards that which is spiritual; first the sacred letter, then the Holy Spirit. The ancient church was fed with the milk of the Word, the modern church needs strong meat: "strong meat belongeth to them that are full of age, even those who by reason of use have their senses exercised to discern good and evil." Instead of burdening the memory with technicalities, Christ provided for the quickening of the moral faculty in man, and thus, in spiritual things, acted in relation to the human soul as in temporal things God had done. God gives man power to get products out of the soil; but instead of saying this must be eaten and that must be refused, he gives the power, call it instinct or reason, which saves him who rightly uses it from noxious plants and animals. It was better to give the faculty of discrimination than to label all the products of the earth. A spirit is better than a catalogue. There are few things in the lower range of life more remarkable than man's instinct by which he discovers what to eat. Every day he is called upon to choose, even so far as the body is concerned, between life and death. The life of the body is exposed to constant risk. In nearly every field there are roots or leaves which might injure or even destroy the health of the body; yet man continues to make a selection adapted to his nature. These poisonous roots are like so many temptations; they are to the body what vices are to the soul; yet speaking generally — for the exceptions only prove the rule — man is superior to them, he refuses if not resists, and saves himself. How is this? Is there not a spirit in man, and doth not the inspiration of the Almighty give him understanding? "This also cometh forth from the Lord of Hosts, which is wonderful in counsel and excellent in working." It may be asked, How has God provided for material civilization? and the answer is, By the spirit that is in man; so it may be asked, How has Christ provided for intellectual expansion, and the corresponding claims which the intellect would present? and the answer is substantially the same. When Christ opened the eyes of the blind, he did not require to create another universe that the vision might have an object to rest upon; the universe was there, waiting to be looked at. So the universe of truth has existed from the beginning, and as there are steep hills, perilous precipices, intricate winding ways, and not a few tangled forest-paths, he has promised the Spirit to guide men into all truth; emphatically to *guide* men, the very word implying difficulty, danger, and constantly new evolutions and combinations; not only to guide, but to guide into *all* truth; not into some departments, but into all; not into external views of truth, but into its very essence, so that men might know truth under every disguise, and be able to eliminate it from every sophism and every heresy. We know what it is to be so far in sympathy with the spirit of a companion as to be able to pronounce an opinion about any of his reputed actions; instantly we say such a charge or statement is true or false; so entire is our mutual accord, that judgment of him is like judgment of our own heart. Our companion, if of a strong character, has put his spirit into us, and instinctively we have come to know whether any report of him is likely to be true or untrue; we know so well his magnanimity that we resent the imputation of any ignoble deed which rumor may connect with his name, or accept with thankfulness any report which details his excellences — in this case our spirit witnesses with the spirit of the report that it is true. In a modified degree this represents the relation of Christians to Christ; that relation is so intimate, so vital indeed, nothing less than consubstantiality having been effected by eating his flesh and drinking his blood, that they can unhesitatingly determine the truth or untruth of any proposition concerning him, and infallibly distinguish between a legitimate expansion of his doctrines and a distortion of them.

The intercommunion between the spirit of man and the Spirit of God, an intercommunion re-established and enlarged by Christ, is the guarantee of purity and progress on the part of the church. By Christ's ministry we are now elevated to the highest plane, and the words of John have a deep meaning: "The anointing which ye have received of him abideth in you, and ye need not that any man teach you." The teaching of the church does not now come from the outside; Christians have *in* them a well of water springing up into eternal life. They judge the preacher and the author by the anointing which they have received of the Holy One, and by their own spirit are able to try all other spirits, whether they are of God. The witness of the Spirit changes the aspect and meaning of all outward things. The Christian writings themselves are valuable in proportion as the spirit of the reader is enlightened by the Spirit that dictated them. The dead man is heedless of the sumptuous banquet: the dead soul is as heedless of the richer banquet of revelation. There must be two witnessing spirits. The sun is nothing to the blind man: give him vision, and the sun becomes his day. Christ thus provides for details by providing for universals. He gives life, and he gives the Holy Ghost to guide life; and in these two, yet indivisible gifts, all things necessary for human cultivation are included. The world had no adequate notion of *life* until Christ came; in fact, so vast is the volume of life which he offers, that it may be almost literally said that Christ brought life and immortality to *light*, as things not known before; not only life and immortality as future blessings, but as present and immediately available realities.

The speculative life of the church is marked by an immense variety of results. Hardly any two thinkers have adapted precisely the same conclusions. How is this to be accounted for, if they have been illuminated and directed by the same Spirit? Easily and satisfactorily. Life is not to be judged by formal logic. Ask two travellers who have completed the same journey to describe the course they have taken, with all the incidents. They have traversed the same road, on the same day, under the same conditions, yet the statement of the one is meagre, the statement of the other minute. How so? They walked under the same light, and the great volume of the landscape lay open before them. The difference is in the mental habitudes of the observers. The eye of the one was trained; the eye of the other was uneducated. The same thing is illustrated in the reading of a book: one reader is instructed, another disappointed. And this diversity, when the spirit of censoriousness is excluded, is fruitful of good. It provokes to deeper and more continuous investigation; it saves the intellectual world from monotony, stagnation, and death; it creates a generous interest in the gifts of fellow-inquirers. There is even a higher benefit: it shows that no one man has all the truth; it breaks up monopoly, it destroys infallibility. There is a truth on every side of polemic theology; and just as men of every clime and race are necessary to make up the entire of God's idea of humanity, so every degree of truth, and every aspect of truth, must be brought together, if we would see the totality of God's doctrine. One nation has caught its poetry, another its logic; one has condensed it into maxims, another has elaborated it into most complex philosophies; no two of them are agreed as to nomenclature; still the doctrine, like its author, is One, though now it is as steady as a star, and anon it heaves like the billows of the sea.

But these are speculative differences merely; it still remains to inquire how moral aberrations are to be accounted for. The answer is, that they are to be accounted for on moral grounds. Paul admonishes men not to grieve the Spirit, and not to quench the Spirit. The Spirit is a "guide," not a tyrant. The Spirit remains with any man only so long as that man is a consenting party. The Spirit may have taught the right way, yet the heart may have rejected the teaching. "Video meliora proboque, deteriora sequor." Christ said to the Pharisees, "If ye were blind, ye should have no sin: but now ye say, We see; therefore your sin remaineth." The same principle is asserted by an apostle who lays down the doctrine: "To him that knoweth to do good, and doeth it not, to him it is sin." So long as man is man, he must have the power of resisting God; and so long as God is God, he must wait until the heart-door be opened from the inside. Omnipotence itself cannot force hearts.

By laying down a few universal principles, sketching a kind of river-map, and giving the Spirit of Truth to be a constant indwelling guest of the soul, Christ is as truly, as potentially, present with this age as he was with his immediate followers in Judæa. This, indeed, is not the whole of the fact. Of every great man it may be justly said that he is more influentially present after his death than during his life. Shakspeare exerts a wider influence to-day than in the days of his flesh; so does Milton; so does Luther; but not so Hannibal, or Cæsar in his military aspect, for destroyers must decrease, but creators must increase. Men's names are kept up with men's sayings. It is remarkable, as an eminent observer of human nature has said, that the question is not only what is said, but *who* said it? So that the saying is associated with the person; and if the saying be strong enough to keep pace with the march of the generations, its author may be said to be with men "even unto the end of the world." What is true in degree of thinkers is true, in an absolute sense, of the man in whom dwelt all the fulness of the Godhead bodily. Notwithstanding the fierce iconoclasm of the age, a hard statement bearing the name of Milton will secure a more reverent hearing than if it were pronounced anonymously. This is right. In the heat and prejudice of controverted times it is well to withhold the name, but whoever speaks a word that goes to the world's heart will quicken an eager desire on the part of those whom he has benefited to have his personality identified. Christ will never be dissociated from Christ's sayings, and in this way he will be with his people unto the end of the world, but in a still deeper way — deeper because the words will receive continually broadening interpretations by the Holy Ghost, and be more urgently and powerfully applied to human experience. The first reading cannot bring out all the meaning of the words. It flows like the oil which the prophet blessed. The few words of Christ have expanded into libraries; the poet has sung them, the painter has painted them; and to-day unnumbered thousands are eating the bread which is distributed by his hand. Seminally, at least, everything in morals can be found in Christ. No man has spoken truths so deep, so far-reaching, and with this remarkable circumstance in addition — he was the first speaker upon the themes which he discussed, he borrowed nothing, he created all. He outlined the most comprehensive theories; sketched plots which poets might work out; gave rebukes which showed the distance which lay between him and all hypocrites, oppressors, and self-seekers; and uttered promises which have sunk into the sorrowing hearts of all subsequent generations. He is thus, and not thus only, with men unto the end of the world.

Christ said that he came to give men life, and to give it " more abundantly." In this latter expression he hinted his relation to the great question of human development — showed that man would never outgrow him, and, in fact, that there was no growth apart from his own vitalizing energy. A generous sophism lurks in the supposition that one man is as good as another, or even that one man is as much a man as another. Manhood varies — varies in volume and purity. Man grows from his original condition — by imperceptible increments, indeed — yet he still grows, if the true life be in him, so that two becomes four, and five ten; and as certainly as he grows he becomes liberated from the obscurity and humiliation which marked his starting-point. Human nature is, of course, primordially the same, but its possible degrees of development are infinite; and it cannot but be a fact of immense importance in this argument, that in those countries where most about Christ is known, every science and every art is most liberally patronized. The light which Christ sheds upon the world has never been proved to be unfavorable to the highest intellectual cultivation, but *has* been proved — and, in fact, is being proved every day — to be in the highest degree favorable to all that can be legitimately classified under the term progress. As a simple matter of fact, Christ is to-day increasing the life of the world. Take a common case: An English Arab is taken off the streets by a Christian philanthropist, and placed under religious instruction; he is taught, for the time, something of his nature and something of his destiny; according to his capacity the instruction is continued to him; by and by he comes to feel that in some little degree he is human, that he has wonderful powers, that he may *be* good and *do* good: so far the philanthropist has given him "life;" — still the culture proceeds, ideas take a wider range; the philanthropist conducts him from point to point in the circumference of knowledge, hoping to find the point most adapted to the youth's capability. At length it is found, and the quondam Arab becomes an explorer, or scientific student, or a man of letters, and so has not only "life," but "life more abundantly," — precisely as Christ promised. Who called him from the dead, and made him a revealer of life to others? Can the scantest justice hesitate as to an answer? There are, however, we may probably be reminded, many men illustrious in science who are not, in the generally accepted sense of the term, or perhaps in any sense of the term, " followers of Christ;" — in what relations do they stand to the Life-giver? They may come under Christ's own classification, " They that are not against us are for us." But what if they are " against" Christ? Then they certainly should not require to be reminded that the whole atmosphere is, so to speak, Christian. All the forces of modern civilization have taken effect under decidedly Christianized conditions, and the more truly scientific mind will be the last to doubt the remote, subtle, and most penetrating influence of what may be termed *moral climate*. The whole air in which the intellect moves is charged with Christian elements; and no scientific man would be speaking *secundum artem* if he denied, at least, their probable influence on the whole current of opinion and practice. There may be a difficulty, in some minds, in tracing the connection between Christian thought and purely scientific pursuit; even Aristotle confesses that it is " difficult to say how a weaver or carpenter would be benefited, with reference to his own art, by knowing the self-good;" yet reflection may be able to trace even this apparently remote relationship. Whatever liberates the mind from low and self-seeking purposes, whatever brings it into more intensely conscious contact with the absolute, gives the whole man a wider and firmer mastery over all that is below and around him. The idea is illustrated partially by the admitted effect of high classical culture upon the discussion of general questions of political and literary life. The man who has been thoroughly drilled in ancient literature will, other things being equal, be better able to discuss subjects of common interest, to trace their bearings and forecast their consequences, than the unlettered man; not that there may be any very patent connection between philology and politics, but because of the severe intellectual discipline and consequent self-mastery which such drill necessitates. Even allowing that Aristotle is right in suggesting the difficulty of seeing how a weaver or carpenter could be benefited in his own art by knowing the "self-good," it is obvious that the more any man knows of any great subject, the less likelihood is there of his continuing in the position of a weaver or carpenter. Intellectual vitality signifies social elevation; and though some may be disposed to raise the grave question, "How could society dispense with its weavers or carpenters?" yet our business relates primarily to the higher considerations, forasmuch as the *man* is of more importance than the *weaver*. When manhood rises, the industrial arts will feel the effect of the elevation.

The inquiry is, "How did Christ propose to make himself not only the contemporary, but the king of all ages?" To this inquiry our answer has been, (1) By a personal ministry; (2) By a fully delineated Judgment; and (3) By the gift of the Spirit of Truth, whose peculiar function it is to take of the things of Christ, and show them unto the church. It has been admitted by the latest writer on the life of Christ, that Christ could, even after his personal withdrawment, visit his people " in refreshing inspirations and great acts of providential justice ; " this admission really covers the whole question of Christ's contemporaneousness with all ages, for if he can visit his people at all in " refreshing inspirations and great acts of providential justice," he is necessarily (if faithful to himself) the chief factor in human development on the Christian side.

CHAPTER XIII.

THESE SAYINGS OF MINE.

CHRIST was pre-eminently a talker. "Never man spake like this man," was the testimony of his enemies. After reading the doctrines of Plato, Socrates, or Aristotle, we feel that the specific difference between their words and Christ's is the difference between an Inquiry and a Revelation. We feel as if at any moment they might push a speculation too far, or suddenly turn off at a wrong angle — as if they were groping their way along dim and perilous paths, throwing gossamers over the dark rivers, and tempting men to walk over the unsubstantial bridge; again and again they run the risk of exalting a riddle into a problem, or settling a definition into a law. With this the method of Jesus Christ most strikingly contrasts. There is, account for it as men please, an authority in every tone; his language is clear, and if short, it is final; it never betrays the faintest sign of hesitancy on the part of the speaker; if it were an immediate revelation from Heaven, there could not be a sharper outline or a firmer emphasis. Thus much may be said simply as a matter of criticism, without any prejudgment of the doctrine. It has been suggested that he spoke with " the authoritative tone and earnestness of a Jew," but this suggestion, if meant for an explanation, is pointless: Christ was not the only Jew who had spoken; and if "authoritativeness of tone" be characteristic of Jewish teaching, it should be borne in mind that Christ was openly and repeatedly *contradicted* by men who spoke with "the authoritative tone and earnestness of a Jew," — by the doctors of the law, by the teachers and leaders of the people, by men who held the historic parchments of the land; so that in all fairness " tone " should be set against " tone," and it should then be explained how the " tone " of the peasant overpowered the " tone " of great councils or solemn sanhedrims. The case, too, is more strongly in favor of Christ, when it is remembered that he abrogated institutions which had existed for ages under the special sanction of God. Moses, it will be allowed, spoke with " the authoritative tone and earnestness of a Jew," yet Christ abolished much that Moses had inaugurated. Isaiah, Jeremiah, and Daniel spoke with " the authoritative tone and earnestness of a Jew," yet they spoke of another, not of themselves; but Christ was his own theme and his own expositor. His immediate disciples would not be wanting in " the authoritative tone and earnestness of a Jew," yet every one of them did his wonderful works, not in his own name, but in the name of Christ. Looking, therefore, simply at the facts, it must be admitted, even in a fuller sense than that conveyed by his enemies, that " never man spake like this man," — not even Moses, not the great seers of Israel, not Elijah on Carmel, not John in the wilderness, nor the contemporary disciples; — he was what he distinctly claimed to be, — separate from all, because greater than all.

The manner in which Christ's followers have reported him is truly marvellous, — a point which calls for serious thought on the part of all who wish to go carefully through the incidental and tributary evidence. In our own day it is so common to have reports of speeches, that we think little of them; though in many cases so wonderful, yet they have come to be regarded as matters of course. But the disciples were not shorthand writers; we do not find that one of them was elected clerk, and that in the evening of each day he made entries in a common journal which all could read and revise; yet they report his discourses often in the first person, and preserve all the sharpness and vivacity of dialogue, retort, extemporaneous definition, and appeal. We feel throughout that we are reading the words of a talker, not of an author; all the sharp edge of free speech is singularly preserved; so much so that with the least effort of imagination, we can be present at the delivery of every discourse, or at every passage at arms, between Christ and his opponents. A strange, yet pleasant feeling of *nearness* to the event steals over every reader of the evangelic story; no lengthening shadows of distance diminish the reader's interest; everything is at hand! In reading *The Laws* we are always conscious of the presence of an artist. Plato has, indeed, arranged all the parts taken by the Guest, Clinias, and Megillus with great skill, determining the proportions and balancing the conversation with a very fine appreciation of the requirements of the dialogue; yet throughout the elaborate production, we feel that it is all *art*, all the work of one master, who in the retirement of his home apportioned and decided everything so as to work out the particular object he intended to compass. On the other hand, in reading the Gospels we feel that everything is life-like, spontaneous, and unfinished, yet suggestive and provocative of thought beyond anything that has ever come from the tongue or pen of man. Yet these Gospels contain no prepared speeches, no formal compositions — nothing but "sayings," often jagged, broken, unconnected, yet singularly full of life. The youngest author could make a better mechanical arrangement, but the oldest could utter no such electric words. Plato's Definitions are practically forgotten, but the Nazarene's words intermingle with universal civilization; and this is the more remarkable as they were not formally arranged. A great composer said that he was spending a long time over his work because he intended it to live long, but this Galilean peasant talks extemporaneously, as if simply answering the question of the hour; yet his words float over all generations, and are prized by men to-day as if they had been addressed exclusively to themselves. This is, perhaps, the most wonderful characteristic of the words of Jesus. Can this be accounted for by "the authoritative tone and earnestness of a Jew"? Is it not rather to be accounted for by "the authoritative tone and earnestness" of the Son of *Man?* These "sayings" are not local lamps, but suns set in the firmament commanding the range of all nations. The Nicomachean Ethics are certainly distinguished by a marvellous comprehension of the peculiarities of human nature; yet who will say that the words of Aristotle are quick with the same intensity of life that is characteristic of the "sayings" of Christ? They are, no doubt, wise, critical, and often most practical; yet the minuteness of definition and the tedious redundancy of detail give them a scholastic air which is little adapted to the tumultuous life of all nations. The best philosophies of the ancient civilization descend so much into detail as to leave no scope for the play of life on the part of the reader. Everything is numbered, labelled, docketed, — there it is, take it, or be a fool. Plato, as before pointed out, was so voluminous in his details, going from statesmanship, philosophy, science, and rhetoric to early rising, hunting, dancing, money-lending, and Sicilian cookery, as to give one the idea that he undertook to do the work of a domestic gasfitter rather than to bring men into the light of the sun. He is so minute as to place a lamp at the corner of every street, at the entrance of every house, and in every room of every habitation. He was a very skilful gasfitter, and very careful; he ran his trial-light over every tube and every tap, but it may be doubted whether, after all, he was more than a painstaking gasfitter, — a high character, too, considering the general darkness of his time. Now, Christ, instead of intermeddling with artificial or secondary light, at once, with something more than "the authoritative tone and earnestness of a Jew," announced himself as "the Light of the world," — not Holman Hunt's "Light of the World," who resembles a belated and forlorn traveller carrying a lantern, but a man who had the light *in* him, and through whom it gleamed like the sun through a summer cloud. Plato lighted his age with gas, Christ lighted the world with the sun; the one was local, the other universal; the one changeable, the other permanent. The heathen philosophers gave directions, Christ gave *life*. Aristotle expounded diametrical conjunction; Christ said, "As ye would that men should do unto you, do ye even so unto them." Cicero wrote excellent advices on friendship; Christ said, "Love thy neighbor as thyself." Plato wrote wise prescriptions for particular diseases; Christ infused his own life into men. The Pythagoreans wrote for favorite circles; Christ sent his gospel to "all nations." Aristotle quotes from Plato, Plato refers to Homer, and the pages of Cicero abound with quotations and allusions; but Christ quotes immediately from the Father, and by so much speaks the universal language.

Christ does not appeal to men as the heathen philosophers did. They ask opinions, court criticism, and even the wily and garrulous Socrates gives men an opportunity of differing from him; but Christ, with "the authoritative tone and earnestness" of the Son of God, says, "This is absolute; believe it and be saved, or reject it and be damned." He says that he came from the Father, that he speaks the word of the Father, and that he is returning to the Father. So there is nothing between him and God; immediately behind him, though invisible, lies infinitude, and he sets himself up as the medium on which the voice of the Infinite is broken into human sounds. When a man says, "I came forth from the Father, and am come into the world; again I leave the world, and go unto the Father," he simply excludes controversy;

there is no common ground between him and his interlocutors; and, when his words are sustained by such mighty deeds as abound in the life of Christ, one of two conclusions is inevitable — either the man is speaking the most sublime truth or he is uttering the most awful falsehoods. He cannot occupy any middle position. No man may make himself "equal with God," and yet pass in society merely as a good man. The morality of language would be violated. All human relations would be disorganized. The term "God" might be used to palm off the most infamous charlatanism, and all exactness of language would be supplanted by the exaggerations of an inflamed and incoherent ideality.

At the risk of speaking paradoxically, it may be said that the sayings of Christ are divine because they are so human, and are human because they are so divine. "He knew what was in man," and this knowledge of human nature was his great weapon alike of attack and defence. The intense humanness of Christ's life is perhaps most seen and felt in his never-failing sympathy with all the conditions of human experience. When he tells men not to think about what they are to eat, it is because he himself is thinking about that subject for them, and is prepared to feed them with his own hand: when he calls men to courage, he means them to draw upon his own power: when he says, "Seek first the kingdom of God," he is prepared to make up all that is wanting for the daily life. He repeatedly referred to his miracles in order to stimulate the faith of his followers; — " How many baskets full of fragments took ye up?" He thus made recollection the ground of hope by teaching that divine power was not exhausted by the performance of a single miracle. There is a kind of power which exhausts itself in one great effort, but it is not *living* power; it is mechanical, not dynamical; and, though it be seen in human history, it is a spasm of weakness, not the throb of a healthy heart. Christ told men that the power which had worked one miracle could work another, and that what was given was but a hint of the resources that were untouched. This could not but substantially aid the effect of his teaching respecting that all-exciting and ever-pressing subject — TO-MORROW. To most men "to-morrow" had been a spectre, but Christ showed how it might be an angel. When men looked forward to it with fear, Christ inquired, with the slightest tremor of reproach in his tone, "How many baskets full of fragments took ye up?" Christ never held history in contempt. He made yesterday the prophet of to-morrow. All this personality of appeal, combined with all this practical demonstration of carefulness for human comfort, showed that Christ never talked *at* men, but always *to* them. His humanness was his power. Apart from it he never could have been so great a talker. Men would have become weary, but in his company they were insensible of the flight of time. Men that heard him only on one set of subjects left him, but those who had heard him on the deepest questions said, "To whom can we go? Thou hast the words of eternal life." The heart lived on such music.

There is one peculiarity about the "sayings" of

Christ which is not claimed by the great philosophers, and which cannot be accounted for by "the authoritative tone and earnestness of a Jew;" that is to say, Christ's "sayings" determined the destiny of all who heard them, and this peculiarity he specially pointed out as enduring forever. To have heard these "sayings" is to have incurred the gravest responsibility. A man may read the Ethics of Aristotle, and treat the reasoning with contempt without endangering his fate; but no man can read Christ's "sayings" without finding "saved" upon one side and "damned" upon the other. Is this dogmatism on the part of Christ? Undoubtedly. God must be dogmatic. If God could hesitate, he would not be God. Do we stumble at the solemn words, "He that believeth shall be saved; he that believeth not shall be damned"? Why should we? An agriculturist says practically, "Go ye into all the world, and say to every creature that there is a particular season for sowing seed: he that believeth shall be saved — shall have a harvest; he that believeth not shall be lost — shall have no harvest." There is thus a gospel of agriculture: why not a gospel of salvation? Men's disbelief of God will damn them in farming; why not in religion? Does God speak decisively in the one case and hesitatingly in the other? There must be a climacteric point — a point of saving or damning — in all the declarations of God, because he has spoken the *ultimate* word on all the subjects which he has disclosed. The *truth* upon any matter, high or low, is the point of salvation or damnation. The man who merely points out the right road to a traveller is in a position (with proper modification of the terms) to say to that traveller, "He that believeth shall be saved; he that believeth not shall be damned:" in other words, "Go thus and you will reach the object of your journey, but go so and you will never reach it." This is the position which Christ assumes, "He that believeth me hath life; he that believeth not me hath not life." Is such a projection of his personality consistent with his being simply one who spoke with "the authoritative tone and earnestness of a Jew"?

In the "sayings" of Christ special prominence is given to a peculiar form of teaching known as Parables. The entire history of religious thought might be written under the twofold division of Dogma and Parable. We are passing through what may be emphatically characterized as the *parabolic era*, taking its tone and order of procession from the transitional and most excited state of the intellectual world. In periods of intellectual quiescence, it is found that the religious world is settled firmly upon theological dogma; but, in periods of great intellectual agitation in scientific and philosophical inquiry, the religious idea passes into what may be called the *parabolic phase;* not that dogma is, or can be, destroyed, but that the mental nature is engaged upon problems rich, truly or deceitfully, in their promise of results. This is illustrated vividly in Christ's own method of teaching. First he gave doctrine, then he gave parable; the first met the positive want of the *religious* nature, and the second stimulated all that was best on the ideal side of the *intellectual* nature. In this manner Christ escaped the stern and cold finality which is characteristic not only of all exclusively dogmatic teaching, but of all teaching that is narrow, shallow, and vulgar. In Christ's "sayings" there was always something beyond, — a quickening sense that the words were but the surface of the thought; there was nothing to betoken conclusion, much less exhaustion; there was ever a luminous opening even on the clouds that lay deepest along the horizon, which invited the spectator to advance and behold yet fuller visions. The dogma was decisive; but the parable set the heart longing for closer intercourse with the parabolist. The dogma marked the distance which had been travelled; the parable pointed to the distance which lay far ahead; dogma was finished like *yesterday*, parable had about it all the haze, yet all the promise and allurement, of *morrow*. It was thus that in a unique sense Christ brought out of his treasure " things *new*," and maintained his hold upon the ages, filling and satisfying their entire capacity of vision and desire. The parable takes the inquirer farther along the line of truth than the dogma does. It stands in relation to dogma as poetry to prose. Even the dogmatic arithmetician calls in the aid of the parabolic algebraist at a certain point in the science of numbers; and, from what may be described as the parabolic side of truth, pushes his inquiries farther than he could have done by the narrow dogmas of simple arithmetic. He is carried forward by symbolism which is founded on dogma, yet which reaches, ideally, farther than dogma; and, when the symbolic arithmetician says, "Let x represent the unknown quantity," he says in his own special sphere of inquiry what Christ says in his loftiest region of research when he says, "The kingdom of heaven is like *unto* —." The kingdom of heaven is the "unknown quantity" which Christ came to reveal, and he helped men to follow him in his wonderful processes by saying, "Let a grain of mustard seed, let a costly pearl, let a man sowing good seed in his field, let leaven, which a woman cast into three measures of meal, let a net cast into the sea, represent the unknown quantity." Religious symbolism gives scope for all that is most profitable in fancy, speculation, or the great dramatic element which is in every man. It provides for the enthusiasm of the renewed nature, for that "madness" which Plato declares to be essential to poet and prophet. It gives such an idea of the unexplained range of thought and the possibilities of mind, as goes far to explain and justify the bold saying of the ancient Sophists, that " probabilities were more to be valued than truths."

> "True fiction hath in it a higher end
> Than fact; it is the possible compared
> With what is merely positive, and gives
> To the conceptive soul an inner world,
> A higher, ampler heaven than that wherein
> The nations sun themselves."

In connection with his parabolic teaching Christ uttered one most remarkable "saying" to his disciples. He had been indulging in most varied and vivid symbolism, and as he concluded he said, "Have ye understood all these things? They say unto him, Yea, Lord. Then said he unto them, Therefore every scribe which is instructed unto the kingdom of heaven is like unto a man that is an householder, which bringeth forth out of his treasure things new and old." Here is the liberty of the Christian teacher: can any charter be more comprehensive? It comprehends all that is past and all that is to come; it is as old as time, yet new as summer. Thus interpreted, Christ becomes, as was said in the last chapter, not only the contemporary, but the leader of every age. He has the old truth for the heart, and the new phase for the eye. He meets the simple and trustful with "old things," and encounters the doctors of all temples with questions they cannot answer, and symbolism which, while it challenges their admiration, puts to the severest test their genius for the interpretation of signs. Christ proceeds upon the principle that the world must be educated by enigmas, pictures, and problems, and he has commissioned his Church to educate it on this basis. He shows that all human life is a parable, and that to understand it men must follow him now as his disciples did aforetime, and ask him to "declare unto them the parable." The difficulty of our agitated time is to find men who combine the dogmatist with the parabolist; the chasm has occasioned very urgent, ungenerous, and bitter strife. It is forgotten that the Dogmatist may be right so far as he goes, and that the Parabolist may be equally right; what is wanted is completion by amalgamation; but where, in the present chaos of religious questions, can we hope to find a perfect education? The reverent inquirer, though he be a sceptic (not a derisive and self-idolatrous buffoon), may after all be a brother who has, by the very bent of his mental constitution, begun his studies rather on the parabolic than on the dogmatic side of truth, and who yet will descend from the quaking and lightning-girt hill of symbolism with two tables of very stern and decisive dogma.

This recalls the fact that men proceed even in religious inquiry according to the base of their intellectual nature. Some men are prepared for dogma at once, and beyond dogma they can never move. To them, Christian theology (we will not say Christian ethics) is little better than an embalmed mummy hidden in the solemn pyramid of the past, to be visited on Sabbatic occasions, looked at, admired, and left in awful solitude and silence until the next visit. To men of another and better mould, "the kingdom of heaven is *like unto*" all that is elevating in life, or permanent in beauty, or pure in love, or satisfying in truth. What wonder if such men fail to understand one another, or if the word of strife be heard in the discussion of subjects which belong to the innermost shrine of the Temple of Peace? The cause of such strife is not so much to be found on the side of religious inquiry as on the side of human nature. Man does not understand man when separated by one degree of latitude; nay, man may speak a foreign language even to his own brother. Now it is distinctly stated that Jesus "knew all men, and needed not that any should testify of man, for he knew what was in man;" that is to say, he had a perfect knowledge of human nature, and in his teaching he set "the kingdom of heaven" at every variety of angle, so that all men might get that particular view of it which would most successfully meet their wants. This could be done only by a teacher who had a perfect knowledge of the nature which he undertook to educate. No mental characteristic escaped him. Every mood of the soul elicited from him the proper response. The consequence was, that he was not followed by any particular class of men, but all men went after him — the multitude after the multitudinous man. His disciples are of course but fractional men, and the power of the Christian ministry is proportionately impaired. The preacher's accent often makes him a stranger to his hearers. He is of course limited by his own individuality, and how can the shallow river of his thought carry the merchandise of the world? The preacher's power must always be in the ratio of his knowledge of human nature. The more of *man* he has in him, the more he will command the attention and homage of men. He is but a learned fool who knows everything but himself. His teaching will be confined to a few self-contained dogmas; it will never give signs of that prophetic fire which shrines itself in poesy or parable. In discoursing upon rhetoric, Socrates wisely touches upon this subject of human nature. He tells Phædrus that, "since the power of speech is that of leading the soul, it is necessary that he who means to be an orator should know how many kinds of soul there are." And again he says, "Unless a man has reckoned up the different natures of those who will have to hear him, and is able to divide things themselves into species, and to comprehend the several particulars under one general idea, he will never be skilled in the art of speaking so far as it is possible for a man to be so;" a most marvellous illustration of the power of him who spake as never man spake, who needed not that any should testify of men, for he knew what was in man. He varied the prescription according to the diagnosis. To one man he said, "Sell all thou hast;" to another, "Ye must be born again;" to a third, "Keep the two commandments of the law:" he took the wise in their own craftiness, and upon the vision of the dreamer he opened such glories as had never shone from the artificial heavens of the poets.

We may claim for Christ's "sayings" an originality, a compass, and living energy such as have not been rivalled by any speaker. This would probably be admitted even by the more self-controlled class of sceptics. Assuming this to be so, we are thrown back upon an old inquiry, "Whence hath this man this wisdom and these mighty works? Is not this the carpenter's son? Is not his mother called Mary, and his brethren James, and Joses, and Simon, and Judas? And his sisters, are they not all with us? Whence, then, hath this man all these things?" That question remains to be answered by those who deny his Godhead. Viewed from the human stand-point, how could Christ's contemporaries be other than confounded by Christ's wisdom? Can any man rise above the normal conditions of his race? Is there a secret way from the nethermost stratum of society up to the eminence of superhuman wisdom? How is it that only one man has ventured on the giddy ascent? His "sayings" have no charm of style; poetic surprises are never attempted; nearly everything is curt, abrupt, and barely allusive, yet to-day, as in the days of his flesh, all who weigh his words come to the conclusion that "never man spake like this man." Is there no argument in this?

CHAPTER XIV.

ETERNAL PUNISHMENTS.

IT is held by many to be a hard thing that any man should be damned for not believing "these sayings of mine." This conclusion must have been reached through a most incomplete apprehension of the term "belief." In the course of this argument, we have had repeated occasion to state that a man's belief is that by which his whole life is governed, — the foundation of his character, the very vitality of his manhood. It can hardly be repeated too often, that belief is not a mere mental assent to a proposition, but the resting and consequent risking of the whole life upon the truth of that proposition.

By setting aside, for the moment, the term "belief" on account of the narrow theological associations which have been unjustly gathered around it, the point may to some extent be elucidated by another word which has no such associations attaching to it, — that word is *character*. Now, as we have found ourselves at liberty, on the authority of Christ himself, to reason from the human towards the divine, let us in a familiar manner try what can be done by an analogical process. Is there anything in the constitution of human society which will throw at least an edge of light around the awful mystery of endless punishment?

It will not be denied, at the onset, that there are many persons whom a virtuous man would not admit to his confidence or hospitality. Ask the reason, and the answer will be, " The persons have lost their good character, — they are dissipated, vicious, and altogether unworthy of respect or confidence." Here, then, is a point to begin at. It is conceded by this answer that purity of character is the indispensable qualification for admission into virtuous society, and by so much it is shown that a bad man is " damned," ostracized (or soften it into unrecognized), solely on the ground of vice. But what is vice? Is it not the practical side of *belief?* The man believes in vice as a principle, or a policy, or an enjoyment, and therefore he pursues it. But by pursuing it he becomes socially a condemned man; he that believeth not (he that is not virtuous) is damned. It may be urged that a man may have many heterodox notions about religion, and yet his social repute may be irreproachable; and on the other hand, that a man's notions about religion may be orthodox, while his life is sinful. This is true, but it merely throws us back upon a definition already laid down, viz., that belief is not intellectual, but moral: " with the *heart* man believeth unto righteousness; " so that religion is not a question of mere notions, but the expression of the entire spiritual life. It would be as logical to contend that a man is going a journey because he can explain the construction of an engine as to contend that a man is going to heaven because he can correctly answer theological questions. Salvation turns upon spiritual vitality, and spiritual vitality is represented by the right use of the term *faith*. It must never be absent from the mind that religion is not a set of opinions, but life in Jesus Christ. So far, then, we find society doing precisely what God does, viz., drawing a broad line of demarcation between the virtuous and the vicious, — in other words, *establishing a system of rewards and punishments based exclusively on morals.* Society has found this to be necessary to its own preservation and prosperity, for all history has gone to show that, apart from every theological system, the *moral element* has always determined the true value of civilization. Virtue has meant safety; vice has meant danger. This is a fact of immense value in an inductive inquiry respecting rewards and punishments.

It is now proposed to show that, in the matter of endless punishment for sin, society does, in its degree, precisely what Almighty God is declared in the Christian writings to do. If God punishes the finally impenitent forever, man does the same thing, and does it *necessarily* — necessarily because of the demands of the moral universe without, as well as the exactions of the moral principle within. In other words, the very constitution of the moral universe demands and necessitates the endless punishment of the impenitent. How we may work our way to this conclusion will now appear.

It is objected that there is no proportion between time and eternity, and, consequently, that to punish man eternally for doing wrong in his short lifetime is inequitable. While it is not denied that punishment is merited, it is contended that there should be some proportion between the crime and the penalty.

In answer to this objection, let us examine the law of proportion in the light of social laws. Does the idea of proportion amount roughly to this, that a day's crime should be met by a day's punishment; that a man who does wrong to-day should be punished to-morrow, and restored to confidence the day after? The objector will probably say, "No, not exactly that; but say that a day's crime should be met by a month's punishment, or a year's; only let there be some proportion between the crime and the penalty." The answer does not relieve the difficulty. What is the moral proportion between one day and a month, or one day and a year? Does nothing depend on the nature of the crime? For example: a man commits a petty larceny; would the objector say that a month's imprisonment would be enough? Another man, say, commits murder; would the objector say that a year's punishment would suffice? But why should the one criminal be punished a month and the other a year? It is urged that the nature of the crime determines that. Let this be granted; then it will appear that the proportion is really not one of time, but of *turpitude*. In reality society proceeds upon the principle that the extent of time occupied in the perpetration of a criminal act is not to be taken into account in considering the punishment which is to be awarded. Nor ought it to be accounted of. Less time may be occupied in taking away a life than in committing a burglary; but, on the principle of strict proportion (which sophistically proceeds on the idea of mere duration), the burglar should undergo a longer punishment than the murderer. But society will not allow this; its moral instincts overrule its sentimentalities, and demand that the gravity of the crime should determine the gravity of the punishment.

An illustration may be useful here. Thirty years ago, let it be supposed, a criminal forged the reader's name to a check for a thousand guineas. He did it in a few moments; a stroke or two of the skilled pen, and the deed was done. The criminal never confessed the act; never uttered a penitential word; he suffered imprisonment for ten years; and now for twenty years he has been at large. Has the reader forgiven him? Has he restored him to confidence? Has he invited the offender into his family circle? Has he replaced him at the commercial desk? The reader says, "No." But what becomes of the argument of proportion? Let it be remembered that the criminal was imprisoned ten years for a crime committed in less than ten minutes. Was not the punishment sufficient? Think of ten minutes being multiplied into ten years, and then say whether more can be reasonably demanded. But it may be urged that the criminal is impenitent; he never owns his sin, never asks forgiveness, and treats the injured man as if he himself had been injured. The injured man is so far philanthropic as to say that he will meet the criminal on the first sign of contrition — he only waits an acknowledgment of the guilt and promise of better behavior. Nothing can be more humane, — nothing more reasonable; and the point to be specially remarked is, that this is the very principle upon which the divine government in relation to sin proceeds: "If we *confess* our sins, he is faithful and just to *forgive* us our sins." Man's own heart being witness, he proceeds upon the very principle of adjudication which he condemns in the government of God.

The sum of the answer is this: if a criminal continue to be impenitent respecting any crime, he is as guilty of that crime on the last day of his life as he was in the very hour of its committal, though he may have survived that hour fifty years. Time has no mitigating influence upon guilt. The question between the criminal and society is not one of *time*, but of *penitence*, and, so long as he is impenitent, society must, by a compulsion deeper than all formal law, mark and avoid him. Society does this. If particular members of society do not do so, they are immoral — connivance with unrepented guilt being an affront to the spirit of virtue. Society punishes (more or less lightly, more or less directly) all impenitent offenders against its laws, and punishes them throughout their *whole lifetime*, which is as much of eternity as its retributive influence can encompass. In very grave cases, indeed, society will not allow the penal shadow to pass from the reputation even after death; so truly is this the case that there are names which cannot now be pronounced, though they represent long extinct lives, without bringing a frown upon the countenances of all who hear them. Is this eternal punishment, or is it not?

The question of proportion may be looked at in another light. A citizen who has maintained a good reputation for half a century as a pure, upright, noble man; who has figured on subscription lists as a generous benefactor of the poor; whose name obtained the highest credit on the Exchange, — has been proved guilty of a crime: the crime was being perpetrated in imagined secrecy; the criminal had no idea that any eye was upon him; the fact, however, becomes known; and the question is, how does society treat the tower which was fifty years in building? Society razes the very foundations, and forgets half a century of unchallenged life in one day's discovered villany. But where is the law of proportion? Why not deduct one day from the fifty years' reputation, or regard the crime but as a spot on the disk of a brilliant life? The law of proportion founded on mere duration would, if strictly interpreted, require this deduction; but society happily forgets its formal logic when under the influence of high moral inspiration, and in its own arbitraments reproduces the government of God.

The argument of proportion as to time is obviously fallacious. No crime is self-contained. All actions are influential. What is done in an hour may affect society through many generations. Long after the pebble is at the bottom of the lake, the circles multiply and expand on the surface. The lifting of a hand sends a vibration to the stars.

A second objection will afford an opportunity of still further exposing the fallacy of the argument of proportion. It has been urged that, as virtue is its own reward, and vice its own punishment, the criminal is sufficiently punished while upon earth, and need not, therefore, have hell superadded. The argument, if valid in relation to hell, is equally valid in relation to heaven; hence, as virtue is its own reward, the virtuous man is sufficiently rewarded on earth, and needs not a superadded heaven. By parity of reasoning this latter position is impregnable. The logic which closes hell annihilates heaven. Without, however, pressing the sophist too severely to accept the results of his premises, the whole answer may be included in one fundamental and fully-illustrated principle — viz., that *punishment is not regenerative.* All penalty is negative. It may appease the more public demands of society without making any good impression on the moral nature of the criminal. Take an instance: a felon who has undergone a term of imprisonment may leave the prison as great a criminal as he entered it. The mere fact of having been in jail for a series of months or years does not make the criminal an honest man. The law could touch his body only; so that at the very moment of his keenest smarting under the penal rod he might be plotting deeper schemes of crime. Punishment *per se* is not a regenerator. Hell itself, if intermediate instead of final, could not convert men to Christianity. It might terrify them; it might impose strong restraints upon them, originating in the lowest and most uncertain motives; but, as to regeneration, it might be as impotent as a passing storm. Virtue founded on fear is only vice in a fit of dejection.

Does not the objector himself proceed upon the principle that *punishment is not regenerative?* Imagine the objector seated in a public vehicle. He is holding pleasant intercourse with a fellow-traveller; he likes the man, is pleased with his intelligence, frankness, and civility: at one point of the journey, however, he is given to understand that his interlocutor is a ticket-of-leave man; does he during the remainder of the journey feel as comfortable as he did at the beginning? Does he, or does he not, involuntarily lay his hand upon his property? Is there, or is there not, a development of suspicion? But why? The criminal has, indeed, broken the laws of his country, but he has suffered the legal penalty, or escaped a portion of it by his creditable conduct; why, then, should not the objector invite the well-behaved convict home, and introduce him to the confidence of his sons and daughters? Why should the convict be punished forever? Where is the proportion between a day's crime and life-long infamy? The objector's philosophy succumbs to his moral instincts. He begins to think of contamination, and mentally to run over all the possibilities of his having had something like friendly intercourse with a returned convict. Yet he would have God's infinite holiness do what his own faded morality cannot do. He would have the sun overlook defects which his own rushlight brings into startling prominence. He fails to see that the case appeals not to benevolence, not to philosophy, but strictly to the moral sense; and if man, whose moral faculty is so liable to perversion, recoils from the idea of confiding in an impenitent convict, how can God look with complaisance on an unclean heart? Does the objector say that, if he knew the returned convict to be a truly penitent man, he would give him another chance in life? Then let him recall the words just quoted — "If we *confess* our sins, he is faithful and just to forgive us our sins."

The objector seems forgetful of the fact, that the

doctrine of vice being its own punishment is necessarily overridden in all the penal arrangements of society, otherwise society would be insecurely guarded against outrage. If vice be its own punishment (not only individually, but *socially*, in a full degree), why should the thief be imprisoned or the murderer executed? Why not leave each to the tormenting remorse of his own conscience? Why not be satisfied with the scorpion sting of memory? The fact is, that there is a practical sophism in the doctrine that vice is its own punishment in an imperfect state of society. By repetition of crime conscience is hardened, so that actually he who has done most is punished least. The young thief, trembling in inexperience, hesitates as he approaches the lock at midnight, but the veteran burglar is as steady in darkness as at noonday. The criminal, therefore, would have merely to repeat his crimes to escape their punishment; for he who now blushes in anger may one day be calm in murder! Vice is its own punishment only when all alleviating circumstances are removed, as will be the case in the next world. There nature will be so quickened, and so thoroughly thrown back upon itself, that vice will in the fullest sense of the term be its own tormentor; but, as earthly society is now constituted, there would be so many counterbalancing influences brought to bear upon the criminal that his reflections might be modified or entirely overpowered. The same principle has its obvious bearings on the doctrine that virtue is its own reward.

A third objection urges that God should issue a universal amnesty,— open every prison door in the universe, — say to devils, "You are forgiven," and to lost men, "Be free." This would be considered so magnanimous as to be worthy of God. The objection is not without plausibility. Two things, however, appear to be forgotten. (1) That an amnesty could not, in itself, work any moral change. Look at the case from a national point of view. Suppose that the monarch were to proclaim a universal amnesty: would the thief, the murderer, the incendiary, or any other criminal, be thereby constituted a virtuous member of society? Such an amnesty, instead of being a blessing, would be a curse; liberty would degenerate into licentiousness. If the insane idea of a universal amnesty were seriously proposed, all virtuous men would protest against throwing back the flood-gates and liberating torrents of crime. What, then, would God's amnesty do? Would a demon be less a demon on one side of a prison door than on another? Does the door make the demon? The second thing that is forgotten by the objector is, (2) That forgiveness requires the consent of two parties. The term "forgiveness" is often used with a most inadequate conception of its meaning. An enemy cannot by any act of so-called forgiveness be turned into a friend. The philanthropic man may even love his enemies, bless them that curse him, and pray for them that despitefully use him and persecute him, and yet not *forgive* them in the right sense of that term. The man may excuse an offence against himself, but he has no power to excuse an offence against righteousness; that is to say, he may rise superior to the mere *personal* consideration, and no doubt will do so; but, if he trifle with the demands of morality, which alone can make personal considerations of any consequence, his so-called forgiveness is a sin, and his supposed magnanimity is a violation of God's prerogative. It comes to this, then, that even God himself cannot forgive a sinner apart from certain conditions, which the sinner himself must supply. Is it (if the supposition may be allowed) anything merely *personal* which God condemns in the action of the sinner against himself? Can the sinner do *God* any harm? Can the mightiest chief in all the armies of hell pluck one star from the sky, or keep back the light of the sun, or bind the sweet influences of Pleiades, or loose the bands of Orion? God is not, so to speak, alarmed for his *personal* government. The offences against his *power* cost him no concern, but the offences against his *holiness* afflict him with great sorrow. The parent cares nothing for the mere blow of the child's tiny fist, but the passion which prompted it breaks his heart. God has to maintain the public virtue and order of the universe. He fears no stroke of power; but if, for mere convenience of expression, we may distinguish between his personality and his attributes, we may say that offences against his person are forgiven, but offences against his attributes cannot be forgiven apart from confession and repentance on the side of the criminal.

It has been suggested that annihilation would better harmonize with the divine attributes than the infliction of eternal misery. This, however, is a sentiment rather than an argument. God does not inflict the eternal misery; he simply points it out as the resultant of certain courses. Men often complain as if the misery were superimposed by God: it is not; it comes out of the man, not from God. God says to his moral creatures, "You are immortal: right means immortal glory: wrong means immortal infamy." In this representation on the part of God there is nothing arbitrary — it simply points out the inevitable operation of cause and effect. When a parent warns a child to beware of the fire, he does so in love, not in anger: he does not inflict the pain of burning; he merely points out that such pain will be the result of disobedience. So with God: he does not inflict the punishment; the punishment is the effect of a cause. It is easy to pronounce the word *annihilation*, but has its meaning been fully considered? There need not be any hesitation in reverently declaring that *God cannot annihilate a moral agent.* If he could, would he not have annihilated the devil that vexed his beloved Son in the wilderness? So far as we can gather from the sacred writings, what has been the attitude of God in relation to the devil? He has degraded his position in the universe; he has taken away the lustrous robe with which he was originally clothed; he has caused him to wither into the most awful and repulsive deformity; on every side the most tremendous pressure has been brought to bear upon him; but no force can touch the *life;* diabolism is nothing but abused divinity, and can God be annihilated? All moral creatures are such by virtue of a divine element in their nature. But cannot God withdraw that divine element? Let us pause. What would he make of it after he had withdrawn it? Could he absorb the poisoned element which for a lifetime had been given up to the devil?

It must not be forgotten that there is a broad distinction between a penalty and a consequence, as those terms are commonly understood. When Christ said, "He that believeth not shall be damned," he announced a consequence, he did not threaten a penalty in the usual acceptation of the term. A consequence is the direct and inevitable result of certain processes, partaking of their very nature, and inseparable from them; but a penalty may possibly be something different, something arbitrarily superadded, regardless of adaptation or measure. Being chilled is a consequence of exposure to cold air; but being flogged for such exposure is a penalty. Eternal punishment is the consequence of rejecting the Gospel, not a penalty (in the low sense of revenge) attached to a crime.

In the Phædo, and also in the Gorgias, we find a theory which seems to meet some of the difficulties, but which in reality meets some at the expense of others. It appears, according to the Platonic dream, that persons who have passed through life without bringing any special disgrace upon themselves suffer for their evil deeds, and are then rewarded for their good works. On the other hand, those who are incurable are cast into Tartarus, where they remain forever. The class lying between receive different treatment. In the first instance, they are cast into Tartarus; but, after remaining there a year, they are cast forth, the homicides into Cocytus, the parricides and matricides into Pyriphlegethon. With a most singular accuracy, the very principle of confession being the basis of pardon, and the consent of two parties being required in order to an act of complete forgiveness, it is declared in the Phædo, that when the members of this intermediate class are borne along to the Acherusian lake, they invoke those whom they murdered or injured; and, if the aggrieved parties relent, the sufferers are permitted to go out into the lake, and thus to escape further suffering; but, if the aggrieved parties do not relent, the sufferers are remanded to Tartarus. The same doctrine is taught in the Gorgias. Rhadamanthus examines the souls, without knowing anything of their identity, and according to their nature he dismisses them either to Tartarus or to the isles of the blessed. The points common to the Platonic and Evangelic theories are (1) that there are two conditions after death, and (2) that eternal punishment is the consequence of unpardoned guilt. In the "beautiful fable" related by Socrates in the Phædo, we have the principle of a purgatory affirmed; that is to say, some sinners are punished for a time and then sent forward to everlasting rewards. The Christian doctrine is opposed to this; it knows nothing of intermediate distinctions; its classification is dual; in referring to destiny, it recognizes two terms only,— heaven and hell.

The moral effect is higher than that of the Socratic fable. No license is given to the criminal; no uncertainty beclouds the anticipations of the good man. Virtue is recognized as a principle, not judged by deceptive shades. Socrates, in concluding his fable, well said that it would not become any man of sense to affirm positively that the things were exactly as the fabulist had pictured them. But Christ makes no such reservations; he speaks with the authority of one before whose eyes all things stood in the clearest light: it is a revealer, not an inquirer, who sees that the bad man cannot rise and the good man cannot fall in the day of judgment. Why be startled by the announcement that the bad man shall "go away into everlasting punishment"? Society has actually affirmed the principle in its own penal arrangements; why, then, be shocked at its own moral instincts? The shock is occasioned by the word "eternal" rather than the word "punishment;" yet why so? If punishment can be endured at all, why not forever? Beings can suffer only according to their capacity. The suffering will be mental, not physical,—an eternal self-reproach for having given God the lie.

This gives us a view of the redemptive work of Christ which could not have been otherwise obtained. It presents, too, an impressive aspect of human dignity. To save man from such consequences, Christ undertook the work of mediation,—would Christ have died to save an insect which could be crushed into nothingness? According to the Christian writings, man stands in a salvable relation to Christ's work only during his continuance on earth; throughout the whole of that period he is importuned by the most earnest persuasions to avail himself of the benefits of Christ's mediation; and if, in defiance of all such importunity, he determinedly persists in a criminal course, how can he possibly escape the effects of that course? The question is, how *can* he? If punishment is not regenerative; if selfish fear is not a moral agent; if a moral creature *cannot* be *annihilated;*— then how *can* the criminal cheat God, and find a way into heaven? Is it suggested that a second probation might meet the case? A second *probation* is an impossibility; but even assuming the possibility, where would be the equity? Give men to know that there would be a second probation, and how many of them would care for the first? And if they neglect the first, they are so much weaker in moral nerve to encounter the discipline of the second. And if there should be two probations, why not three?

> "But say I could repent, and could obtain
> By act of grace my former state; how soon
> Would height recall high thoughts, how soon unsay
> What feigned submission swore! ease would recant
> Vows made in pain, as violent and void."

How do men regard this probationary idea as it comes up in the concerns of daily life? There is one seed-time in the year; an indolent farmer neglects it, and then sets up the theory that to have only an annual seed-time is ridiculous! When poverty comes as "an armed man," does society pity or reproach him? It may be suggested that possibly the sufferings *might* have a good effect upon the lost; it might cause them to reflect; it might bring them to repentance. It is forgotten, however, that everything has been done for them which even God could do: they have resisted the whole system of redeeming love; thrust away the bleeding and dying Christ; and, if mere suffering will save any man, God has made a stupendous mistake in sending his Son to save sinners. Hell would then be more successful than the Son of God.

In the most appalling of his parables Christ represents a rich man as lifting up his eyes in hell, being in torment. Parables are not always to be pressed into literal evidence, but this parable is absolutely pointless if it does not teach (1) that there *is* a hell, and (2) that those who are in hell are *conscious* of their position. This parable contains an incidental confirmation of Christ's picture of the judgment. The rich man neglected Lazarus, — that is the principal fact we know respecting his outside relations: the next thing heard of him is, that he is "in hell." So in the judgment the goats go away into everlasting punishment because they have neglected the hungry, the thirsty, and the sick, — that is positively the only charge brought against them. But what are the terms of the preaching commission? Not he that is *philanthropic*, but — "He that *believeth* shall be saved." Are the terms, then, altered? The alteration is nominal, not essential. No man can *believe* without being a philanthropist; no man can be a *philanthropist* without believing, — that is, without going out of himself, resting on something better than the pivot of individualism. Philanthropy is the man-ward aspect of faith in Christ. "Pure religion and undefiled before God and the Father is this, To visit the fatherless and widows in their affliction, and to keep himself unspotted from the world." The basis of arbitrament, then, is not changed, but an enlarged conception of faith is given, and by so much is disclosed a fuller view of the enormity which brings upon itself "everlasting punishment;" for it appears by this definition of faith (a point often overlooked in the discussion of the subject), that the criminal outrages alike theology and humanity, — God and man. Those who " go away into everlasting punishment " are expressly said to have *neglected their fellow-creatures;* they are condemned on *human* grounds, — not because they had an heretical creed, but because they had no love towards *man,* — " and if a man love not his brother whom he hath seen, how can he love God whom he hath not seen ? " *Misanthropy alone* necessitates hell.

So much for an outline of argument. We are not unaware of the pleadings of mere sentiment. All good men would unite in the expression of generous hopes were they at liberty to deal with the sentimentalism of the subject; but, as all the arrangements of society show, the moral instincts of the world protest against a forgiveness of the criminal apart from suffering and contrition. If temporary punishment in hell will bring men to God, why send Jesus Christ to die a sacrificial death, or any death at all? Why not put all men into hell at once, and save by fear those who refuse to be saved by love? Is it because we have pleasure in contemplating the suffering of criminals that we have spoken thus urgently of future punishments? We know that we subject ourselves to such a taunt; it may be, however, that a frank statement on the affirmative side of the question may be conceived in a more delicate and tremulous tenderness than the utterance of vapid generalities of hope. We are bound to point out that nowhere in the sacred writings is hell referred to as exerting a remedial influence on the criminal; if it does exert such an influence, it was an inexcusable oversight not to dwell upon the fact specifically. On the other hand, it is distinctly taught by Jesus Christ, that, if men will not avail themselves of such moral advantages as are at their disposal, they would not " be persuaded though one rose from the dead." Men are apt to think that something which has not been tried, specially something startling and sensational, would succeed in saving the obstinate. Are they wiser than God, or tenderer than Christ? Others, again, refer to the heathen, and to those within our own civilization who have never heard the Gospel, and they ask, " Are such to be eternally punished?" This horror is uninformed and unreasoning. No man will be condemned for not believing what he never heard. It is the man who *believeth not* that is to be condemned, and the very terms imply that the case has been laid before him. As for others, they are in the hands of God, and will be adjudged righteously. " It is better to fall into the hands of God than into the hands of men." Why preach the Gospel at all then? some may say. The answer is, (1) Christ commanded it to be preached, and (2) the very nature of the Gospel demands proclamation; the truth will not be silent. The appeal which most concerns us is addressed immediately to those who have heard the Gospel, seen Christ in his word and works, and had an opportunity of accepting eternal life. If men have insulted God, poured contempt upon his Son, counted the blood of the covenant as an unworthy thing, grieved and quenched the Holy Spirit, what can possibly remain of a remedial kind? The inquiry is one on which reason may expend its powers. What remains after *God* has been exhausted? Those who plead against eternal punishment often talk as though no mercy had been shown to the sinner; as if mercy were an orb reserved to shine upon the uttermost darkness to show the way to heaven. Such a suggestion is a grave reflection upon the plan of salvation; it plainly, though indirectly, charges that plan with incompleteness, and violently enlarges the period of human probation. As if God's mercy were less than man's pity! We attempt not to read the unpublished decrees of God; in our present sphere, with our present means of judging, reason itself binds us to accept the conclusions of consciousness and revelation in preference to the plausibilities of mere sentiment.

CHAPTER XV.

THE CROSS OF CHRIST.

THE Cross is the culmination of the mystery. It is now proposed to view it not so much in its place in systematic theology as in its relation to Christ's personal history. Pilate's superscription is easily read, but there is another writing more difficult of interpretation. The one word which we have succeeded in deciphering is *love*, and we have ventured on the not improbable inference that such a word must have kindred words around it.

The death, and its attendant circumstances, was not an unexpected event to Jesus Christ, — it was preceded by many demonstrations of ill-regulated excitement on the part of the people, plainly showing unsteadiness of aim on their side; but the heart of Jesus Christ was fixed by a great design. He had been living the kind of life which, viewed from the outside, seemed inevitably to lead to a violent death; yet his control of the element of time in the completion of his purposes is most significant. The baffled revolutionist, whose schemes have overweighted his resources, has no power over the apportionment of his time; but Jesus Christ spoke of his "hour" with the precision and calmness of conscious mastery. It seemed as though he would not allow history to be made immaturely, — as if there was a law by which events come to a crisis, and which could not be accelerated by the wildest impatience or the most violent determination. Early in public life he began to talk of his " hour ; " repeatedly he said that his hour was " not yet ; " and not until he offered his intercessory prayer, which escaped from his breaking heart like a long sigh of sorrowing love, did he plainly say, " The hour is come." There were two forces in operation ; the force of a malign intent on the part of the Jews, and the force of a control which times all events to a moment. Passions cannot hasten the time of heaven. Every hour has its work, and every work its hour. There was no reader of the signs of the times so quick and so correct as Jesus Christ. He saw the fields " white unto the harvest" sooner than his nearest followers did ; and while superficial men were reading the skies he chided them for dulness in reading the more important tokens of the world's condition. All this is in harmony with his anticipation of his " hour." He knew the laws which regulate the tides ; he was not misled by the foam with which the winds bespattered him ; he knew that not the winds but the worlds touch the tidal springs. He foresaw the last swell of the great deep, and encountered it in an attitude of prayer.

This anticipation of his " hour " is noticeable as a side-illustration of the purpose which ran through the life of Jesus Christ. The cross was not an accident. The cross was not an after-thought ; its shadow came up from eternity, and was first visible to men in the manger of Bethlehem. The most cursory view of the powers which he wielded during his life is sufficient to show that Jesus Christ was perfectly able to repel the ruffians who undertook to compass his death. He was no weakened Samson who had given up the secret of his power; he was still the wonderful man whom the winds and the sea obeyed; yet he consented to be led as a lamb to the slaughter, and as a sheep before her shearers is dumb, so he opened not his mouth. He had been accustomed to the idea from before the foundation of the world. Even in his earthly course he was never separated from the cross; it varied in form, never in nature; it was only less prominent, not less real, at Bethlehem than at Calvary. The cross was never dissociated from the life; he brought it with him; he carried it in his heart long before the mob laid it on his shoulder, and had suffered all its agonies before the nail was driven into his flesh. But the gross-minded world could never have known this apart from the sight; it measures the sorrow of the soul by the suffering of the flesh; it weighs the tears that it may know the weight of the woe, as if all woes could make their way through the eyes. The giving up of the flesh was nothing; external force could have overcome any mere bodily resistance; the concurrence of the spirit was essential to the value of the offering in the sight of God. The poverty which is caused by irresistible forces is one thing, the poverty which comes of self-sacrifice for the good of others is another.

The cross means love, but what does love mean? Can lexicography explain that word? We must go back to the life for hints of interpretation. Jesus Christ is the answer as well as the enigma. In no case did Jesus Christ work for himself. He only received that

he might give; he only asked that he might distribute.
As he did not live for himself, so he did not die for
himself. That melancholy cross must bear other stains
than those of murder; he who might have turned it
into a throne, and waved from it the sceptre of the
world's dominion, must have had some object in view
worthy of the generous life which preceded it. The
course of beneficence would not be broken off just before the end. Jesus Christ will be consistent throughout; for *you*, not for *me*, will be his watchword to the
end. How can a good man make death give the lie
to his life?

The method, too, of leaving the world is consistent
with his method of living in the world. The cross is
a wonderful counterpart of the manger. There were
no violent discrepancies in the life; only once, and
that on the top of a mountain, did the Godhead visibly
burn in the poor shrine of his flesh, — a sight which
Moses had seen prefigured at Horeb. From beginning
to end there was one line of humiliation. The child
of the manger is the man of the cross; the youth who
was about his Father's business in the Temple was doing his Father's will on Calvary. There were other
plans of leaving the world than that of crucifixion.
Why not go up into the skies at midday, amid a great
lustre, welcomed by the voices of angels, and the peal
of trumpets? Why not make a great demonstration
of power rather than a saddening spectacle of weakness? Think of what might have been done! Yet
he was numbered with the transgressors; his name
was pronounced as a felon's; and even they who knew
him best left him as if he had wronged their souls.

The very method of departure is fraught with deep significance. The suffering itself must have had a meaning. When he could have taken the wings of the morning, or called around him the angels that excel in strength, or gone up from Calvary as he ascended from Olivet, and yet became obedient unto death, even the death of the cross, the very manner of the dying must have interpretations which separate it from all other deaths.

Now, we may approach the cross without any light except that of natural reason, or we may avail ourselves of the suggestions of the sacred writings. Before we attempt to interpret, let us come to some understanding as to canons and standards. With regard, first of all, to natural reason, it may be enough to remind ourselves that the whole history of Jesus Christ removes itself as far as possible from the court in which natural reason presides. We have had occasion to point this out incidentally in former chapters; let us now stand and calmly look at it as a fact likely to help our further inquiries. Is there any point in the whole development of Christ's person and ministry at which we can say, "*This is just as we thought it would be*"? Or is there not everywhere something like a studied upsetting of foregone conclusions and logically-arranged anticipations? Given a world that has lost its moral standing, to know how God would recover it; and we venture to say that the New Testament answer would never suggest itself to natural reason. That answer, then, stands by so much at a disadvantage; the whole stress of reason is against it; it has every inch of ground to make for itself, for reason will not allow it so much as a foothold. Reason, on being pressed for an answer, would probably betake itself to elaborate demonstration; its customary notions of the proportions which means should bear to ends would force it to set up a most imposing breastwork of superhuman appearances and interpositions. Probably some such plan as this would be accounted reasonable: — The world having lost its moral standing, God himself, in undisguised personality, must speak to it from the heavens with a voice of awful power; the guilty world must see him robed with fire, crowned with a diadem in which a thousand suns flash their commingling glories, and encircled by unnumbered squadrons of the seraphim; all men must hear him lamenting the apostasy, and offering instantaneous and universal pardon; the great Deceiver must be publicly destroyed, and his track obliterated from the face of the earth; and, to prevent the possibility of further falling, the whole family of man must be translated to heaven. — This would suit the reason that is fond of demonstrativeness. Other forms might be suggested that would suit the reason that is prone to philosophical speculation. But among them all the New Testament idea would never come up. Pain, sorrow, humiliation, death, resurrection, stand off beyond the reach of natural reason. It is not saying too much to say that such a process is offensive; it is foolishness; it is a stumbling-block. What we have to suggest is this: that by so much as the Gospel method is removed from the probabilities which natural reason would affirm, it is unlikely that natural reason conceived it. That method is not merely here and there contrary to expectation, but throughout, from end to end, there is not a solitary point which satisfies natural reason. Was ever reason so unreasoning? Did reason ever so far exceed the limit of probability? A partial excess might have been understood, an occasional obscurity might have been accounted for; but the mystery is unbroken, the lamp of reason nowhere touches the great darkness. Instead of foreclosing the inquiry, this should quicken reverent investigation. Originality is not madness. What if God should be greater than man has thought him to be? What if the Infinite cannot be measured by the finite? We are thrown back upon analogous inquiry respecting God — his universe is around us; how does he work in that? History is at hand; how has he mingled with men? Man's own personality is a witness. How has God created it, individualized it, kept it from absorption in the boundless ocean of contemporaneous life? Is God easily understood everywhere but at the cross? Is he a common riddle which any child can guess? Or is he still an unsolved problem — the problem of all problems? Is he an exhausted theme; or does he enlarge before our reverent and wondering vision? These collateral inquiries may help to set reason in its proper attitude before the cross. The sight which Moses saw at Horeb may be reversed at Calvary; Moses saw the God of Abraham in the God of nature — what if we see the God of nature in the God of Abraham? Nature itself offers a thousand perplexities to reason; out of the whirlwind God has rebuked the complaining and dissatisfied Jobs of the race: "Where wast thou when I laid the foundations of the earth? declare, if thou hast understanding. . . . Hast thou commanded the morning since thy days, and caused the dayspring to know his place? . . . Hast thou entered into the springs of the sea; or hast thou walked in the search of the depth? . . . Gavest thou the goodly wings unto the peacocks; or wings and feathers unto the ostrich?" With a peremptory voice God thus shuts out human wisdom and power from nature; what wonder if the same voice should chide self-sufficiency when it pronounces on "the mystery of godliness"? As the very impossibility of man making any one thing in nature is regarded as a proof of God's power, why should the utter impossibility of man conceiving the New Testament idea of salvation not be regarded as a proof of God's wisdom? There is a point at which reason leaves nature, unable to make further way; it does not consequently deny the universe: why not treat with the same trust the greater mystery of which the most mysterious nature is but the background?

The Scriptures are not silent respecting the meaning of the cross. If we credit the Scriptures as to the fact of the cross, why doubt them as to its meaning? Do they tell the truth in history, and tell lies in doctrine? We put it thus frankly, because, if the professedly divine word is modified, he who modifies it must be wiser than God, or it bears itself a forged signature. What, then, do the Scriptures say respecting the cross? To the inquiry, Why was Jesus Christ given up? they answer: "He was delivered for our offences." To the inquiry, Why did he suffer? they reply: "Christ hath once suffered for our sins, the just for the unjust, that he might bring us to God." We inquire for what purpose he suffered, and they answer: "He gave himself for our sins, that he might deliver us from this present evil world, according to the will of God and our Father." If we ask what practical effect the offering of Jesus Christ should have upon us, the Scriptures reply: "Who his own self bare our sins in his body on the tree, that we, being dead to sins, should live unto righteousness." When we ask, Did he die for himself or for others? we are told, with the utmost precision, that "Christ died for the ungodly." This is the testimony of Scripture. We get the doctrine where we get the fact. Can we obtain better answers elsewhere? The responsibility of rejection lies with the reader. It is easier to blow out a light than to create one. Here is a great historic event which is to be explained; we may exercise the speculative faculty in balancing guess after guess, or accept the testimony which is avowedly of God. Let us see in which direction this testimony goes.

The Scriptures declare plainly that the cross stands in direct relation to *sin*. Sin necessitated a condition which love alone could meet. Holiness never caused death. All that comes within what may be called the sphere of death (pain, misery, disappointment, tears) is due immediately to moral decay. Throughout the Scriptures this principle is constantly affirmed, but nowhere is it seen in full force of demonstration but on the cross. It could not have been a trifle which started the great drops of blood from the body of Jesus Christ in Gethsemane, or that caused him his exceeding sorrow on the tree. Great natures cannot weep blood but on great occasions. There must, then, have been something terrible about this moral putrescence which is called *sin*. It was no speck on the surface; it was poison in the blood. The tones heard at Golgotha are not the harsh tones of vengeance; there is no scream of fury; no thunder of cursing: there is a wail of sorrow, deep, loud, long, as if the very heart of God had broken. It is the agony of love; it is the paroxysm of a lacerated and dying spirit. It was love that had failed in life, determined to succeed in death. It was dying innocence struggling with dead guilt. And does not every man repeat in his low degree the same great tragedy? Can any man forgive without suffering? Can a man take back even his own wicked son without first stretching his fatherly heart on the cross? When a father sheds tears over his rebellious child he carries his anger to the sublimest point. God's hatred of sin is best seen, not in his frowns, but in his tears. Hell does not afford the most impressive view of God's estimate of sin. When Christ said, "My soul is exceeding sorrowful, even unto death," he did more to show the horror in which he held sin than could have been shown in all the fire that glows and blazes throughout the universe. We best know the intensity of human anger when it settles into deep human sorrow; so we see God's hatred of sin more in the storm of grief which Christ endured than if the angry heavens had shot lightning into every point of space. God suffered more than the sinner can ever suffer on account of sin. Does not the parent suffer more than the sinning child? The sinner by his very sinfulness lessens his own capacity of suffering, while virtue is shocked through every sensibility.

What, then, was the relation of the cross to sin? It meant more than condemnation. The mere condemnation of sin was not worth all this expenditure of the finest fibre of life. The thunder or the whirlwind might have sufficed for anathema, had that been all that the case required. There was, however, not only a curse to pronounce, but a blessing to offer; — not only was the devouring beast that had committed such havoc in the flock of God to be destroyed, but that flock was to be protected, saved! This could not be done by mere power. The hand of the Lord is omnipotent, but omnipotence can work upon the heart only with the heart's consent. We say reverently, but with deep conviction, that when omnipotence is weak, then it is strong; broken, bleeding, dying on the cross, Jesus Christ is mightier than if the armies of heaven had fought in his name. In the hour of its majesty omnipotence may strike terror into human hearts; but when omnipotence allows itself to be mocked, defied, wounded, and broken on the cross, it gets hold upon the heart deep as the roots of life. The cross, be it repeated, goes deeper than mere condemnation; it shows how the holiest suffer most, and how without suffering even the holiest cannot forgive. It shows the tenderness of God. He cannot look with indifference upon fallen humanity; he suffers with it, that through suffering he may renew his hold upon it, and recover it to himself. So the cross comes to have a great power in interpreting the essential dignity and value of human nature. In God's suffering we see man's worth. Man was cut out of the very heart of God. His erectness, faculty of speech, dominion over inferior life, and power of reasoning upon the future, have a strange light of divinity lingering upon them even now. Man is as a fallen god upon the earth. In his wildest talk there are accents and snatches of expression which must have come from heaven; his magistracy is a blurred reprint of an ancient charter; his thinking is the dim light which struggles through an eclipsed genius. He does not know himself as a fallen member of the heavenly hierarchy: he gropes and flounders as though he had lost something; and now and again there come through his daily life gushes of tenderness and glitterings of mind which have a deep meaning, a meaning which makes the heart sore and sad as it vainly tries to piece itself into wholeness and render the ciphers into intelligible language. The cross tells man what he is, and what he may be. It tells him what a sinner he is, and what a son of God he may become. *All that*, look at it! to lift man up, a cleansed, pardoned rebel! Tears could not reach his case, only blood could; — "without shedding of blood there is no remission of sins." Only life could reach death. Only God can sound the depths of the human fall. Christ said he would draw all men unto him when he was "lifted up from the earth;" they would see what he was, and what they are, and the revelation would have a resurrectional effect upon them. Not that they would escape suffering on that account, but rather that they would suffer more when they saw what he suffered for them. In the midst of his sin, man does not see the enormity of his own guilt; in the midnight revel, in the eager pursuit of forbidden pleasure, in the whirl and thunder of excitement, he does not see the case as it is; but, when he sees the agony of a holy woman as she pours her burning tears over the recollection of his misdeeds, he begins to feel how great must have been the sin which has wrought such sorrow, and learns from a broken heart how far he has gone astray. In some such manner, with infinite extension of the proportions, men see their history best at the cross; on the background of Christ's innocence, as he hangs there in mortal pain, they see how black, how ulcerous, how deadly is their own sin. They never could have seen it otherwise. No man could have shown it to them. Only Jesus Christ could reveal the exceeding sinfulness of sin.

There is still more in the cross than God's view of human guilt. There is all that is meant by a word which is almost over-familiarized — *salvation*. It shows not only what man is, but what man may be; not only the withered and decrepit rebel, but the robed and crowned saint. There are yet great possibilities in manhood. The sun was a finished creation, as large and bright on the first morning as he is to-day; but primæval man was a germ, — little as a grain of mustard seed, compared with a gigantic and overshadowing tree. The worm laid hold of the root, and all the juices were so poisoned that no summer dew or light can expel the corruption. Christ did what was required, and now every fibre feels the energy of his life. As out of the dead Christ upon the cross came the Mediator who is now in heaven, so out of all who die with him shall come a renewed and glorified manhood.

The cross was an expression of God's love to the human family,—not his justice, or vengeance, or wrath: these are but fractional words—the integral word is love. "God so loved the world that he gave his only-begotten Son." All love must *give*. Only one love rose to the highest point of sacrifice. The cross means justice, law, and satisfaction, only as elements or aspects of love. Yet sacrifice, we have said, is in the very nature of love: it is the last expression of love; we only love any being in proportion as we are prepared to suffer for his sake,—not one whit more; we may never be called upon to undergo the suffering, still the willingness to suffer is the precise measure of the love. If love be represented by a straight line, sacrifice is the last point of it,—not something beyond it, but something *in* it, something *of* it. All love, then, is strictly sacrifice,—counting nothing its own while its object is unattained. We thus get a glimpse of God's love towards man; he loved him to the shedding of blood—not the blood of inferior life, but the blood of his only-begotten Son. The point of sacrifice is indicated by the word *only*,—a word which intimates that there was nothing left behind, no spared treasure,—all was given; not the hand only, but the heart,—not the heart's sigh, but the heart's blood. He who gave this might well say that he *loved the world*. To give one out of many would have been nothing; to have only one, and to give it, was as much as even God could do. Out of all this comes once more the idea of the value of human nature. The ideas of Christ's life and man's worth are inseparable; they so interpenetrate as to explain the apparent contradiction that Jesus Christ was alike Son of God and Son of man. What was to prevent God allowing the human family to fall into utter darkness, and to be forgotten forever? Nothing but *love*. He had made man in his own image: how could he withhold from him his own Son?

But is there not a great practical difficulty? Man's relation to the cross is a different thing to the relation of the cross to man. In the latter we have God's declaration; what have we in the former? Man has the power (necessary indeed to being a man) to treat the cross with indifference, to join those who wagged their heads, and uttered taunting words, and to see in the cross nothing but an ignominious failure. God did not set up the cross merely that he might win a victory, but that he might express a sorrow. If not a man be moved by the display of affection and grief, the cross has not failed altogether of its purpose. The parent weeps even over the child that will not be recovered, and the weeping shows at once the agony and the love. It relieves him even to open the door which may never be entered by the wanderer. What if this be a hint of the feeling that is in God? What if his great sorrow must have an outlet, and if that outlet be the cross?

It is not uncommon to represent the sacrifice of Jesus Christ as being a satisfaction to divine justice, an appeasing of the divine anger, a quenching of the fire that is in God. There is a sense in which these terms are true, but the terms have been most foully abused and most disastrously applied. The cross was not a satisfaction to *divine* justice as if that were a *special kind* of justice; it was quite as much a satisfaction to what may be termed *human* justice, — to justice itself, whether in God or in man. Human nature, quickened into perfect consciousness, would itself affirm the necessity of a basis upon which one attribute would not be upheld at the expense of another. If it was simply the *penal* side of justice that required to be satisfied, then the cross did not meet the case, and nothing could have met it but the instant and utter destruction of the human family. For God to take mere vengeance upon his Son on account of a race that had sinned, would have been entirely inconsistent with his nature. It is an unjust justice that is satisfied with the suffering of an innocent being; but a most holy and righteous justice that cannot pardon sin without the humiliation of confession and the sorrow of penitence on the part of the offender. Christ's sacrifice, consequently, was a satisfaction to the *spirit of justice* alike in God and in man; it protested that the original law was right; it guarded the divine wisdom from the charge of having laid down a wrong law; it made the law honorable, and so preserved the consistency and majesty of God's moral government. See what would have been the effect if no such sacrifice had been offered: let it be supposed that God could have indifferently regarded every violation of his law, and that he had virtually said, " If you don't like this law, try another, — if my requirements are too exacting, modify them." In that case, he would have simply surrendered his Godhead, for no moral law can be modified — to break a letter of it is to break it all; right can never be less than right, wrong can never be more than wrong; and the moral law was not a law superimposed upon moral beings without any regard to their own nature. On the contrary, it was in perfect harmony with man's moral constitution; so that when man offended the justice of God, he also offended his own, and no sacrifice could avail that did not satisfy the whole claim of abstract justice. This case could be met only by an uncorrupted Being, — a Lamb without blemish and without spot; and such a Lamb was found in the only-begotten Son of God. The mere affirmation of the sanctity of justice would not have been sufficient; it might have been enough for God himself to have thundered through the universe that he hated sin and still maintained his law; but it would have left man where he was, for no man can repair his yesterdays, or pay the arrears of his life. The crisis was met by the gift of the Son; so that not only may God be just, and yet the justifier of the ungodly, but man can receive the justification without feeling that his innate sense of justice is dishonored. He can truly say that the law was good and right; that from the beginning God was just, and that he alone was guilty and helpless before the Most High. He feels that God has not trifled with law, but that mercy itself is an aspect of justice. The human is satisfied as well as the divine. Was, then, the punishment all Christ's, and the favor all man's? Certainly not. Man's punishment is even now according to his sensitiveness; not only at the crisis which is popularly designated his repentance, but throughout his life he suffers on account of his sins. The good man's life is one unbroken repentance; repentance is not the act of an hour, — it is the constant experience of the soul. What, then, of joy? It is contemporaneous with repentance. It is inseparable from it. The joy that is born of sorrow is the only joy that is enduring; not a transient gleam, but lifelong light.

We have not followed the analysis of the scientific theologian, but have rather come abruptly upon such points as have been thrown up by the biographers of Jesus Christ. Our purpose may not lose anything by this, as the plan of this work does not admit of much regard being paid to Polemical Divinity, to whose mischievous course we can never refer without a feeling of intense dissatisfaction. We have the Cross before us as the chief fact in all known history; and as there is suspended upon it a Man with whose life we have now become reverently familiar, we wish to know the exact relation which subsists between the life as a whole and this its final and most melancholy act. Throughout the life we have constantly seen an endeavor to *save* men; never to destroy them. Is the cross in keeping with this noble aim! We have, too, seen the most perfect unselfishness. Does the cross sustain the impression which such unselfishness has made upon the heart? Does the cross start a new and unexpected chapter in Christ's life, or is it of a piece with all that has gone before? By so much as it is accordant with the tenor of the antecedent course, it is a purpose, not an accident; — by so much does it represent a sacrifice, not a martyrdom; an atonement, not a murder. If Jesus Christ had no power to resist the cross, then he was a mere martyr; but if he could have overturned the purpose of the Jews, he was entitled to say of his life, "No man taketh it from me, but I lay it down of myself; I have power to lay it down, and I have power to take it again." There is here the authority which was present in the working of miracles. What if all the other miracles were about to be eclipsed in the miracle which he wrought upon himself? Was not the Resurrection a gathering up and reproduction of the miraculous element which pervaded Christ's whole life? Was it not a healing of the diseased, an opening of blind eyes, an unstopping of deaf ears, a strengthening of withered limbs, — in short, a magnificent recapitulation of the eloquent argument of miracles?

So far as God the Father was concerned, what did the cross signify? It signified all that can be comprehended under the term *love*. So far as Jesus Christ was concerned, what did the cross signify? Its interpretation runs thus: I die that men may live; I encounter the storm of sin that men may live in the calm of holiness; I show how submission may be conquest; I show the utmost verge and boundary of *love;* I honor a broken law and establish a basis of gracious communication between God and man. He makes all other woes light. Men forget their miseries in the sob of his overwhelming sorrow. So far as man was concerned, what did the cross signify? It signified his guilt, his self-helplessness, his entire dependence upon God for pardon, purity, and all the blessings of salvation. It was the return-way to God; too strait for selfishness, but wide enough for penitence and trust.

Are sacrifice and atonement equivalent terms? Not necessarily. Atonement is the possible result of sacrifice, when looked at from the human side. The atonement, practically considered, may be regarded as the application which the sinner himself makes of the sacrifice of Jesus Christ. This may be illustrated by a reference to the typical ritual: "Aaron shall bring the bullock of the sin-offering which is for himself and for his house, and shall kill the bullock of the sin-offering which is for himself. Then shall he kill the goat of the sin-offering that is for the people, and bring his blood within the vail, and do with that blood as he did with the blood of the bullock, and sprinkle it upon the mercy-seat and before the mercy-seat. And this shall be an everlasting statute unto you, to make an atonement for the children of Israel for all their sins once a year." The sinner is not saved simply because Jesus Christ died upon the cross, but because he accepted that death as his own expression of the necessity of sacrifice for the pardon of guilt. He thus becomes, in a secondary though most practical sense, his own priest; so to speak, he offers Christ continually as his sacrifice; he confesses his poverty, and pleads the worthiness of the Lamb. This is not inconsistent with the scriptural doctrine of Christ's priesthood, for we find that Jesus Christ was both priest and sacrifice, — "once in the end of the world hath he appeared to put away sin by the sacrifice of himself," — and thus the marvellous duality which we have traced through the whole argument is present at the very end of the life. The sinner can only offer himself as a *living* sacrifice, after he has partaken of the benefits of Christ's offering; but a *living* sacrifice does not meet the necessities of the case, for " without shedding of blood there is no remission of sins." A man might offer himself, but *suicide* is not sacrifice. He must go out of himself for help; and if he go elsewhere than to Jesus Christ, he incurs the responsibility of counting the blood of the covenant an unholy thing. He impugns the wisdom of God. "He that despised Moses' law died without mercy under two or three witnesses: of how much sorer punishment, suppose ye, shall he be thought worthy who hath trodden under foot the Son of God, and hath counted the blood of the covenant, wherewith he was sanctified, an unholy thing (κοινόν, a common thing, the blood of a common man), and hath done despite unto the Spirit of grace?" The Lamb of God has been offered for the sins of the world, and thus an atonement has been made; yet, unless every man accept that offering on his own account, and, as it were, present it in his own name, it will be no atonement for him, — rather a witness against him, and a most sure ground of condemnation. If the sacrifice of Jesus Christ were to take saving effect without an appropriating action on the part of man, the moral constitution of the universe would be overridden; man would be saved apart from his own will, and thus his moral liberty would be mocked and set at nought. Jesus Christ distinctly proceeds on a different principle; in working out the basis of man's salvation, he respects the fundamental conditions of manhood, leaving it perfectly possible for his cross to be misunderstood and despised. "If we sin wilfully after that we have received the knowledge of the truth, there remaineth no more sacrifice for sins, but a certain fearful looking for of judgment and fiery indignation which shall devour the adversaries."

CHAPTER XVI.

RELATION OF THE CROSS TO THE LAW.

THE Cross, which we have just been studying, must have produced many deep moral effects. It is proposed now to look at its relation to the principal educational agent which had been operating in society until the time of its appearance. That educational agent was *Law;* a term, however, which has been used in so many senses, that it may be necessary first of all to fix the meaning which we attach to it in this chapter with some approach to precision. Even in the sacred writings the term " law " is employed in various senses: for example, it sometimes comprehends the whole doctrine of revelation, — thus, the "delight" of the "blessed man" is in "the law of the Lord, and in his law doth he meditate day and night." Sometimes it is limited to the Ten Commandments, thus, "I had not known lust, except the law had said, Thou shalt not covet." Sometimes it describes the principle or tendency within men which is known as "the law of their being;" thus, "I see another law in my members, warring against the law of my mind, and bringing me into captivity to the law of sin which is in my members." Occasionally, it is used to signify the sense of right and wrong which is in every man, apart altogether from written statutes and formal sanctions: thus — " When the Gentiles, which have not the law, do by nature the things contained in the law, these, having not the law, are a law unto themselves: which show the work of the law written in their hearts, their conscience also bearing witness, and their thoughts the meanwhile accusing or else excusing one another." This is the innate law to which every other law, either of God or man, must make its appeal, — a law without which even the commandment of God would be a dead letter; it is as the eye of the soul, apart from which all light would be shed upon the moral nature in vain. Then there is what has been termed the law of love; that sublime concentration and urgency of the soul in all loving homage and service, which cannot be regulated by written orders, or formal stipulations, but is a delight, a holy rapture, a hallowed, self-forgetful, and all-surrendering passion. This is the law of the unfallen angels, and the spirits of the just. They serve with an ardor which can never be enkindled by any statutes which could be written with ink, or engraven on stones. There are several other, perhaps minor, senses in which the term " law " is employed, but the main use is that which Paul makes of it, when he includes under it all the outward system of commands, prohibitions, checks, rewards, and penalties which was divinely established to meet the apostasy of the race. Now, in relation to this system of imperative edicts, the author of *Ecce Homo* well says that the work of Jesus Christ operates in a manner at once of ratification and abolition. Paul says we are delivered from the law, that being dead wherein we were held; that we should serve in newness of the spirit, and not in the oldness of the letter. Paul is most precise and clear upon this point; he never hesitates about it; anticipating anything like objection to the width of liberty which he claimed, he said, "The law of the Spirit of life in Christ Jesus hath made me free from the law of sin and death." He stood in a new relation towards God and man; he was no longer pressed and checked, like an undisciplined child, but had entered into what in one of his exultant moods he called the glorious liberty of the children of God. How has he attained this freedom? What is the signature, and what the date of his charter? In prosecuting the inquiry, we hope to come upon the meaning of the words, "The law came by Moses, but grace and truth by Jesus Christ."

Man must stand in one of two relations to law; either to law as an outward declaration of divine authority in a rebellious sphere, or to law as an inward principle of love, trust, and self-surrender to the divine Father. Take the principle into the family for practical elucidation. Law, as an outward authority, is established in the family, to meet ignorance on the one hand, or disorder on the other. So long as the household has worked harmoniously, the head of the house does not feel called upon to write commandments, and publish edicts; he truly says, "It is better to have spontaneous expressions of interest and love, than forced submission;" but when family order has been set aside, he feels that where love has been defective, law must be made stringent; as the moral impulse is weak, the outward prohibition must be emphatic. Legal restriction is in proportion to moral feebleness. The stronger the written law, the weaker the unwritten dictate of love. The ignorant or self-opinionated man, especially the guilty man, must have law thrust upon his notice, thundered into his ear, sometimes, indeed, scourged into his flesh. By an inverse process we may read a nation's (or a man's) moral history by studying its penal code. The legislators and magistrates are constantly, though it may be unconsciously, writing the spiritual history of the country. Many criminal laws simply mean much crime. So with the family,— where there are many commandments, there is moral incapacity, or moral turpitude, on the part of the household, or a miserable littleness, and pitiful conceit of authority, on the part of the domestic legislator.

Outward law is necessarily consequent upon tainted or defective loyalty. God owed it to his own perfections, at least to *publish* what was due from the creature to the Creator. Silence on his part would be tantamount almost to connivance, and would certainly have degraded the dignity and authority of right. He can, up to a given point, only meet defection on the part of moral agents by an instant, emphatic, and universal proclamation of what is due to himself. It is the same in the family; in the case of domestic insubordination, either the rebellion must be ignored, or a stern commandment, adequate to the occasion, must be proclaimed; but God cannot, by his very nature, connive at rebellion: he must therefore declare and establish a law. A cultivated man knows what it is to be driven to *tell* certain insensate people what is due to himself or to his position; actually to put it into plain words: the coarse-grained cannot see it without a law of common courtesy be laid before them in letters of the most demonstrative magnitude, and the refined man is pained at being driven to do what natural sensitiveness ought not to have required. All outward law, then, except such as shall be presently explained, is a reflection upon man's inconstancy of homage and love. Thus the Decalogue itself is a history of man's deep shame. Every one of the commandments is really an indictment against the human family. To think that such things as are named in the Decalogue should have been forced into human speech! Such things as idolatry, unnaturalness, adultery, theft, covetousness! Such words could only have been extorted from the lips of the Holy God under a tremendous pressure. That ever *he* should have been driven to say to the very being whom he fashioned in his own likeness, "Thou shalt have no other gods before me;" or to say to a being that was once lustrous with his own purity, "Thou shall not commit adultery"! How it must have tortured him — how necessary that at the time of saying it he should be encircled with flames of fire! He was not so encircled in Eden; there he smiled, but on Sinai he blushed.

A distinction must be made between a regulation and a law, and between a consequence and a threatening. Take the terms on which Adam began life — "And the Lord God commanded the man, saying, Of every tree of the garden thou mayest freely eat; but of the tree of the knowledge of good and evil, thou shalt not eat of it: for in the day that thou eatest thereof thou shalt surely die." This, we have said, is a regulation or stipulation, simply pointing out cause and effect, and is therefore a display of grace rather than a formal legal appointment. Everything was new; as the finite is necessarily limited, God graciously pointed out the limit; did not *make* the limit in an arbitrary spirit, but pointed it out as the simple necessity of all created or conditioned life, and this he did in full recognition of Adam's integrity.

Law, then, may be looked at in relation to the human constitution generally, and so far may be described as educational, regulative, and disciplinary; or, viewed historically, it may be regarded as a moral protest, a declaration of affronted righteousness, a demand of dishonored justice, and so far it is penal, coercive, and retributional. The law of Eden was informational and regulative; the law of Sinai was retrospective and penal. By considering the law given in Eden as purely regulative, we get a new and satisfactory view of the so-called probation of Adam. The terms of interdict were not threatening, but explanatory; they contained simply an announcement of consequences, — "in the day thou eatest thereof thou shalt surely die." God did not threaten man with death as an arbitrary punishment; it was not a matter of graduated offence and penalty, otherwise death would have been an excessive punishment for a first offence, — it was an inevitable consequence, spoken of and warned against, in no spirit of threatening, but with all the care and tenderness becoming the divine Father. Why, Adam could not have understood *threatening!* Think of it! *We* know the meaning of angry tones and menacing gestures, but what could Adam know of them? Threatening in the very first conversation with God would have been the most self-evident anachronism! When a parent says to a child, "In the day that thou takest poison thou shalt surely die," he does not mean that death is a punishment, but a consequence; hence his statement is not severe, but merciful — not a threatening, but a revelation. Nor can the child complain of disproportion between the act and the effect as an arbitrary appointment: it is the outworking and inevitable result of a natural law. This gives what we conceive to be the right view of Adam's probation. It is not uncommon to represent that probation as being arranged upon arbitrary conditions, as if God had set a snare for the being on whom he had left the impress of his own image; it is entirely forgotten in such a representation that there cannot be two infinities, that the finite must be limited at some point, and that trespass upon God's province is necessarily followed by death. We re-state this view because it is important in the present connection.

To show that something more than a system of mere restraints and penalties was necessary to meet the wants of fallen men, it is only requisite to look for a moment at the necessary limitation and weakness of all outward law, whether indeed it be educational or penal. The householder may compel every member of his family to be present at the hour of domestic worship, but he cannot compel one of them to *pray.* He may be so infatuated as to make a law that they *shall* pray, but they can in the very attitude of prayer mock the law and the lawgiver. The converse of this is also true: he may make a law that his children shall not pray, yet while his frown is darkening upon them their souls may be holding fellowship with God. How inoperative, then, is formal law! Its words are high-swelling, but the heart is its own master; it may threaten much, but the soul shuts itself in from the storm. The Legislature may restrain men from stealing, but the Legislature cannot make men honest. Law may compel men to close places of business on Sunday, but law cannot compel men to keep holy the Sabbath day. Law may imprison rebels, but law cannot raise rebels into patriots. We thus get, again and again, a glimpse of what is meant by the scriptural expression, "What the law could not do in that it was weak." It has no mastery over the heart. It sets up prisons, penal settlements, instruments of vengeance, and writes an elaborate code; but, after all its efforts to encompass a great result, it is confessedly "weak." Law had long ages in which to show what it could do; under its stern and righteous rule the earth never became much brighter than a prison-house, and human life had a deep melancholy gloom of conscious servitude about it. Law stood at the outside. Its balance was faultless, its sword was strong and sharp; no felon could escape it, no casuist could outwit it, no hypocrite could cheat it with empty promises; yet it was "weak," there was always something beyond which baffled, or mocked or despised, its propositions and its penalties.

The powerlessness of penal law as a morally resurrectional and regenerative agent may be seen from a detail of personal experience given by the Apostle Paul, in the seventh chapter of his Epistle to the Romans: "But sin, taking occasion by the commandment, wrought in me all manner of concupiscence; for without the law sin was dead." The man was living in a kind of moral chaos; but in proportion as law was set up in the chaotic state, he was not merely put on the defensive in an argument, but the worst passions of his nature took arms against the invader. The Milanese hermit is reported to have boasted that he had not travelled beyond the city walls for sixty years; but immediately that a royal order was given that he should not go beyond the boundary of the city, he was seized with an irrepressible desire to extend his travels. The child is often most strongly tempted to open gates which have been specially interdicted. If nothing had been said about them, probably he would not have cared to open them. "Thou shalt not" often quickens what it was meant to allay or restrain; so that again and again we are thrown upon the expression — "What the law could not do in that it was weak." Why then have any law? Because without it chaos and death are inevitable; but with it, notwithstanding the strife which it necessitates, there may come a moral quickening which may lead to the restoration of men. To save one man from death is a victory worth all the battles which God has fought. Any movement towards life is better than the miscalled peace of death. Miscalled, indeed; peace is a compound term, including intelligence, purity, order, moral satisfaction, not one of which is found in death.

Milton puts the case graphically: —

> " Therefore was law given them to evince
> Their natural pravity, by stirring up
> Sin against law to fight; but when they see
> Law can discover sin, but not remove,
> Save by those shadowy expiations weak,
> The blood of bulls and goats, they may conclude
> Some blood more precious must be paid for man,
> Just for unjust, that in such righteousness,
> To them by faith imputed, they may find
> Justification towards God, and peace
> Of conscience, which the law by ceremonies
> Cannot appease, nor man the moral part
> Perform; and, not performing, cannot live.
> So law appears imperfect, and but given
> With purpose to resign them in full time
> Up to a better covenant; disciplined
> From shadowy types to truth; from flesh to spirit;
> From imposition of strict laws to free
> Acceptance of large grace; from servile fear
> To filial; works of law to works of faith."

Now all this weakness and failure of outward law goes to show that, if ever the world is to be lifted up, the elevation must be wrought by a higher force than written statutes. The law has been doing a kind of vexatious work; there has been a good deal of schoolmastering about its tone and method; everywhere there has been pressure, or correction, or sharp humiliation; nothing genial, sympathetic, or alluring, has appeared in its whole course. What was to follow? Law had long carried its codes in one hand and its iron rod in the other; what should displace it?

Paul answers, — "What the law could not do in that it was weak, God sending his own Son in the likeness of sinful flesh, and for sin, condemned sin in the flesh, that the righteousness of the law might be fulfilled in us who walk not after the flesh, but after the spirit." Law was to give place to Life. "God sent forth his Son, made of a woman, made under the law, to redeem them that were under the law, that we might receive the adoption of sons." Law could not reestablish the filial relation between God and men; it could at best only put men in the position of scholars and servants. "For the law made nothing perfect, but the bringing in of a better hope did; by the which we draw nigh to God." Sonship, then, was the divine idea in starting the corrective remedial measures which are classed under the respective designations Law and Gospel; not mere servitude; not mere innocence; but a holy, hearty love of God as the Father of mankind. If man could have been made by law as undeviating in his course as the star in its orbit, such constancy would have been a failure, unless it had been the result of an intelligent and enthusiastic love of God, — such a love as law can never inspire, — a love which could be born only of a greater love.

This throws us back upon the weakness of law: God has had no trouble with the worlds, but his children have cursed him to his face! Was it not a great risk (we put the inquiry with trembling reverence) to create any existences that came so entirely within the conditions of God's essential nature? In fashioning planets, in quickening vegetation, in creating brutes more or less bright in instinct, he was, so to speak, a long way from himself — far out of the awful circle which is specifically divine; but, when he set his hand to the fashioning of *man*, a creature that should be distinctively *in his own image and likeness*, he confined himself within the interior of that circle! Think of what he proposed in making man: the creature was to be made in his own image, inspired with his own breath, and admitted to his very presence for fellowship. Now came the awful problem, — *How much can man contain of God without seeking to contain more?* The sun could not seek to extend his empire; the stars never mutinied against their King; in all the uproar of the seas there was no tone of discontent: but this creature, this God in miniature — will he ever plot against his Maker, will he make confusion amid the peaceful order of the universe? The higher the life, the higher the difficulty. Ascension means complication. Man has less difficulty with dead wood than with living wood; less difficulty with vegetable life than with animal life; less difficulty with a beast of burden than with the child that reflects his own image. So with God. His difficulty, so to speak, was at the top, not at the bottom of creation. It was a child, not a beast, that broke the boundary. What was to be done, then? In the first instance, prior to the trespass, while the glory of the Divine image lingered on the human countenance, there was law regulative and educational, — law that would have been a defence of liberty, and would have promoted a continual and blessed growth in divine strength, favor, and honor, — law that would have restrained only as a father's loving grasp would restrain from the edge of the chasm, or the nest of the serpent. After this came law judicial and penal. God said in deeds what he said in the first commandment from Sinai. He showed that there could be but one God, and taught the ambitious rival that the power which created him could limit his functions, and burn him in unquenchable fire. It must have been hard for God to say this to his human child; the words affect us as we see them on the page — what must their utterance have cost the heart of God? It was necessary to say them. God could not vacate the throne, and leave the universe to be overrun by the anarchic spirit. A protest must be forthcoming. Hence came all that elaborate, stern, magisterial *law*, back of which lies the never-dying worm.

The history of ages is at hand, so that no difficulty need be felt in estimating the effect of this law upon the moral growth of man. To do this, in outline, will help to illustrate the value of the cross, and to dispel illusions respecting a merely legal service. The question resolves itself into one of evidence. How does the testimony of the acutest students of human nature tend? A citation or two from the Christian writings will answer the inquiry: " By the deeds of the law there shall no flesh be justified in his sight;" " The law having a shadow of good things to come, and not the very image of the things, can never, with those sacrifices which they offered year by year continually, make the comers thereunto perfect;" "If there had been a law given which could have given life, verily righteousness should have been by the law." What is this but a repetition of the expression, " What the law could not do in that it was weak"? Is any man at liberty to treat the verdicts of history with contempt, and to try to live by the law as if its weakness had never been proved?

Now arises the important question hinted in the title of this chapter — What is the Relation of Christ's Cross to the Law? Have those who have put their faith in Christ no more to do with law of any kind? Is the Christian life anarchic? This class of inquiry seems to have occupied the attention of Paul a good deal, and while discussing the subject he makes copious citations from his own experience: thus he tells the Romans — " The law of the spirit of life in Christ Jesus hath made me free from the law of sin and death." There are two laws here spoken of, — the one is said to make free from the other, — the law of life liberates from the law of death. The same writer speaks of two services, respectively termed " the oldness of the letter" and "the newness of the spirit," and rejoices that he is an able minister of the New Testament, " not of the letter, but of the spirit, for the letter killeth, but the spirit giveth life." This shows somewhat of the new relation in which Christ's cross has set Christians towards law. They no longer work from the outward commandment, but from the inward impulse; the *shalt* of law gives way to the *must* of love, — a mightier tyranny, mightier because making no pretensions to might. The difference between the letter and the spirit as regulating service is seen in common life; the hireling says, " It is my *duty*," the child says, " It is my *delight;*" the hireling asks, " Is it so nominated in the bond?" the child says, " It is more blessed to give than to receive." Duty weighs and measures all its services; love can never do enough,—it knows nothing of quantity; it proceeds upon the principle that nothing has been given where aught has been withheld.

What, then, is meant by being delivered from the law? Take one of the commandments, say — "Thou shalt not steal : " — is the Christian delivered from that, — is it no longer binding upon him? Certainly he is delivered from it in the sense of not keeping it " in the oldness of the letter," but he can never cease to keep it "in the newness of the spirit." Obviously, this command, in its literal expression, could apply only to such as are in the very lowest moral condition; it goes as low down in the moral scale as possible,— down to the elemental line. So with all the other commandments. "These laws (against robbery and murder), to be sure, were not obsolete, but the better class of men had been raised to an elevation of goodness at which they were absolutely unassailable by temptations to commit them." * Christ's cross delivers Christians from what may be termed moral drudgery; they are not oppressed and pined serfs, but freemen and fellow-heirs, serving their Lord Christ with all gladness of heart. Let a Christian be told as he is proceeding with the business of the day that he must not *steal*, and at once he will regard the remark as an affront or a pleasantry. His *soul* is *honest;* not honest merely in the rough sense of not picking pockets, but in all the finest shades of that honesty which will not withhold a good opinion where it is due, which will not strain a

* *Ecce Homo*, p. 200.

word to the injury of any human creature, which will not steal any man's reputation, or plunder any man of his righteous claims to consideration and honor. The man who is truly possessor of "the spirit of life in Christ Jesus" *cannot* have any other gods but his Father in heaven; *cannot* commit adultery; *cannot* bear false witness; *cannot* kill; *cannot* steal. Such a man comes down upon all the exercises and avocations of life from a high altitude of wise and loving homage to the Son of God, and expounds practically the saying of an apostle — " Whosoever is born of God sinneth not, but he that is begotten of God keepeth himself, and that wicked one toucheth him not." If it be urged that many professing Christians do break the Commandments, notwithstanding high public pretensions, the apostle just quoted gives the only true answer — " If a man say, I love God, and hateth his brother, he is a liar," — and there is an end of *that* hypocrisy. Paul, too, designates such professors " enemies of the cross of Christ," and " weeps " as he writes of them in his letter to the Philippians.

The meaning of Christian freedom from "the law of sin and death," can be approached only when the heart is in the highest ecstasy of love, when the soul rises into the unclouded light of full communion with God, and forgets all other boasting in glorying in the cross. Such experiences are rare, by reason of the weakness of the flesh; the body could not long endure such a strain as the highest joy puts upon it; yet, in the moment of passionate love, when the soul is at its full stretch of rapture, we feel how chilling and inadequate is the service required by written statutes: the heart spurns the niggardly dole, and cries, with no poetic license, but with literal simplicity of meaning, "I count all things loss for the excellency of the knowledge of Christ Jesus my Lord." It does not require to be taken to "the mount that might be touched" that it may learn its duty towards God; it has condensed the Ten Commandments into one word, and that word itself but a syllable, "LOVE is the fulfilling of the law." This love, which subdues and tones the whole life, never could have been inspired by *law*. Legal enactments leave no scope for the play of the affections; they show the particulars and the aggregate, and demand payment to the uttermost farthing. Love comes from personal contact with the all-loving Christ, who gave himself a sacrifice unto God for man's sake. Love can be learned only at the Cross. Strange as it may appear, the loving apostle has marked this love as a corollary. He says, "We love him because he first loved us:" how delicate is that logical form! Does this love, then, exempt us from keeping commandments? By no means. But now we come upon the commandments in another spirit and from another point. "This is the love of God; that we keep his commandments, and his commandments are not grievous;" they demand no servile obedience, they are done by the heart and not merely by the hand. "If a man love me, he will keep my words, and my Father will love him, and we will come unto him, and make our abode with him." Amid such love how can it be otherwise than that the yoke should be easy and the burden light? Under the inspiration of such love, instead of avoiding commandments we inquire diligently for them; constantly the heart is asking, "Lord, what wilt thou have me to do?" "And whatsoever we ask, we receive of him, because we keep his commandments, and do those things that are pleasing in his sight."

Law regulative and educational, and law judicial and penal, is an expression of the divine purpose accommodated to human limitation and human guilt. All incomplete life must be placed under tutors and governors, under formal statutes and decrees. Young life lives by the senses, and must, therefore, have corresponding arrangements made for its defence and edification; appeals must be made to the eye and the ear, and, if need be, the flesh must feel the sharpness of the penal rod. All this comes of incompleteness. Life is not spheral; at first it is but an arc, and law assists in the extension of the periphery, and corrects, sometimes severely, every aberration of the unsteady or unwilling hand. This external adaptation to human incompleteness is not required by those who are in Christ, for in him "dwelleth all the fulness of the Godhead bodily," and we "are complete in him," complete in every sense; complete beyond the small entirety which the dreams of technical theology have comprehended. This is what Jesus Christ came to fulfil. "I am come that they might have life, and that they might have it more abundantly;" might have it completely; might so have it as to be beyond the reach of death; might so have it as to bring "the power of an endless life" to bear upon "the things which are seen and temporal." This great bestowment of life — in other words, this vast increase of manhood — was rendered possible only by the cross of Christ, and the crucifixion which we endure upon it: "Our old man is crucified with him, that the body of sin might be destroyed, that henceforth we should not serve sin." Christ said that he would "draw all men to him," "if he was lifted up from the earth;" draw all men to him to be crucified with him, for men cannot be men in the highest sense until they have undergone crucifixion. Paul said: "I am crucified with Christ." No man can be morally crucified without Christ; he alone made crucifixion possible; and only by joint crucifixion with him are we made free from "the law of sin and death," and from that "other law warring in our members," for "they that are Christ's have crucified the flesh with the affections and lusts," and can understand the apostle when he inquires, with somewhat of amazement if not of anger in his tone, "If ye be dead with Christ in the rudiments of the world, why, as though living in the world, are ye subject to ordinances?" He means that, if they had been "planted together in the likeness of his death," they would have been planted "also in the likeness of his resurrection," and so have had much life, which means much liberty. The whole is a question of *life*, — the vitality of man had run down to a minimum, and could be increased only by the infusion of Jesus Christ's life; and as that began to operate each could say, "I live, yet not I, but Christ liveth in me." "I can do all things through Christ which strengtheneth me."

Here, then, we obtain an idea of the influence of Christ's cross upon the law which God gave to the earlier generations. It magnifies that law and makes it honorable, yet delivers those who accept Jesus Christ as their Saviour from the bondage of the letter. The law of Sinai, comprehending, as it did, worship, natural affection, self-discipline, and all social virtues, received a deeper and wider interpretation from the work of Christ. It ceased, in the case of the true Christian, to be a formal externalism, and became a living and gracious power in the heart. It so far, too, quickened and strengthened man's power of understanding the nature of God, that man needed not to study the letter with painful desire to reduce its meaning to the utmost so as to accommodate his own weakness, but inspired him with a heroic and unconquerable determination to " know nothing among men but Jesus Christ and him crucified," and to " spend and be spent " in the service of the Son of God. Instead of throwing the commandments into contempt, it gave them a higher moral status, and even Sinai itself was shorn of its greatest terrors when viewed from the elevation of the cross. Love was really the reason of the law, though the law looked like an expression of anger. We see this, now that we love more; love is the best interpreter of God, for " God is love."

A practical point arises here: the cynic hears of an ideal, and contemptuously contrasts it with the actual life of Christians. With the scorn which only cynical natures can feel or simulate, he points to the errors and weakness of men who profess to be in Christ, and asks if these are the fruits of the law of the Spirit of Christ Jesus. It is the inquiry of a man who mistakes an atom for a globe. The experience of Paul is the best reply: " I delight in the law of God after the inward man, but I see another law in my members, warring against the law of my mind, and bringing me into captivity to the law of sin which is in my members." A distinction must be made between the sins which have the full consent of the mind and those which arise from the weakness of the flesh; these will be conquered as the spirit becomes stronger. Paul anticipates the possible use which cynics and hypocrites may make of his reasoning, and inquires, "Shall we sin because we are not under the law, but under grace?" If any objector should imagine that Paul grants liberty to sin, let him ponder Paul's words: "Let not sin therefore reign in your mortal body, that ye should obey it in the lusts thereof, neither yield ye your members as instruments of unrighteousness unto sin, but yield yourselves unto God, as those that are alive from the dead, and your members as instruments of righteousness unto God." Thus liberty is guarded; thus an unholy use of privilege is forbidden, and the libertine must go elsewhere than to Christ's Gospel if he would bow down to the bad sovereignty of his own passions.

CHAPTER XVII.

RELATION OF THE CROSS TO PRACTICAL MORALS.

ARE men at liberty to live as though the cross of Jesus Christ had never been introduced into human history? Or does the very fact of the existence of that cross involve responsibility on the part of men? This inquiry leads to the consideration of the practical aspects of Christ's work.

We have said that Christ's morality was the active side of his theology; — not something added to it, or made to be collateral with it, but essentially part of it, so essentially as to have no existence without it. This position is amply sustained by the Sermon on the Mount. One expression in that sermon seems to govern the whole doctrine; the expression occurs again and again, with so much gravity that the hearers must have felt themselves in immediate contact with the divine mind: the words are — " Father which is in heaven." It is interesting to mark with what ease Jesus Christ finds his way from the commonest subjects of his discourse to his Father, and how he varies the expression from *my* Father to *your* Father, as if he were addressing his younger brothers. For example, when he teaches the love of enemies, he gives as the reason — " That ye may be the children of your Father which is in heaven ; "— when he refers to the dispositions and courtesies of the Christian life, inculcating a deeper love and a wider salutation than the publicans exemplified, he says, "Be ye therefore perfect, even as your Father which is in heaven is perfect;" — when he teaches respecting alms, and fasting, and prayer, he warns his disciples against so acting as to "have no reward of your Father which is in heaven;" — and when he refers to the conditions of entrance into the heavenly kingdom, he states explicitly that "not every one that saith, Lord, Lord, shall enter, but he that doeth the will of my Father which is in heaven." This lofty expression can alone interpret the morality of the Sermon on the Mount; it is a heavenly morality; the sources of its inspiration and the rewards of its practice are divine. There is nothing earthly in the tone; there is nothing earthly in the motive; there is nothing earthly in the result.

Look for a moment at the complete unselfishness of the manhood that would be trained by such doctrine. From beginning to end, the discourse leads man away from himself; and to what does it lead him? It leads him to the *cross:* throughout we have discipline, self-denial, crucifixion. The cross of Christ was as truly, though not as visibly, set up on this mountain as on Calvary. Christ graduated the revelation of the cross so wisely that at first men did not see it, but after the full revelation came, every introductory word acquired its true meaning, and was seen in its relation towards the great end. A few references will show how the cross was to be the agent in discipline, and how the whole life of man was to be constantly tried by the test of crucifixion. The offending right eye is to be plucked out; the offending hand is to be cut off; the man is to go to the offended brother, not to wait for the offended brother to come to him; the natural love of display is to be mortified, so that giving, fasting, and praying may be done in secret; thought of life is to be given up; perishable treasures are not to be amassed; and men are to prepare for a strait gate and a narrow way. What is all this but the cross? What but the spirit of crucifixion can bring a man to unresisting suffering, to give his cloak as well as his coat, to go two miles instead of one, to give and lend to those who ask and borrow? These "sayings" cannot be understood until crucifixion has been endured. They were, therefore, hard words with which to open a mission among selfish men, and their utterance at an early period in his ministry instead of its close shows incidentally how Christ came to put the first last and the last first. It has been said that what is known as the evangelical element is absent from the Sermon on the Mount; but no misconception can be greater. Let any mere theorist attempt to " *do* these sayings of mine," and he will find that through every step of the process he will require the help of Jesus Christ, and to feel *that* is to be conscious of the necessity of the evangelical element. At this point of consciousness the dominion of self is broken up; the theorist feels his weakness, and reaches the crisis when his destiny is determined, — he must then build his house either on the rock or on the sand. It is to be observed that Jesus Christ does not offer his sermon as a theory of morals, but as a moral code which is to be embodied in actual life; so long as men look at it as a theory, they will expose themselves to all the dangers of partial and misguided speculation, but when they attempt to *do* it, they will be driven to ask the speaker himself how it is to be done, for he only can show how a man can conquer his own nature and set at defiance the bad influences of unchristian society. The first thing, therefore, that is done in any honest attempt to carry Christ's doctrines into practice is to fight a decisive battle with one's own selfishness. We begin where Christ began; he began at the cross, and, from that eminence of suffering love, taught that self-denial was the indispensable condition of membership in his society.

But is the motive suggested by Jesus Christ sufficient to enable a man to overcome opposing forces?— or is man called to an impracticable morality? Christ suggests one motive,—*the reproduction of the nature of God:* "Be ye therefore perfect, even as your Father in heaven is perfect;" "that ye may be the children of your Father which is in heaven." He thus says that the man who attempts to carry out his morality will be moving towards God, will be getting away from the earthly and advancing towards the heavenly; and lest the man should fail as he thinks of his own ignorance and weakness, Jesus Christ tells him that all the resources of God are at his disposal; he has but to ask, that he may receive,—but to seek, that he may find; and if any misgiving should arise as to the willingness of God to help him by heavenly gifts, he is chided by these words: "If ye then, being evil, know how to give good gifts unto your children, how much more shall your heavenly Father give the Holy

Spirit to them that ask him?" Now, is it worth while to be like God? The great issue which Jesus Christ puts before men is, go higher, or go lower; be the children of your Father which is in heaven, or grow away from him into more and more hideous moral decrepitude; — if you do these sayings of mine, you shall be like God; if you do them not, you shall be carried away by the floods and the storm.

In general terms, the case may be put thus: In the Sermon on the Mount, Jesus Christ lays down the doctrine of complete unselfishness as the cardinal doctrine of his kingdom, and assures all who wish to learn that doctrine that they may look to God for every help they can ever require. The term unselfishness, as here employed, is used in the inclusive sense of mortifying bad personal instincts and extending to others the most magnanimous and beneficent consideration. Man comes to the latter through the former. God has no occasion to do the former; his nature is love, and every motion towards love is consequently a motion towards himself. This is a general view of the Sermon on the Mount; it may be useful to sustain it by going a little into detail.

The description of the "blessed" with which the sermon opens is a magnificent display of conquest over *self*. The "poor in spirit" are first blessed; they are empty of pride, of self-defence, of self-satisfaction; they see themselves in their precise relation to God, and before him they utter no boast: the mourners, the meek, and the merciful are entirely unoccupied with self. When a man is his own god, why should he mourn? When a man is sovereign, why should he be meek? When a man is self-enclosed, why should he be merciful? They who hunger and thirst after righteousness plainly declare that they drink not of their own well, but go out of themselves for spiritual satisfaction: the pure in heart and the peacemakers happily combine reverence for God with goodwill towards men, both of which are incompatible with self-idolatry; and "they which are persecuted for righteousness' sake" are evidently superior to selfish indulgence and comfort. Meekness, mercy, purity, and peace; self-poverty, mourning, desire after righteousness, and uncomplaining suffering for Christ's sake, — all lie quite beyond the sphere of common attainment; yet Christ calls them, so to speak, and them alone, around him, to be crowned openly with his blessing. Is there a single stain of selfishness in any one of them? All the blessed men are good men; all the good men partake of the very nature of him who blesses them. The Beatitudes constitute a complete delineation of Jesus Christ himself: he was poor in spirit; he mourned; he was meek, merciful, pure in heart, and peaceful: his meat and his drink were to do his Father's will; and he was pre-eminent among those who were persecuted for righteousness' sake. His power was thus derived from his own enjoyment of blessing, so that he could, in the deepest sense, say, "The words that I speak unto you, they are spirit, and they are life." The blessed man himself told how other men might be blessed. He preached, not a sermon that he had learned, but a sermon that he had lived. What would be the effect if society were composed of such men as are described in the Beatitudes?

This is Christ's aim, and its loftiness warrants his followers in claiming for Jesus Christ's doctrine the most practical moral design.

The manner in which he calls his disciples to the accomplishment of this design is marked by the highest wisdom. With what appears to us as a most startling abruptness, he tells them that they are the salt of the earth, and the light of the world; what more, then, could be required of them? Instead of abusing them, he told them what high things were expected of them, and by so much he gave them power to achieve them. He first recognized the dignity and force of manhood, and then with inimitable grace remarked upon the uses to which high powers might be put. He said, "Ye are the salt of the earth, but remember that salt may lose its savor; ye are the light of the world, but remember that a candle may be put under a bushel." Here is a beautiful distinction between the essential and the accidental, — between the capacities of human nature and the uses to which those capacities may be put. Men are first to be encouraged, then to be directed; their native dignity is to be saved from bad applications; and they are to feel the responsibility of possessing a great nature. Men are not to be trained by being scoffed at, nor are they to be stimulated by any attack confined merely to their practical abuses. Christ begins with the word of honor, and then passes to the word of caution: he says, "You are great, don't prostitute your greatness; you are influential, don't lose your influence." What would be the effect of such teaching upon the moral development of society? It would give men a right conception of their powers, and prepare them for divine counsels as to their occupation. This is what Jesus Christ himself proposes to do. He saves the savor of the salt, and puts the light where it can give light to all that are in the house. Do the non-Christian moralists purpose any higher work? It can only be for want of careful examination of his purposes and methods, that they hesitate to take their places in the school of Jesus Christ. It should be remembered, too, that Christ does not throw discredit upon the dispensations which he came to fulfil and supersede. He would not have it thought that he came to destroy the law or the prophets, nor would he have one of the least of these commandments set at nought. Still, the righteousness of the Scribes and Pharisees was to be exceeded, otherwise the kingdom of heaven could not be entered. In this twofold representation, Jesus Christ honored human nature, and honored the means of educating it, which had prevailed from the giving of the law and the ministry of the prophets. He did not accuse them of error; he pointed out their incompleteness. He would not allow men to start off on the plea that if the law had been better they would have been better too: the law was held in its integrity; it was good for the whole period in which God designed it to be operative; still it was only a schoolmaster to bring men to Christ, and now the higher teacher began the higher education.

The base of that education was intensely spiritual; — uncaused anger he declared to be murder, lustful desires he set down as adultery. He gave, too, deeper interpretations of the maxims and laws on which human intercourse had hitherto proceeded; and the noticeable feature throughout is that of *elevation*, — nothing is relaxed, nothing diminished, the whole scheme of training is raised to the highest level; not only are the hands to be clean, but the heart is to be without a stain; not only must outward law be satisfied, but spiritual law must be honored. The stream was to be cleansed by the purification of the fountain. The fruit was to be made good by first making the tree good. Can the non-Christian moralists excel this idea of the reformation and advancement of human society and human interests? If men please, they may attempt to make a watch keep time by altering the hands, but the only wise plan is to correct the internal action. Jesus Christ went to the mainspring of human life; while the Pharisees washed their hands, he sought to cleanse men's hearts; while others criticised the action, he pronounced upon the motive.

The results of this spiritual education were to be seen in the entire course of life; to be seen, for example, in the common use of language; words were to be the truthful expression of the heart. " Let your communication be Yea, yea; Nay, nay: for whatsoever is more than these cometh of evil." Men had so distrusted one another that only an oath could be accepted as a pledge of sincerity —

" Kneel with me — swear it — 'tis not in words I trust,
Save when they're fenced with an appeal to heaven,"

was the rough creed of nearly every class of society. This was to be thrown away, and men were to hold frank, unselfish, and reliable intercourse with each other. No mental reservations, or Jesuitical subtleties, were allowed by Christ; words had a moral value assigned them, so that by his speech a man was to be justified or condemned. In perfect accordance with this simplicity of fellowship are the directions respecting secret almsgiving, secret fasting, and secret prayer. The processes are to be marked by the most intense sincerity, so much so that even God's eye may not see wrinkle or flaw upon them. Can the non-Christian moralists excel this idea of purity of social honor, — this test of homage and service? These directions upset all that is false in speech, and all that is insincere in action; and set men in a right attitude towards each other and towards God. They are fundamental in spirit, and consequently universal in application, and by so much they prove themselves to have come from one who spake with "authority, and not as the Scribes."

All the objections which have been urged against Christian morality proceed, apparently, upon a very partial collation or a strange misunderstanding of scriptural statements. An eminent political economist has expressed himself in terms of no ordinary stringency; and, if his indictment be valid, an instant revision of Christian ethics would take place. He says, "Christian morality (so called) has all the characters of a reaction; it is, in great part, a protest against paganism. Its ideal is negative rather than positive; passive rather than active; innocence rather than nobleness; abstinence from evil rather than energetic pursuit of good. In its precepts (as has been well said), 'Thou shalt not' predominates unduly over 'Thou shalt.'

In its horror of sensuality it has made an idol of asceticism, which has been gradually compromised away into one of legality. It holds out the hope of heaven, and the threat of hell, as the appointed and appropriate motives to a virtuous life; in this falling far beyond the best of the ancients, and doing what lies in it to give to human morality an essentially selfish character, by disconnecting each man's feelings of duty from the interests of his fellow-creatures, except so far as a self-interested inducement is offered to him for consulting them." How much latitude may be claimed for the parenthetic " so called" is not stated, but, unless it saves the moral reputation of Jesus Christ and all the Christian writers, who alone *could* teach Christian morality, the description is a caricature and a lie. If men persist in accepting as Christian morality what was never taught by Christ and his apostles, they simply prove themselves immoral. We submit, too, that it would be fair in impeaching Christian morality to cite the particular passages to which objection is taken. A general charge cannot be grappled with, and if a parenthesis be skilfully thrown into that general charge the difficulty is increased to an impossibility. In the quotation just given it is alleged that the ideal of Christian morality is "negative rather than positive, passive rather than active." Then what is the meaning of such words as "Let your light so shine before men, that they may *see your good works;*" "Whosoever shall do and teach these commandments, the same shall be called great in the kingdom of heaven;" "But be ye doers of the word, and not hearers only, deceiving your own selves;" "What doth it profit, my brethren, though a man say he hath faith, and have not works? Can faith save him? If a brother or sister be naked and destitute of daily food, and one of you say unto them, Depart in peace, be ye warmed and filled, notwithstanding ye give them not those things that are needful to the body; what doth it profit?" Is this negative rather than positive, passive rather than active? It is further charged that " its ideal is innocence rather than nobleness." Is this true of the morality taught by Christ and his apostles? "Love your enemies, bless them that curse you, do good to them that hate you, and pray for them which despitefully use you and persecute you;" "If thine enemy hunger, feed him; if he thirst, give him drink; for in so doing thou shalt heap coals of fire on his head." Is this innocence rather than nobleness? Christian morality is further charged with inculcating "abstinence from evil rather than energetic pursuit of good." How do the Christian writings testify on this point? "Prove all things; hold fast that which is good;" "Believe not every spirit, but try the spirits whether they are of God;" "To the law and to the testimony; if they speak not according to this law, it is because there is no light in them;" "Abhor that which is evil; cleave to that which is good;" "Hold that fast which thou hast, that no man take thy crown." Is this a "mere abstinence from evil"? It is further charged that "'Thou shalt not' predominates unduly over 'Thou shalt.'" This complaint is unjust. Christian morality legislates for society as it is, and not for society as it might have been,—for real, not ideal man. Christian morality had not only to enlighten ignorance, but to restrain evil. We venture to say that, in family training, " Thou shalt not" occupies a larger share of the daily instruction than " Thou shalt," according to the age of the children. It should be remembered, too, that Almighty God himself pronounced the "shalt" and "shalt not" of the Decalogue; and if he gave the one "undue" prominence over the other, he was unqualified to give any moral commandments. In connection with the moral legislation of the sacred Scriptures, it cannot be too clearly remembered that it was addressed to a fallen race, consequently there was a great negative work to be done; and if " Thou shalt not" was much required, the objector should blame the immorality which necessitated it, and not the morality which it was intended to recover. This allegation against the negative aspect of Christian morality can be accounted for only on two grounds: first, upon an ignorance of human nature, which reflects not that legislation should be adapted to the age and capacity of those who need the law; and secondly, an ignorance of the fact that, though the form of the legislation is negative, the reasons of the legislation are positive. The objector may forbid his child to enter a certain house: the child sees only the negative aspect of the command, not the positive reason of the commander; nor could he understand that reason, however the parent might attempt to explain it. The first thing to do is not to quarrel with the legislation, but to have faith in the Legislator; and then his word, how difficult soever of explanation, will be received with confidence and honor, and the time of interpretation be waited for with patience.

An objection has been taken to Christian morality from the purely political side. It has been said by the writer already quoted, that "while in the morality of the best Pagan nations, duty to the State holds a disproportionate place, infringing on the just liberty of the individual, in purely Christian ethics that grand department of duty is scarcely noticed or acknowledged." If we mistake not — and we have read the purely Christian ethics with some care — this is a superficial and unjust opinion. It should be borne in mind that "the State" is an expression which means different things in different countries; or, if it means the same thing substantially, there are endless modifications in the practical use of the term. Purely Christian ethics have a deeper application than the political codes of particular countries; and probably, while saying less about the State than Plato does, they are all the while affecting State life more powerfully than all the formal political treatises that could be written. The "purely Christian ethics" address themselves to *man*, and not to particular nationalities; when men reduce the purely Christian ethics to practice, their political relations will feel the advantage. Purely Christian ethics say, "Thou shalt love thy neighbor as thyself:" "Honor all men; love the brotherhood; fear God; honor the king:" "Husbands, love your wives; wives, be in subjection to your husbands:" "Render unto all their dues, tribute to whom tribute is due, custom to whom custom, fear to whom fear, honor to whom honor:" "Render under Cæsar the things which are Cæsar's, and unto God the things which are God's." The vital operation of these principles in the intelligence and conduct of any community, would inaugurate a healthier political era than could be introduced by the most exact statistical tables, and the most elaborately detailed political creed. They leave all variations of the State just as the genius of statesmen may determine; but they go to the heart of the people, and give its impulses and resolutions the highest and purest tone. What if purely Christian ethics had been occupied in advocating one form of government against another, in putting monarchy against democracy, or despotism against constitutionalism? The influence of purely Christian ethics would have been limited, and limitation in moral advantage is essentially opposed to the bounty of the grace of God. We take this political objection to be rather a commendation than a reproach. Politics may be local, but ethics must be universal: a man may be a democrat or a king, a Czar or a serf; he may follow Cæsar or Brutus, without endangering his destiny by bad character; but the moment a man attempts to accommodate ethics to personal prejudice or passion, he is dangerous to any State. Jesus Christ commanded his disciples to preach the Gospel in " all nations," — a thing which would have been impossible had the Gospel embodied a special political creed; but wherever the Gospel is received, the less is comprehended in the greater; better men become better politicians; larger hearts conceive larger measures; holier consciences call for purer statutes; and as kings and citizens are drawn toward the Great Ruler, a new vitality and wider freedom characterize statesmanship and all the relations of public life.

The same writer expresses himself in language more decisive still, if possible; he says, " I am as far as any one from pretending that these defects are necessarily inherent in the Christian ethics, in every manner in which it can be conceived, or that the many requisites of a complete moral doctrine, which it does not contain, do not admit of being reconciled with it. Far less would I insinuate this of the doctrines and precepts of Christ himself.... But it is quite consistent with this to believe that they contain, and were meant to contain, only a part of the truth; that *many essential elements of the highest morality* [the italics are the transcriber's] are among the things which *are not provided for* in the recorded deliverances of the Founder of Christianity.... I believe that *other ethics than any which can be evolved from exclusively Christian sources* must exist side by side with Christian ethics, *to produce the moral regeneration of mankind.*... It can do no service to blink the fact, known to all who have the most ordinary acquaintance with human history, that a large portion of the noblest and most valuable moral teaching has been the work, not only of men who did not know, but of men who knew and rejected, the Christian faith." *
A little more precision in the use of words would have been useful in enabling the reader to understand this doctrine. If, as the writer distinctly allows, " the many requisites of a complete moral doctrine " " admit of being reconciled with " the Christian ethics,

* Mill, *On Liberty.*

RELATION OF THE CROSS TO PRACTICAL MORALS. 287

it does not quite appear how " many of the essential elements of the highest morality" are not provided for by the Founder of Christianity. How can the "complete" be "reconciled" with the "not provided for"? When " many essential elements of the highest morality" are wanting, how·can there be a "reconciliation" between such a deficiency and "the many requisites of a complete moral doctrine"? At best, the reconciliatiou can only be partial; partialness is incompleteness; and incompleteness in moral teaching is a grave charge to bring against Jesus Christ; it is not incompleteness in merely theoretical or doctrinal teaching, but incompleteness in moral comprehension. Look at the possible consequences of such incompleteness. Those who listened to Jesus Christ received from him an incomplete morality; by so much as their morality was incomplete their lives might be immoral; by so much as their lives were immoral responsibility must be fastened on their teacher. If they had known better, they might have done better; Jesus Christ did not teach them better, and upon Jesus Christ the responsibility must rest. If it be contended that the incompleteness was merely in statement, not in principle, the plea cannot be accepted, because it is distinctly alleged by the objector that "many essential elements of the highest morality are not provided for in the recorded deliverances of the Founder of Christianity." Suppose, then, to apply the case to the present time, that any man should accept Jesus Christ as his *only* moral teacher; that his whole life should be built upon the sayings of Jesus Christ: it must follow, since he has nothing but " the recorded deliverances of the Founder of Christianity " to go by, that his life will be destitute of " many of the essential elements of the highest morality ; " yet Jesus Christ promises that those who " do " his " sayings " shall be saved, and declares that those who " do them not " shall be lost: but if " men who knew and rejected the Christian faith " have favored the world with " a large portion of the noblest and most valuable moral teaching," where is the equity of saving men who are destitute of " many essential elements of the highest morality," and condemning men who have given society " the noblest and most valuable moral teaching "? And if the equity be challenged, what does there remain in the teaching of Jesus Christ? The men who have " rejected the Christian faith " must (1) have had access to higher moral sources than were available to the Founder of the Christian faith ; or (2) have had finer and larger moral capacity than Jesus Christ; or (3) must have been endowed with what for want of a better term may be called a more powerful faculty of moral statesmanship so as to enable them to legislate more comprehensively than the Founder of Christianity. Under any of these assumptions it is clear, from the objector's point of view, that Jesus Christ is superseded by a higher order of teachers, and that his morality must go down with other narrow dogmas which were adapted to semi-barbarous ages.

But is it true that " many essential elements of the highest morality are among the things which are not provided for in the recorded deliverances of the Founder of Christianity "? What are the essential elements of the highest morality? Would intelligent and loving reverence for God be admitted to be one of them? If so, it is provided for in the recorded deliverances of the Founder of Christianity. Is the highest veneration of human nature worthy to be ranked as one of them? If so, it is provided for in the recorded deliverances of the Founder of Christianity. Is the loftiest disinterestedness, or the most generous magnanimity, an essential element of the highest morality? If so, it is provided for in the recorded deliverances of the Founder of Christianity. Do justice, mercy, forgiveness, and peace, find any place among the essential elements of the highest morality? If so, they are provided for in the recorded deliverances of the Founder of Christianity. Is philanthropy, as shown in loving care for all men, alike as regards the body and the soul, in any way related to the highest morality? If so, it is provided for in the recorded deliverances of the Founder of Christianity. We have not been able to discover one essential element of the highest morality which is not provided for in those deliverances, and we have waited with unrequited patience for specific references on the part of the objector. In a general way the author says, " It is in many points incomplete and one-sided; and unless ideas and feelings not sanctioned by it had contributed to the formation of European life and character, human affairs would have been in a worse condition than they now are." As not one of these " many points " is given, we have no case before us. We know not to what " ideas and feelings " not sanctioned by Christian morality European ideas are indebted for not being " in a worse condition than they now are," but our conviction is strong that if

Europeans had done unto others as they would that others should do unto them; if they had fed their hungering enemies, and overcome evil with good; if they had done justly, loved mercy, and walked humbly with God; if they had abhorred evil, and cleaved to that which is good; if they had not believed every spirit, but tried the spirits whether they were of God, — that their "affairs" would have been so much the less voluminous by the absence of every knavish intrigue and every unrighteous war. We cannot see what is meant by calling upon Christian morality to interfere in European affairs in any other manner than that in which it interferes with the affairs of the whole world. On this point we have already expressed an opinion. Christian morality is not elaborated like a table of statistics or an Act of Parliament; it gives the moral spirit, and in that it gives everything that can be required. The sun will not do any gardening, but without it no gardening could be done. The dew will sow no seed, but without it seed would be sown in vain. The greater the agent, the less of detail will it attempt; the greater the spirit, the less of literal law will it dictate. So it will be found, that where the Spirit of Jesus Christ is, the morality of Jesus Christ will follow: that Spirit determines the whole course of life; and it should be remembered by all who represent the Christian ethics, that, if any man have not the Spirit of Christ, he is none of his. It is, therefore, positively immoral on the part of objectors to drag in Christ's name as responsible for all moral systems which ignorant men may set up.

The author now under consideration can hardly

escape this charge. He occasionally confounds the teaching of Jesus Christ with "religious education," and the " Calvinistic theory." For example, he affirms that " in the morality of private life, whatever exists of magnanimity, high-mindedness, personal dignity, even the sense of honor, is derived from the purely human, not from the religious, part of an education, and never could have grown out of a standard of ethics in which the only worth professedly recognized is that of obedience." This may be a serious charge against the "religious education" that was inflicted on the objector; but it is not therefore a true charge against Christian morality. We have no intention to be flippant when we say that we accept the objector's own account of the "religious education" which he received, for most truly he has done his utmost to bring dishonor upon the morality which would have had a happier effect upon him than the dogmas which he has mistaken for Christian ethics. Does the objector know where "the purely human" part of education ends, and where the "religious" part begins? Can he inform us what would have been the condition of mankind, not to speak merely of European affairs, if Jesus Christ had never appeared on the earth? Does " the purely human part of our education" itself owe nothing to the inspiring and expansive genius of Christianity? Has Christianity done nothing to promote the intellectual culture of mankind? Has the voice of Christianity never been heard pleading for liberty, defending weakness, and assailing despotism? Is Christianity altogether a dumb morality? Is it mere declamation that has represented that her trumpet rang the clearest and loudest blast in every call to war for truth and virtue; that her hand was the strongest and steadiest in all conflicts; and that her white banner was never borne off the field in shame? Is there any truth in all this, or is it but a frenzied imagining on the part of Christ's dupes? No wonder that the objector should have come to some such conclusion respecting Christian morality when we find him confounding it with "the Calvinistic theory," which he thus describes: "According to that the one great offence of man is self-will. All the good of which humanity is capable is comprised in obedience. You have no choice; thus you must do, and no otherwise: 'whatever is not a duty is a sin.' Human nature being radically corrupt, there is no redemption for any one until human nature is killed within him. To one holding this theory of life, crushing out any of the human faculties, capacities, and capabilities, is no evil: man needs no capacity but that of surrendering himself to the will of God; and if he uses any of his faculties for any other purpose but to do that supposed will more effectually, he is better without them." We may leave Calvinists to deal with this passage, as we cannot profess to know their case so well as they may know it themselves. We venture, however, to suggest that the term "human nature," as employed in this quotation, is probably used in a different sense to that in which Calvin employed it, and therefore the sanguinary representation of "*killing* human nature" is by no means the murderous deed which the objector would have his readers suppose. We know not how weak may have been the Calvinists with whom the objector may have come in contact, but we own to certain recollections, not quite so distinct indeed as we could wish them to be, of periods in European history in which Calvinists have not shrunk from battle, or prison, or hunger, or death, that they might break the sway of oppressors and enthrone Liberty in her rightful elevation. All this, however, is of comparatively small concern to us. We are more careful to point out the slanderous remarks which the author has inferentially, we hope not intentionally, made respecting the character of God. Even allowing the "Calvinistic theory" to be exactly as he puts it, his view of God is most degrading, not to say blasphemous. The author speaks of "the will of God" in a manner which shows that he entertains a doubtful opinion of that will. Practically he contemns the idea of that will being the rule of human life. We can conceive of one ground only upon which such contempt can be sustained, and that is, the ground of *imperfection on the part of God.* The writing of these words costs us no little feeling, yet they are not too strong to express the simple fact of the case. If God is an imperfect Being, submission to his will may be a profound mistake; but if he is infinite in wisdom, infinite in holiness, infinite in love, then submission to his will must be the brightest and noblest end of life. The decision turns wholly on the character of God; and that being determined, we shall have a correct interpretation of "obedience," a term which is apparently an insuperable stumbling-block in the author's way. What is *obedience* as viewed in the light of the true character of God? The objector clearly regards it as implying an affront to human reason, and indeed to all the attributes which are characteristic of manhood. He imagines obedience to be equivalent to a renunciation of personal thought and a surrendering of personal liberty. He would be right if the obedience were demanded to any being in the universe but God. The finite can never be humbled in accepting the will of the Infinite; indeed, all human life, if properly directed, is spent in one continuous effort to reach a higher standard than it has yet attained; what if that effort be called *obedience*, and that standard be called *God?* It sounds very arbitrary to say, "You have no choice; thus you must do, and no otherwise:" but the fact is that every man has a choice; every man may walk in the light of his own wisdom; every man may shut out the sun and light his own torch; or, any man recognizing the uncertain, the ever-changing conditions of human life, may seek the wisdom which is divine, a wisdom which rouses the intellect into fuller vitality, and leaves unimpaired every faculty of manhood.

Let us, however, suppose a state from which "the religious part of our education" is totally excluded. Great care must be taken in this supposition, for, to make the case effective, every trace of God and Jesus Christ must be entirely avoided. We cannot allow the objector to avail himself even of incidental obligations to the Divine or Christian element, because his declarations upon the general question necessitate a choice between positive Divine government and practical atheism. He has said that "many essential elements of the highest morality" are wanting in Christianity; that "a large portion of the noblest and most valuable moral teaching has been the work not only of men who did not know, but of men who knew and rejected, the Christian faith;" that "in the morality of private life, whatever exists of magnanimity, high-mindedness, personal dignity, even the sense of honor, is derived from the purely human, not from the religious, part of our education;" that "while in the morality of the best Pagan nations, duty to the State holds a disproportionate place . . . in purely Christian ethics that grand department of duty is scarcely noticed or acknowledged;" that "it is in the Koran, not in the New Testament, that we read the maxim, 'A ruler who appoints any man to an office, when there is in his dominions another man better qualified for it, sins against God and against the State;'" and, above all, he deprecates the idea of man surrendering himself entirely to the will of God.* Let us, then, accepting these statements for the sake of argument, exclude the religious element entirely from the State. No God of any kind can be allowed; no authoritative standard of morals can be acknowledged; every man must be his own god and his own lawgiver; the sanctions of the future life must be ignored as fictions; the idea of a final and public judgment must be treated as a delusion; veneration, which we have been accustomed to recognize as lying at the base of all great character, must be annihilated; every instinct or recollection that relates to divine things must be destroyed or forgotten. All this being done, we have to fabricate a theory of statesmanship, and to supply bonds of nationality;

* Mill, *On Liberty*.

we have to establish bases of domestic and commercial relationship, and to start the whole machinery of confederated life and activity. We have no suggestion to offer as to how all this could be done in the proposed atheistic state; but we fear that, having got rid of "the religious part of his education," the difficulties of the atheistic politician would be greater than he had anticipated. From one or two hints which we find in the work *On Liberty* we infer that even atheism itself could not quite escape some of the perils which attend society as it is now constituted,— even utilitarianism would occasionally get entangled in the meshes of speculation. For example, Mr. Mill says, "I regard utility as the ultimate appeal on all ethical questions," and yet a few pages afterwards he says, "The usefulness of an opinion is itself matter of opinion; as disputable, as open to discussion, and requiring discussion as much, as the opinion itself." What, then, becomes of Mr. Mill's "ultimate appeal"? Utility is the ultimate appeal, but utility itself is disputable; what, then, is the value of a disputable ultimate appeal? Two combatants agree to remit the question in debate to the ultimate appeal of utility; but, on approaching the tribunal, they are informed that the controversy may be continued, because "the usefulness of an opinion is itself matter of opinion." The difficulty is not much relieved by another dictum of the utilitarian author; he says, "We can never be sure that the opinion we are endeavoring to stifle is a false opinion; and if we were sure, stifling it would be an evil still." It would follow, then, that if we can never be sure that an opinion is false, we can never be sure that an opinion is right; and if we can never be sure that an opinion is right, we can never be sure that an action is right (for all intelligent action must be founded on opinion); and if we can never be sure that an action is either right or wrong, then law is a conjecture and justice is an impossibility. Will it be answered that there are certain opinions and courses of action settled as good and useful, or useful and therefore good? We may ask, Who settled them? Who had any right to settle them? It must be borne in mind that we are conducting the inquiry on the understanding that "the religious part of our education" has been strictly excluded from society; hence the appositeness, and hence the necessity, of asking, Who settled that *any* opinion or *any* course of life is useful and good? Mr. Mill gives what is apparently intended as a solution of this difficulty; he says, "Complete liberty of contradicting and disapproving our opinion is the very condition which justifies us in assuming its truth for purposes of action; and on no other terms can a being with human faculties have any rational assurance of being right." This is somewhat firm for a man who has just laid down the doctrine that we "can never be sure that the opinion we are endeavoring to stifle is a false opinion." Even after it is "completely contradicted," what then? Contradiction simply amounts to setting one opinion against another; and, if the appeal be made to "utility," we are told by the author that "the usefulness of an opinion is itself matter of opinion." The subject is not much illuminated by another deliverance: "The cessation, on one question after another, of serious controversy is one of the necessary incidents of the consolidation of opinion; a consolidation *as salutary in the case of true opinions, as it is dangerous and noxious when the opinions are erroneous.*" We use italics, because we are somewhat startled to find so broad a distinction drawn between opinions that are true and opinions that are erroneous, when we have just been told that "we can never be sure" that any opinion is false!

The practical difficulties' in carrying out Mr. Mill's ideas are hardly less than those of accepting his theories. When opinion is formed, it may, of course, become an active agent; Mr. Mill anticipates this, and lays down the following illustrated doctrine: "An opinion that corndealers are starvers of the poor, or that private property is robbery, ought to be unmolested when simply circulated through the press, but may justly incur punishment when delivered orally to an excited mob assembled before the house of a corndealer, or when handed about among the same mob in the form of a placard." What is the object of an opinion being "simply circulated through the press"? Is it not to create public opinion? Who is responsible for the excitement of a mob? Can those persons be held guiltless of the excitement (supposing it to take an insurrectionary turn) who have simply circulated through the press the doctrine that private property is robbery? Which are the more guilty, the men who taught the lesson or the men who carried the lesson into effect? If the opinion did not lead to action, the doctrine would be harmless; but opinions do lead to action, and the serious question is, Who are responsible in cases of insurrection, the teachers or the taught? The teacher may be less inflammable than the man who receives his instructions; but it seems, from our point of view, just as dangerous to teach the doctrine that private property is robbery as to throw a spark upon a powder magazine. Mr. Mill, as it appears to us, in constructing his atheistic or, if he so please, utilitarian scheme of society, has overlooked the practical aspect of opinion. He apparently forgets that opinions express themselves in action, and that the mental life (except in cases of the grossest hypocrisy) determines social action and influence. Mr. Mill apprehends no more evil from the advocacy of any opinion than from the recitation of the letters of the alphabet or the enumeration of a list of adverbs, provided that advocacy be not associated with such a powerful temptation as that of speaking against corndealers before the house of a corndealer.* If a " placard " against corndealers be given away at the door of a blacksmith the circumstance may not be criminal, but if at the door of a corn-merchant it becomes an indictable offence, though the blacksmith may live immediately opposite the corn-merchant; so great a difference may ten yards of pavement make! Yet Mr. Mill does now and again turn to practical matters; he says that " the liberty of the individual must be thus far limited: he must not make himself a nuisance to other people." What is a nuisance? The man who " circulates through the press the doctrine that private property is robbery " may be making himself a nuisance to his

* *On Liberty*, p. 22.

honest neighbors; the man who sets up utility as the ultimate appeal on all ethical questions may be making himself a nuisance to other people; the man who "simply circulates through the press" the statement that Calvinism "kills human nature" may be making himself a nuisance to other people: it is necessary, consequently, to have a definition of a nuisance before we can limit the liberty of the individual who makes himself a nuisance to other people. The utilitarian must give his opinion of a nuisance, and when he has done so we may remind him that we "can never be sure" whether an opinion is either true or false.

These are some of the difficulties that we have found in the working of the Atheistic Constitution. In the absence of an absolute standard of morals, we have felt it impossible to decide anything. What one of the utilitarians said yesterday is contradicted by another to-day. That which was harmless on a placard has become treasonable in a speech. Utility itself has been pronounced useless, and every opinion has been charged with uncertainty. It may be an excellent constitution for atheists; it may be very satisfactory to men who wish to disclaim personal responsibility; but we confess to a consciousness of deep want which cannot be satisfied with the sophisms of utilitarianism. The quotations which we have made from one utilitarian would seem to justify the opinions which Lord Macaulay pronounced on utilitarians as a body: "We cannot say that we think the logic on which they pride themselves likely to improve their heads, or the scheme of morality which they have adopted likely to improve their hearts;" and again, "The utilitarians have sometimes been abused as intolerant, arrogant, irreligious; as enemies of literature, of the fine arts, and of the domestic charities. . . . But scarcely anybody seems to have perceived that almost all their peculiar faults arise from the utter want both of comprehensiveness and precision in their mode of reasoning."

From utilitarianism we turn to Christianity with a most grateful sense of relief. Whatever mysteries becloud some sides of it, we can at least comprehend its sublime morality founded upon a right idea of God. It descends into no such details as have just been discussed; it simply raises the whole nature of man to its proper elevation, and gives human reason the advantage of Divine guidance. Its teachings are enforced by the highest sanctions; the dignity of manhood is constantly recognized; and the doctrine of responsibility constantly enforced. The greatest mind may reflect with satisfaction and delight on its great principles, while the simplest mind may comprehend its practical directions. Every heart knows the meaning of love, and Jesus Christ makes his appeal to love alike in the name of God and of man. Christianity is addressed to all that is fundamental in human nature; it needs no accommodations to accidental circumstances, any more than the sun needs to adapt himself to the various features of the landscape, or the atmosphere to the changing dialects of the nations.

The words of Lord Macaulay are, to our thinking, so just and forcible that we gratefully avail ourselves of his testimony. Omitting proper names as far as possible, for the sake of brevity, we quote as follows: " The 'greatest-happiness principle' is included in the Christian morality; and, to our thinking, it is there exhibited in an infinitely more sound and philosophical form than in the utilitarian speculations. For in the New Testament it is neither an identical proposition, nor a contradiction in terms. . . . 'Do as you would be done by,' 'Love your neighbor as yourself,' — these are the precepts of Jesus Christ. Understood in an enlarged sense, these precepts are, in fact, a direction to every man to promote the greatest happiness of the greatest number. But this direction would be utterly unmeaning, as it actually is in Mr. Bentham's philosophy, unless it were accompanied by a sanction. In the Christian scheme, accordingly, it is accompanied by a sanction of immense force. To a man whose greatest happiness in this world is inconsistent with the greatest happiness of the greatest number is held out the prospect of an infinite happiness hereafter, from which he excludes himself by wronging his fellow-creatures here. This is practical philosophy, as practical as that on which penal legislation is founded. A man is told to do something which otherwise he would not do, and is furnished with a new motive for doing it. Mr. Bentham has no new motive to furnish his disciples with. . . . To induce men to act without an inducement is too much even for him. He should reflect that the whole vast world of morals cannot be moved unless the mover can obtain some stand for his engines beyond it. He acts as Archimedes would have done, if he had attempted to move the earth by a lever fixed on the earth. The action and re-action neutralize each other. The artist labors, and the world remains at rest. Mr. Bentham can only tell us to do something which we have always been doing, and should still have continued to do, if we had never heard of the ' greatest-happiness principle ; ' or else to do something which we have no conceivable motive for doing, and therefore shall not do. Mr. Bentham's principle is at best no more than the golden rule of the Gospel, without its sanction. Whatever evils, therefore, have existed in societies in which the authority of the Gospel is recognized, may, à fortiori, as it appears to us, exist in societies in which the utilitarian principle is recognized. We do not apprehend that it is more difficult for a tyrant or a persecutor to persuade himself and others that, in putting to death those who oppose his power or differ from his opinions, he is pursuing ' the greatest happiness,' than that he is doing as he would be done by. But religion gives him a motive for doing as he would be done by; and Mr. Bentham furnishes him no motive to induce him to promote the general happiness."

The Ptolemaic theory of morals is superseded by the morality of Jesus Christ. The earth is not the centre of the universe; self is not the centre of life. God is the sun: around him life should constantly revolve, drawing from him light, warmth, beauty, and fruitfulness. A motion round its own axis alone, would mean night, winter, death; but the revolution round the sun means day, summer, immortality. The utilitarian morality is to be classified with the Ptolemaic astronomy. Both have a wrong centre; a centre which necessitates a delusive survey and an incorrect calculation. It may seem a small thing to the hardy utilitarians that Christians should be passive, innocent, and negative; but perhaps the utilitarians consider too little the severity of the process through which Christians have come into the character which is held in such philosophical contempt, and forget that what is now negative may be preparatory to what is affirmative. Jesus Christ himself, looked at on the cross, presents a spectacle of extreme weakness and humiliation; nothing could more effectually excite the scorn of strong-minded utilitarians; yet his weakness may be succeeded by strength; the ear of corn may be dying that it may bring forth a fuller life; so that judgment upon the case may be premature. Does it ever occur to the robust mind of the utilitarian that he may be reasoning upon an incomplete induction? We venture to think that he is never troubled with self-convictions upon this point. But is he not aware that self-restraint is a clearer proof of strength than self-gratification? Who is the strong man: he who seeing luxuries must sate his appetite, or he who can look at them and hold his desires in moderation, — nay, further, who can deny himself of every one that he may dispose of them for the benefit of others? Who is the strong man: he who instantly repays the slights and hurts which have been inflicted upon him, or he who is willing to forgive even where he is able to destroy? Who is the strong man: he who will live so as to gratify every lust, or he who says that, if eating flesh cause his brother to offend, he will eat no more while the world stands? At this point we see what the utilitarians may regard as the weakness of the cross; so far they are partially right; it now remains to show them that crucifixion is to be succeeded by resurrection; that the man who has crucified himself may come to have a rulership wide as the world and lasting as time.

CHAPTER XVIII.

THE POSTHUMOUS MINISTRY OF JESUS CHRIST.

THE resurrection of Jesus Christ will not be called in question by any who pay the slightest regard to the authority of the Christian writings. On this point there is entire consistency and unanimity on the part of the witnesses; and so important is the fact of the resurrection that the stupendous fabric of the Church has been built upon it: "for if Christ be not risen from the dead, then is our preaching vain, and your faith is also vain." It is not proposed, then, to go into the evidence respecting the resurrection, but to inquire, What effect, if any, did the resurrection produce on the spirit and ministry of Jesus Christ? Moments of triumph put a man's spirit to the test. Many men appear to be humble so long as all weapons of war or resources of defence are beyond their reach, who become inspired with desire for revenge when circumstances combine in their favor. How was it with Jesus Christ? Did the voice which sounded over the open grave correspond with the music which announced the lowly birth in Bethlehem? The angels sang of "good will towards men:" did Jesus Christ, after the resurrection, contradict or fulfil their song?

The writer of the first Gospel enables us to answer

these inquiries. The eleven disciples met their Master by appointment upon a mountain in Galilee; their emotions were not unnaturally conflicting, — "they worshipped him, but some doubted." Jesus Christ's first word to them, as recorded by Matthew, reveals the spirit of the Gospel in a most graphic and impressive manner: "All power is given unto me in heaven and in earth"—what then? We thought he had "all power" before, when he wrought his mighty works, — to what use, however, did he put his power? When "all power" is given into the hands of a man who has been exposed to the highest indignities which society can inflict upon him, it may be expected that his enemies will not escape judgment. It is not only interesting, but most exciting, to pause at the expression "all power is given unto me in heaven and in earth," and to conjecture how the sentence will be finished. We know how it is finished, yet so far as it is possible to move the mind back to the critical point the excitement is most intense. The language of doom might come after such an announcement; the "power" might express itself in forms of vengeance, in the overturning of the Roman rule, in the expulsion of every priest who had given his voice for the cross, or in the calling down of fire upon all his enemies. Such are some of the possible uses of power; what is the use which Jesus Christ makes of his omnipotence? Having asserted his possession of all power, he adds, "Go ye therefore, and teach all nations, baptizing them in the name of the Father, and of the Son, and of the Holy Ghost." Jesus Christ thus taught *the true use of all power*. Power is only used truly as it is used *educationally*,—" Go ye therefore and *teach*." They who have must give. No man is at liberty, according to the laws of the kingdom of Jesus Christ, to turn his power to merely personal or selfish uses. His power must be expended for the world's advantage, otherwise Jesus Christ will disclaim his professions of discipleship. The measure of any man's power is the measure of his obligation to educate society,—the power may be intellectual, commercial, social; that is to say, the man may have great thinking powers of his own, or great pecuniary resources, or great influence arising from a lofty reputation; and Jesus Christ claims that "all nations" shall have the advantage of his ability. As he was, so his disciples are to be in the world according to their measure, for it is plainly declared that "if any man have not the spirit of Christ, he is none of his." The spirit of Christ is educational, and therefore willingness to educate is the test of life in Christ. When Paul addressed the elders of the Church of Ephesus, he said, "I kept back nothing that was profitable unto you," plainly showing that he had deeply entered into the spirit of Jesus Christ. This idea of "keeping back" is most expressive. Ananias and Sapphira "kept back part of the price," and we know their fate; Paul "kept back nothing," and we know with what exultancy he looked forward to his "crown;" the goats kept back the bread and water, and they went away into everlasting punishment; the sheep kept nothing back, and they entered into life eternal.

The comprehensiveness of this educational charter is most suggestive. There is the grandeur of the conception; standing with eleven men, poor and unlettered men, upon a mountain in Galilee, Jesus Christ turns the world into a great school, and elects teachers who may constantly draw upon himself for instruction and inspiration. He refers to no difficulties, never provides for surrender or withdrawment, describes no boundaries; but speaks of the world as a unit, of all nations as scholars, and of his Gospel as the theme of every teacher. Before the magnificence of this conception even the miracles dwindle into insignificance. Then there is the implied adaptation of the Gospel to human nature universally. There are no modifications of the subject; the Gospel is one just as the sun is one; and human nature is as essentially one as is the Divine nature. Then there is the determination of destiny, — he that believeth shall be saved, he that believeth not shall be damned. No statesman ever spoke of the affairs of state with so much ease, confidence, and comprehensiveness as Jesus Christ spoke of the world. He looked with the eye and spoke with the voice of the Universal Prince, yet the marks of recent wounds were on his hands and his feet, and no man was ever more unprincely in his visible resources. This must be accounted for by those who deny his Godhead; to those who believe in his Godhead the case presents no difficulty. They would rather accept the mystery of God becoming man than the impossibility of man becoming God.

So far the spirit of Jesus Christ after the resurrection is entirely accordant with all that we have seen in him up to the time of the crucifixion; what difference there may be is not one of nature, but of application;

the benevolence is the same, though the commission now includes the whole world, as well as the lost sheep of the house of Israel. There remain two instances of Christ's posthumous spirit yet to be looked at, in which the world can never cease to be interested. They relate to individuals, it is true, yet those individuals may be regarded as representative so long as doubters and backsliders are to be found in society. Happily, the disciples represented various temperaments, and various intellectual capacities. Had they been elected upon some special principle of inclusion, that circumstance would have excited suspicion; as it was, however, the most opposite characteristics were represented by the eleven disciples, so that the teaching of Jesus Christ had to commend itself to what was essential, and not to what was accidental, in human nature, and this is the more remarkable when it is considered that nearly everything he said seemed to be entirely opposed to the main conditions of human nature generally, and of Jewish society particularly. The two instances referred to are singularly pathetic. The first is that of Didymus. He was absent when Jesus Christ appeared to the disciples on the evening after the resurrection, and when the appearance was reported to him he met the statement with the most resolute scepticism: "Except," said he, "I shall see in his hands the print of the nails, and put my finger into the print of the nails, and thrust my hand into his side, I will not believe." To see his general appearance would not be enough; to hear his voice (which sufficed for Mary Magdalene) would not be enough; he must descend into particulars, and elect his own standards of judgment. How will Jesus Christ treat the doubter? A question of transcendent import! The doubter will come upon every age: on what principle shall he be encountered? After eight days Jesus Christ made a second appearance to his disciples, and the doubter was present; as soon as he repeated Εἰρήνη ὑμῖν, Jesus passed at once to the sceptical Didymus, and said, "Reach hither thy finger, and behold my hands; and reach hither thy hand, and thrust it into my side; and be not faithless, but believing." Instead of resenting the slight which had been cast upon the veracity of his disciples, instead of rebuking an occasional absence from the Christian fellowship, Jesus Christ actually submitted to the very tests which the doubter himself had elected! He was greater in that hour than when he wrought the chief of his miracles. He gave, however, a gentle hint that the time of personal, sensuous revelation was just closing, and that the spiritual era was about to open. He said, "Thomas, because thou hast seen me, thou hast believed; blessed are they that have not seen, and yet have believed." It was an appropriate close of the physical dispensation, a powerful and convincing climax! Any other climax would have been a failure. A hand thrust into the wound finishes with most tragic effect what Simeon so well began when he took the child in his arms and sighed for rest. Thomas Didymus was the first doubter that entered into peace through the wounded Christ, and to-day there is no other plan by which the soul can steady itself but by resting on the same wounds, though in a higher and nobler sense.

Not only was this an appropriate conclusion of the physical testimony, but a most gracious introduction to the spiritual age: " Blessed are they that have not seen, and yet have believed." It was the old word. We heard it first on the Mount of Beatitudes, we hear it last on the way to Olivet, the Mount of Ascension; it was " blessed " at the beginning, it was " blessed " at the close; the changeful anthem, varying from the whisper of a breeze to the noise of a storm, began and ended on the same note. The last man who believed by sight, was not so blessed as the first man who believed on testimony. Each age has been offered a larger blessing than that which was offered to its predecessor.

The second instance is still more deeply interesting than the first. All the disciples forsook Jesus Christ and fled about the time of the crucifixion. The case of Peter was one of special aggravation. He denied his discipleship with an oath. The first to accept Christ's call, he was the most resolute in disclaiming his Master. Can a crime like this be forgiven? Is there compass enough in Christ's love to get round a treason so black, an apostasy so complete? When the sovereign and the traitor meet, what will happen? They did meet. Early in the morning Jesus Christ appeared on the shore of Tiberias, and accosted seven or eight of his disciples, who had been fishing all night without success. With the keen instinct of love, John was the first to identify the Master. Turning to Peter, he said, "It is the Lord." That was enough for the man who carried an intolerable burden on his heart; when he heard it was the Lord, " he girt his fisher's coat unto him (for he was naked), and did cast himself into the sea." We know not what happened in the private interview which succeeded, the interview between the great sinner and the greater Saviour. It is better that we do not know; better that the heart should have its own sweet and secret memories of intercourse with Jesus Christ, — something that should be quite the heart's own treasure. Perhaps no words passed; perhaps only a look; perhaps only a grasp of the wounded Hand! We know the effect of one look; it broke Simon Peter's heart: perhaps the look of the eyes which had slept in death, healed it again. We cannot tell; we wish to know, yet we would not inquire, lest we profane the sanctuary of the soul. Part of the story is told. The risen Saviour dined with the disciples. After dinner Jesus saith to Simon Peter, "Simon, son of Jonas, lovest thou me more than these?" He was once boisterous in his demonstrativeness, — ready for prison, prepared for death, — yet he was convicted of falsehood and profanity! How would he answer now? "He saith unto him, Yea, Lord; thou knowest that I love thee." Again the question, and again the answer; and yet once more; the three denials were lost in the three confessions; and the thrice plighted backslider was thrice charged to feed the flock, — to feed the lambs, and to feed the sheep; no partial ministry; no sign of humiliation attached to the service; the forgiveness was complete, the restoration was vital. In the beginning of his ministry Jesus Christ had said to Simon Peter, "Follow me;" the old words precisely were repeated on this occasion. Jesus foretold the circumstances of

Peter's death, and then said, "Follow me." The broken link was taken out, and this new one put in its place. We know what a strong man Peter became after his restoration, — how he excelled all the New Testament writers in richness of pathos, and how he rivalled even Paul in catholicity and labor. The heart is enriched by its sorrows. Restored men, so often looked upon with suspicion, ought to be the wisest of Christian teachers : wise to guide the sheep, and strong to carry the lambs.

In this charge to Simon Peter, Jesus Christ gives no instruction as to theology or morals. Nothing approaching the nature of a formal creed is hinted at. Yet this would have been the time above all other times, had such a creed been necessary, to enter into details; specially so with Simon Peter, who had fallen into shame. On what, then, was the great mission founded? Simply on *love*. Where there is intense love of Jesus Christ, there is capacity to feed the flock; where this love is wanting, all other capacity is useless. Love is the security of the Christian life, and of the Christian apostleship. Love is the guarantee of morality, for love is the fulfilling of the law. God so *loved* that he *gave;* man, too, must so love as to give. He is not to be drawn with chains of iron; he is to be impelled by love. Consider what love is, and see its sufficiency and power. Love is the term which expresses the purest and intensest enthusiasm of the soul. When that purest and intensest enthusiasm is directed towards Jesus Christ, love attains its noblest development. The whole man is aglow with an ardor which nothing that is unholy can touch and live! The man's vitality is at its highest point; every sensibility is as keen as it can be; every faculty is under pledge to suffering or service. This was all that Jesus Christ required even of the man who had fallen so foully, and shown himself so helpless under pressure. Before the crucifixion he had trusted in himself: the very last element of self-conceit was to be destroyed in him, and henceforth he was to live under the inspiration and guardianship of perfect love. There is no faculty of interpretation equal to love; it has access, so to speak, to every chamber of God's heart, and can speak all languages: nor is there any capacity of suffering equal to it; it accepts suffering as a trial of reality and strength, and wrings great spoil from its unwilling grasp. This we had known before; but Jesus Christ employs a word which calls us to consideration; on being assured of Simon Peter's love, he tells him to *feed* the flock. How can love *feed?* We know how love can stimulate, defend, or soothe; but this new word startles us somewhat. Yet it need not. Love delights in the satisfaction of others. It does not care in any low sense to feed itself; it thrives best when it gives most, and does most for the lambs and the sheep. But which lambs and sheep? Is the fold defined? Yes: Feed *my* lambs — feed *my* sheep — was the command of Jesus Christ: the *love* was Christ's, the *service* was Christ's; nor does Simon Peter appear to have forgotten the charge, or the metaphor by which it was expressed, for long after he wrote, — "Feed the flock of God which is among you, taking the oversight thereof, not by constraint, but willingly; not for filthy lucre, but of a ready mind; . . . and when the chief Shepherd shall appear, ye shall receive a crown of glory that fadeth not away." Love must, by the force of its own nature, feed others,— study them, comprehend their capacity; and satisfy them when they feel

"The curse of a high spirit famishing
Because all earth but sickens it."

Jesus Christ dealt thus with the doubter and the apostate,— gently, instructively, and forgivingly. Not a harsh word was said to either of them: let the church recollect this, and consider how far the servant has followed the Master's example. There may be some standing without who should be called within.

Jesus Christ made a remarkable posthumous appearance to two of his disciples, as they walked to Emmaus. They may be regarded as representing men who have taken an incomplete view of the facts which relate to Christ. If their collation of evidence had been fuller, they would have had less trouble. They saw but a "fragment" of the case; "and as they communed one with another, they were sad." (Luke xxiv. 17.) The interview between Jesus Christ and them was remarkable chiefly for the full exposition of the case which Christ gave from what may be termed the documentary side: "Beginning at Moses and all the prophets, he expounded unto them in all the Scriptures the things concerning himself." This puts the Old Testament in its right position. It is a Christian document. From the beginning of revelation to its close, Christ is the main subject: without him there was nothing to be revealed.

At the close of all, he breathed upon his disciples

the Holy Ghost. This, however, was but preparatory to the full gift which was shortly afterwards received. They were to tarry in the city of Jerusalem until they were endued with power from on high. Thus the epochs merged into one another. John pointed to Jesus, Jesus promised to send the Comforter, and so, after long ages, we have come to the rule of the Spirit. He works deeply though silently. His "going" is not heard in the thunder, or earthquake, or whirlwind. He comes as quietly as the morning, and while unobserving men are exclaiming, "Where is the promise of his coming?" he is actually filling the heavens with light and renewing the face of the earth. Of him it may be said, as was said of Jesus Christ, "There standeth one among you, whom ye know not; he it is"!

CHAPTER XIX.

CONTROVERSIAL NOTES ON "ECCE HOMO."

THE most cursory observation cannot fail to notice the innumerable beauties of this publication. The writer has rendered inexpressible service to the cause of free religious inquiry by his magnificently intellectual discussions of fundamental truth, and has given views of Jesus Christ's Life and Work which must be most useful in many ways. The present writer cannot but thank the author of *Ecce Homo* for the intellectual stimulus and moral inspiration which he has derived from a repeated perusal of its instructive and stimulating pages. It is in no captious spirit, therefore, that the following Notes are submitted to the respectful consideration of the author and readers of *Ecce Homo*. The writer is most anxious that the truth should be vindicated, at what risk soever to all minor considerations. The term "Notes" is employed because what follows is little more than an arrangement of mere marginalia; the subjects themselves have been discussed, more or less, in preceding chapters; what remains is a series of running criticisms or suggestive inquiries.

I. Page 25.

"The conception of a kingdom of God was no new one, but was familiar to every Jew."

True; but Christ came to give that conception a profounder interpretation, and a more intensely spiritual bearing. The Jew had a carnal idea of a spiritual fact.

II. Page 26.

John and Christ "revived the obsolete function of the prophet, and did for their generation what a Samuel and an Elijah had done for theirs."

This is too narrow an interpretation of the term "prophet," and too limited as applied to Christ. A prophet may *teach* as well as merely predict.— Samuel and Elijah spoke of another, Christ spoke of himself. — Christ did not work for a "generation," but for all men through all time. Christ did not "revive an obsolete function," he consummated the purpose of a prefigurative office.

III. Page 31.

"Now under which form did Christ propose to revive it (the ancient theocracy)? The vision of universal monarchy which he saw in the desert suggests the answer. He conceived the theocracy restored as it had been in the time of David, with a visible monarch at its head, and that monarch himself."

Was it merely a conception ("he conceived"), or was it the carrying out of an eternal purpose? Did Christ come *with* a plan or *without* a plan? If with a plan, *when* was that plan formed? This brings up the mystery of the incarnation, the non-recognition of which is the cardinal error of the book. Is there not some confusion of terms in the latter part of the sentence just cited? How can a *man* be at the head of a *God*ocracy? The word "representatively" may be suggested; but in so far as there is any distinctive value in a theocracy, that value is diminished by any qualifying term whatsoever. The Jewish world had already passed through what may be designated a representative theocracy; and if Christ came merely to reproduce this idea (which the perversity of the Jews caused to be a failure), replacing David's name with his own, wherein was the value of his service? When the author of *Ecce Homo* speaks of Christ's being the visible head of the theocracy, has he sufficiently considered the meaning of Jesus Christ's declaration to Philip, "He that hath *seen* me hath *seen* the Father"?

IV. Page 33.

"He saw that he must lead a life altogether different from that of David; that the pictures drawn by the prophets of an ideal Jewish king were colored by the manners of the times in which they had lived; that those pictures bore indeed a certain resemblance to the truth, but that the work before him was far more complicated and more delicate than the wisest prophet had suspected."

From this representation it might be inferred that Christ began his work in a kind of mental vacancy, and waited to observe the current of thoughts and events around him before committing himself to any publicly avowed policy. He came, it would appear, to this conclusion while " meditating upon his mission in the desert." This view of the case is irreconcilably inconsistent with the mystery of the incarnation. It would suit very well the case of a fanatic who had suddenly conceived the insane idea of embodying the features of the predicted "ideal Jewish king," and who was watching an opportunity for self-disclosure in this novel and critical character; but it signally fails to meet the *necessary* idea of the incarnation, — namely, the idea of anterior purpose and arrangement. Could a man begotten of the Holy Ghost find himself in the dubiety necessitated by the above suggestion? Again it may be asked, Did Jesus Christ come *with* a plan or *without* a plan?

V. Page 34.

"It is said that when Jesus Christ called himself a King, he was speaking figuratively, and that by 'King' he meant, as some say, God, as others, a wise man and teacher of morality, but that the Jews persisted in understanding the expression literally."

Christ employed the term "King" in its right sense. If the Jews by virtually deposing God had come to have low and vicious, or carnal and grovelling notions of royalty, that was no reason why Christ should not restore an abused term to its right application; on the other hand, it was in perfect harmony with the genius of his mission that he should recover perverted terms to right uses as well as restore fallen men. He came to seek and to save all that was *lost*. — King is a divine designation, and can be employed among men only as a convenient accommodation of what does not belong to them.

VI. Pages 38, 39.

"Christ announced the restoration of the Davidic monarchy, and presented himself to the nation as their King, yet, when we compare the position he assumed with that of an ancient Jewish king, we fail to find any point of resemblance."

Did Jesus Christ announce the restoration of the Davidic monarchy? Was not the Davidic monarchy, so far as it was untainted by human guilt, or unenfeebled by human infirmity, the prefiguration — very shadowy and incomplete, indeed — of one aspect of his own? The author seems to have inverted the relation between David and Christ, and to have overlooked the *typical* aspect of pre-Christian history. The very fact that "we fail to find any point of resemblance" between Christ and an ancient Jewish king, throws us back for our analogies beyond the older royalty, and compels us to find them in traits of government and purpose which lie beyond the merely political horizon. Christ took the appellation "King," not from the man, but from the function. When did Christ announce the restoration of the Davidic monarchy? If the facts contradict the theory, what confidence can be placed in the theorist?

VII. Page 50.

Christ "did not work his way to royalty, but simply said to all men, ' I am your King.' He did not struggle forward to a position in which he could found a new state, but simply founded it."

This ignores the doctrine of Jesus Christ's pre-existence. He had been working his way by all preliminary dispensations. Aught of suddenness or unpreparedness which appears in the life of Christ must be accounted for on the people's side, and not by immaturity of plan or vacillation of purpose on the part of Christ. — " Simply founded it ;" — quite so ; but why do not other men "simply found" a monarchy with the same ease? God "simply" made the heavens and the earth; "simply" said, "Let there be light;" in the same way, did not Jesus Christ "simply found" his monarchy?

VIII. Page 55.

"Men could approach near to him, could eat and drink with him, could listen to his talk, and ask him questions; and they found him not accessible only, but warm-hearted, and not occupied so much with his own plans that he could not attend to a case of distress or mental perplexity."

To "attend to a case of distress or mental perplexity" was an essential part of "his own plans." He came for the very purpose. He had no "plans" inconsistent with such attention. Attending to a case of distress or mental perplexity is not a circumstance to be separated from his plans, or to be regarded as merely collateral, but as being the great object of his incarnation. It is to be particularly noted that while every man's "distress or mental perplexity" came within the range of his power, his own "distress and perplexity" were beyond the reach of all human sympathy and aid. He suffered alone, trod the wine-press alone.

IX. Page 55.

"This temperance in the use of supernatural power is the masterpiece of Christ."

The Jews had long and justly suffered from supernatural power. Not to speak of anything further, their political position in the days of Jesus Christ was one of deep dishonor and shame. They required, had they but known the day of their visitation, the very aspect of divine power which Christ distinctively revealed, as has been shown in the preceding pages, power not destructive, but constructive. "To save," was Christ's object.

X. Page 61.

"As the new theocracy was to be the counterpart of the old," &c.

Another inversion of relations. The old theocratic form was a prefiguration of the new, not the new a mere counterpart of the old. There had been a prophetic element in all history, a typical element in all teaching, and an acknowledged incompleteness in all legislation: what was the meaning of symbol and fragment? The law came by the servant, grace and truth could come only by the Son.

XI. Page 64.

"We arrive, therefore, at the first distinguishing characteristic of the society into which Christ called men. It was a society whose rules were enforced by no punishments. The ancient Israelite who practised idolatry was stoned to death, but the

Christian who sacrificed to the genius of Cæsar could suffer nothing but exclusion from the society, and this in times of persecution was in its immediate effects of the nature rather of a reward than of a punishment."

Punishment is to be estimated by the nature of the society from which the offender has been excluded. Exclusion from a mere political union may be a very trivial affair. But as, according to the author's own showing, Christ's society was a *theocracy*, how could any punishment be greater than the very punishment which he describes as being, under certain circumstances, somewhat of the nature of a reward? To be excluded from the *God*ocracy, how tremendous a punishment! A punishment, too, singularly in harmony with the *spiritual* character of the society. What is a storm of mere thunder and lightning, compared with the faintest frown that darkens the brow of troubled love? We find precisely the same principle in the Judgment. There are no such external forms of punishment as we associate with the infliction of penalty, — simply a "going away," a turning of the back on the light, an exclusion from the theocracy! The author's argument, moreover, is limited to "the immediate effects" of this exclusion, a most unsatisfactory method of stating the case; for in all *moral* transactions the consequences are co-ordinate with the duration of the actor. We are not sure either, that the word "immediate" is well chosen; if it is intended to mean *external*, it may be appropriate, but surely the heart of the excluded man would feel an "immediate" vacancy, an indescribable poverty, and a terrible sense of loneliness.

XII. Page 65.

"Christ himself never ceased to feel keenly as a patriot."

Where is the proof that he ever felt "keenly as a patriot"? Whatever may have been his personal patriotism, he obliterated, in view of the highest purposes, all ethnic distinctions. Without destroying the special characteristics of patriotism, he carried patriotic heroism up to philanthropy. Jesus Christ aimed at the enlargement, as well as the purification, of human ideas, so that the man who began with a city ended with the world. Apart from the Cross, old nationalities remain; but when men are crucified with Christ, they are denizens of all nations. When they are "lifted up" with him, "all men come" unto them. "Strangers and foreigners" are absorbed in "the whole family" named in and centralized by "the Son in the Father's house."

XIII. Page 69.

"To obey John's call was easy; it involved nothing beyond submission to a ceremony; and when the prophet had acquired a certain amount of credit, no doubt it became the *fashion* to receive baptism from him."

To "obey" *any* call requires faith; and to submit to *any* ceremony implies *want*. This, notwithstanding hypocrites who make an investment of their so-called obediences and submissions.

XIV. Page 82.

"We ought to be just as tolerant of an imperfect creed as we are of an imperfect practice."

The author, as we have read him, here does himself an injustice. The term "imperfect" seems to be used in this sentence and in the context in two senses: imperfection of creed may mean simply incompleteness, but an "imperfect practice" may mean viciousness. This latter seems to be the author's meaning, for he has just been writing of "some very unchristian vices." Now we may be tolerant of incompleteness and weakness (seeing we are all incomplete and weak), yet we are not called upon to be tolerant to vice, — a fact we need not have pointed out but for the ambiguity of the term "imperfect."

XV. Pages 86, 87.

"Now of these prophets Christ was distinctly one and the greatest of all."

Say rather that as they all prophesied of him, they are not to be mentioned comparatively with him. "Greatest" indicates degree, but what of the *nature?* Christ was not a prophet in the same sense that Elijah and Ezekiel and Daniel were prophets. As the author himself has well said — "How the truth came to the prophet he himself knew not;" but Jesus Christ was the inspirer and the inspiration of the prophets: "they wrote of me;" — he was himself the message, not merely a messenger. The monarch is never one of the heralds.

XVI. Page 89.

"We conclude that though it is always easy for thoughtless men to be orthodox, yet to grasp with any strong practical apprehension the theology of Christ is a thing as hard to practise as his moral law."

We cannot see the particular pertinence of the opinion that "it is always easy for thoughtless men to be orthodox;" all things are equally easy to "thoughtless men;" still it ought to be known that though some "thoughtless men" may be orthodox, yet all who are orthodox are not necessarily thoughtless men. Is it not unworthy of the subject to throw out insinuations as to the capacity or morality of opponents? Then as to the doctrine: Why is the moral law of Jesus Christ hard to practise? Is it not because the heart is out of sympathy with his purposes? The light is not distressing to the healthy eye. Why should it be harder to do right than to do wrong? Jesus Christ says that his "yoke is easy and his burden is light." We cannot admit the difference which the author assumes between Christ's theology and Christ's moral law. Christ's moral law has no existence apart from his theology. The theology of Jesus Christ was the Fatherhood of God, and out of that great doctrine came all the practical life which Christ preached and exemplified.

XVII. Page 102.

"It may seem to us that Socrates and Christ were in fact occupied in the same way; certainly both lived in the midst of admiring disciples, whose minds and characters were formed by their words; both discussed moral questions, the one with methodical reasoning as a Greek addressing Greeks, the other with the authoritative tone and earnestness of a Jew."

In the twelfth chapter we have already adverted to the value of "the authoritative tone and earnestness of a Jew." If the author's judgment be correct, then we may well prefer "methodical reasoning" to an "authoritative tone." To put Socrates and Christ together in this manner is simply to ignore Christ's own declaration of divine origin and power. The words of Jesus Christ, as reported by those who heard them, are before us, and they profess to be marked, not by the authoritative tone and earnestness of a Jew, but by the authoritative tone and earnestness of the Son of Man and Son of God. This is their own distinct profession, — not matter of inference, but of positive and literal claim. The author either believes Christ's words or he does not believe them; if he believes them, then he ought not to put Socrates and Christ together as he has done; if he does not believe them, then Christ is not the good man whom he has endeavored to make him out to be. From our point of view, it is a poor and dishonoring thing to say of the Son of God that he spoke with "the authoritative tone and earnestness of a Jew." His enemies, who had daily opportunity of listening to the most authoritative and dogmatic teachers in the world, confessed that "never man spake like this man," a circumstance which alone would warrant the inference that there was a life and a power in his communications which could not be accounted for by "the authoritative tone and earnestness of a Jew."

XVIII. Page 107.

"Socrates holds his place in history by his thoughts and not by his life, Christ by his life and not by his thoughts."

In reply we venture to say — *incorrect*. The vital difference between Christ and all other teachers is this — the perfect identity of his life and thoughts. This consistency alone puts him beyond the range of comparison with any other man. We often find noble thoughts associated with imperfect morality, and spotless morality may be found detached from any marked power of thought; but in Christ the consistency was perfect — a consistency which is itself one of the clearest arguments in favor of his Godhead. All men are self-discrepant; Jesus Christ was self-consistent.

XIX. Page 119.

"This monarchy was essentially despotic, and might, in spite of the goodness of the sovereign, have had some mischievous consequences, if he had remained too long among his subjects, and if his dictation had descended too much into particulars."

A theocracy must be despotic. The sovereign and the monarchy in such a case are inseparable. The sovereign of a theocracy *must* be good — ("in spite of the goodness of the sovereign") — but how he can "remain too long among his subjects" does not appear. The author's view represents Christ rather as a shrewd propagandist than as the Son of God. In all these remarks the author appears to have overlooked the fact that Christ came not *for* a plan, but *with* a plan. If he came without a plan, his " authoritative tone " would hardly stand him in good stead; and if he came *with* a plan, he must have had something more than the " earnestness of a Jew." With respect to the possibility of his " remaining too long," it is forgotten, apparently, that from the beginning he spoke of his " hour." The time was fixed.

XX. Page 167.

" This third feeling is the love, not of the race nor of the individual; it is the love, not of all men, nor yet of every man, but of *the man* in every man."

Say, rather, of *the God* in every man. The author has well pointed out on another page that the normal condition of society in the earliest ages was that of mutual enmity. We honor man most when we see most of God in him. The author has forcibly shown that the idea of immortality gave a new view of injustice and suffering by opening up possibilities of retribution which could not have existed in the limited term of human life on the earth; so, on the same principle, it may be pointed out that in proportion as man recognizes the divine image in man, will he take an enlightened interest in himself and in the destinies of the race. Man has everything to fear from an atheistic view of his own personality and destiny. It is the divine element that gives man his right position.

XXI. Page 168.

" We save a man from drowning, whether he is amiable or the contrary, and we should consider it right to do so, even though we knew him to be a very great criminal, simply because he is a man."

True; but is not this a commonplace? And in so far as it is valuable, is it not valuable by reason of something deeper than is expressed? We save a *horse* from drowning, whether he is vicious, or the contrary, and we should consider it right to do so even though we knew him to have thrown his last rider (and even though that rider be our best friend), simply because he is a horse. What then? Evidently *there is a law of salvation among men*. Anything is saved in proportion to its real or supposed value to *man*. Who would care to save a straw in comparison to saving a letter? Who would risk his life for a floating chip, yet who would not make strenuous endeavors to recover a note-book which had dropped into the river? If we had to make our choice between saving a man or a horse from drowning, we should of course elect to save the man, because of his rank in creation. But take the question upon practical grounds. It is observed that two human beings are drowning; the observer instantly desires their salvation on the simple ground of common humanity; but tell the observer that one of the human beings is his own brother, and instantly we shall have a modification of the principle laid down in quotation 21st. But tell the observer that it is *not* his *brother*, but his own *child*, and then say for whom he will make the most perilous and costly attempts at restoration? The observer would have done much to rescue another man's child, but what effort would he spare when his own son was in question? This may be called selfishness, yet there may not be a particle of selfishness in it. Men would miss the deepest and grandest views of human nature if it were not for the love they bear to their own offspring. When the parent sees his own child drowning he comes to know something of God's feeling in respect to the salvation of man. Man is God's child, and " like as a father pitieth his children, so the Lord pitieth " his suffering child. While, therefore, the above quotation is literally correct in principle, it gives a very inadequate view of the doctrine of human salvation.

XXII. Page 182.

The author represents "the intellectual man" as asking, "What has Christianity added to our theoretic knowledge of morality? It may have made men practically more moral, but has it added anything to Aristotle's ethics?"

Yes; it may be replied in addition to the answer which the author himself has given, It has added *God* to them. Morality is no longer philosophical, it is theological. Aristotle regarded ethics as a subdivision of political science; but in the very midst of his great Ethical Discourse, Jesus Christ said, "Be ye therefore perfect as your Father in heaven is perfect." Aristotle conducted his ethical student from δεινοτης to φρόνησις; Christ leads his disciples from calculation of chances to fellowship with the very nature of God. In his ethical discussions Aristotle ignores any connection between his subject and an ideal or absolute Good; he rather seems to proceed upon the principle laid down by Meno, "that a man's virtue consists in his being competent to manage the affairs of the state, and, managing them, to do good to its friends, evil to its enemies, and to take care that he suffers himself nothing of that kind;" on the other hand, as we have pointed out before, Christ makes morality the practical side of theology: "Thou shalt love the Lord thy God . . .

and thou shalt love thy neighbor." Aristotle's master discussed the question of virtue on a much higher basis. Plato lays it down that virtue cannot be taught, and argues that it is not hereditary, else Themistocles, Thucydides, and other virtuous men, would have had sons worthy of themselves; and adopts the conclusion, that as virtue can neither come by nature nor be taught, that it is bestowed upon certain men by "divine fate." This is good so far, at least, as it recognizes a divine element in virtue, for atheism is corrupt throughout — a fool's theology — a madman's morality! We cannot see the appropriateness of the author's remark, that "Christianity has no ambition to invade the provinces of the moralist or the casuist." (P. 182.) Christianity not only invades them, but revolutionizes them, breaks up their very foundations, and consumes their sophistical quibbling and refinements. Bad morality or casuistry cannot be tolerated by Jesus Christ; how, then, can Christianity be said not to invade the province of either? If it gives no systematic form, it gives the inspiring life.

XXIII. Page 198.

"It was the inspiration, the law-making power, that gave Christ and his disciples courage to shake themselves free from the fetters even of a divine law."

This "law-making power" is to be guarded very watchfully. Though every man may be a law unto himself, yet there must be a common law to which individual legislators should appeal. Euthyphron defined holiness to be "that which is pleasing to the gods," but Socrates soon brought him to confess that the gods themselves were divided about "things pleasing" and "things not pleasing;" that what was pleasing to Jupiter might be odious to Saturn, what was pleasing to Vulcan might be odious to Juno. We should find much of the same difficulty among the law-makers that Plato thus found among the gods, in the absence of common law. We understand that law to be given in the Christian writings. On all questions in casuistry the utmost freedom of personal legislation is allowed; but on all questions of principle the words of the Son of God are final. This is the generally-accepted creed of the orthodox: are they "thoughtless men"? With regard to "shaking themselves free from the fetters even of a divine law," it may be well to note that even in matters of temporary regulation men no more "shake themselves free from the fetters of divine law" than a man shakes himself free from the fetters of his first garments. The man grows out of them; but because he has become too large for a particular set of garments, it does not follow that therefore he must remain naked ever after. It should be noted, too, that he who gave the law gave also the capacity of growth; and as men grow by the favor of the legislator, it may be possible to find some more grateful, not to say more accurate, expression than "shaking themselves free from the fetters even of a divine law." The expression gives the idea of bondage, not of adaptation; of despotism on the part of God, not of temporary incapacity on the part of man.

XXIV. Pages 202, 203.

"It may sometimes strike us that the time which he devoted to acts of beneficence and the relief of ordinary physical evils might have been given to works more permanently beneficial to the race. . . . He might have left to all subsequent ages more instruction if he had bestowed less time upon diminishing slightly the mass of evil around him, and lengthening by a span the short lives of the generation in the midst of which he lived."

There is more in this, we imagine, than, as the author suggests, "that Christ merely reduced to practice his own principle" "of a positive rather than a negative service of man" (p. 203). Jesus Christ never relieved physical diseases without pointing out, by the very condition required, that they were the result of moral causes. He saw more than the leprosy on the body; he saw the deadly ulcer on the soul. Not only so, he had readier access to the body than to the spirit, and so, as we have had repeated occasion to say, he began at the most accessible point, and worked into the deeper nature. We conceive, therefore, that the author's argument is untenable. As to the value of affirmative service there cannot be two opinions, but affirmative service is not confined to the body; an idea is certainly of greater value than a restored hand, but if the sufferer refused permission to his soul, and could barely exercise faith enough to bring his body into a right relation to Jesus Christ, the Healer could begin only on the offered terms, yet with the hope that the healed hand might prepare the way for the healing of the moral nature. We do not consider the author as suggesting to Jesus Christ that he did not make the best use of his time; the author would undoubtedly shrink from so immodest (not to say profane) a protrusion of his own wisdom; he is, as we take it, simply expressing the feeling of a reader who looks at Christ's life from a purely human stand-point.

XXV. Page 207.

"The enthusiasm of humanity in Christians is not only their supreme, but their only law."

This is bold, certainly; on what proof does it rest? Allowing this to be precisely as the author puts it, why should the effect be dissociated from the cause? Love of man is put by Jesus Christ as the consequent of love of God — the enthusiasm of God first, then the enthusiasm of humanity. Who ever knew anything of the enthusiasm of humanity, in its true sense, until Christ revealed the Father? Throughout the teaching of Jesus Christ the *paternal idea* runs as a stream of life; it is because men are the children of one Father that they are related to one another. The Christian writings on this subject seem to reveal two things: (1) That there is a spurious enthusiasm of humanity, and (2) that the true enthusiasm of humanity is inseparable from a filial love of God. There is not only an enthusiasm of humanity, but there is a fanaticism of humanity. Sympathy with God is the life of the former. Jesus Christ never could have been Son of *Man* if he had not first been Son of *God;* — why should we not follow *his* law and development of enthusiasm? He proceeded from the divine to the human; can we proceed by a better way? It is affecting, and not a little instructive, to watch how he retires again and again from the multitude, that he may renew his enthusiasm of humanity by secret communion with God. It will be admitted that the enthusiasm of humanity never reached such perfectness and intensity as in Jesus Christ; but how did he repair the daily exhaustion which it involved? Do not his nights of prayer best explain his days of toil? Does not his constant reference to his Father's will show that the law-making power in man is truthful and safe only so long as it renews itself at the divine source?

XXVI. Page 211.

"Prevention is better than cure, and it is now clear to all that a large part of human suffering is preventible by improved social arrangements."

True; but this is in perfect harmony with the morality of Christ. Is there not, however, a good deal of confusion in the use of the terms "prevention" and "preventible"? We cannot "prevent" the great fundamental fact in human history, viz., the Fall. We have to work upon a "lost" humanity, therefore "prevention" has no part whatever in the business of salvation. Prevention can be applied only to details, and so far its application is undoubtedly useful. Had we to map out a course for pristine man, we should probably be no wiser than God himself, but begin precisely where he began; that is to say, at *prevention*. It is a fact not sufficiently considered, that prevention was actually tried in Eden, and failed; yet moralists and economists bring up the idea of prevention as if it had not dawned on mortal genius until these latter days!

XXVII. Page 218.

"And if the progress of science and civilization has put into our hands the means of benefiting our kind more and more comprehensively than the first Christians could hope to do — if, instead of undoing a little harm, and comforting a few unfortunates, we have the means of averting countless misfortunes and raising, by the right employment of our knowledge and power of contrivance, the general standard of happiness — we are not to inquire whether the New Testament commands us to use these means, but whether the spirit of humanity commands it."

The great, the inexcusable error in this statement is the implication, that possibly the New Testament may be less philanthropic than "the spirit of humanity," and this we take to be an insult to the Son of man. The author apparently ignores the fact that Christianity proposes to deal with a sick man, not with a healthy man; "they that be whole need not a physician;" Jesus Christ repeatedly said that he came to call *sinners*, and not the righteous, to repentance — that he came to seek and to save that which was lost. He did not come with a theory of prevention, but with a scheme of salvation; he did not propose to "comfort a few unfortunates," but to save the world. What is the use of a theory of prevention in a churchyard, so far as the dead are concerned? Weeds may be prevented growing on the graves, but of what advantage is this to those who are in the graves? Resurrection, not prevention, alone can benefit the dead. The author appears to ignore not only the statements of revelation, but the testimony of consciousness as to the moral condition of human nature, and to be more concerned for a law of philanthropy which will "avert countless misfortunes" than for a salvation which encompasses the whole case. The physician is not called upon to decide between prevention and cure; the patient is sick, and must be cured if possible. Jesus Christ had not to consider the case of unfallen beings, but of men who had lost their moral status. "Science and civilization" have enabled us to decorate the sick man's room, and to make all outward circumstances more pleasant to him, but not to touch his disease. If the New Testament, recognizing the urgency of the case, does not dwell upon mere preventives, but points at once to the seat of the malady, and indicates the only possible restoratives, who shall say that it is deficient in "the spirit of humanity"?

It would be a great mistake to imagine that the pre-Christian philosophies troubled themselves even to "undo a little harm and comfort a few unfortunates," much less to "avert countless misfortunes." On this point the words of Baron Macaulay are well worth repeated perusal. "The ancient philosophy disdained to be useful, and was content to be stationary. It dealt largely in theories of moral perfection, which were so sublime that they never could be more than theories; in attempts to solve insoluble enigmas; in exhortations to the attainment of unattainable frames of mind. It could not condescend to the humble office of ministering to the comfort of human beings. All the schools contemned that office as degrading, some censured it as immoral. Once, indeed, Posidonius, a distinguished writer of the age of Cicero and Cæsar, so far forgot himself as to enumerate, among the humbler blessings which mankind owed to philosophy, the discovery of the principle of the arch, and the introduction of the use of metals. This eulogy was considered as an affront, and was taken up with proper spirit. Seneca vehemently disclaims these insulting compliments. Philosophy, according to him, has nothing to do with teaching men to rear arched roofs over their heads. The true philosopher does not care whether he has an arched roof or any roof. Philosophy has nothing to do with teaching men the uses of metals. She teaches us to be independent of all material substances, of all mechanical contrivances. The wise man lives according to nature. Instead of attempting to add to the physical comforts of his species, he regrets that his lot was not cast in that golden age when the human race had no protection against the cold but the skins of wild beasts, no screen from the sun but a cavern. To impute to such a man any share in the invention or improvement of a plough, a ship, or a mill, is an insult. 'In my own time,' says Seneca, 'there have been inventions of this sort, transparent windows, tubes for diffusing warmth equally through all parts of a building, short-hand which has been carried to such perfection, that a writer can keep pace with the most rapid speaker. But the inventing of such things is drudgery for the lowest slaves; philosophy lies deeper. It is not her office to teach men how to use their hands; the object of her lessons is to form the soul. Non est, inquam, instrumentorum ad usus necessarios opifex.'"* So much for the ancient philosophy, and we very much doubt whether what the author of *Ecce Homo* calls "the blessed light of science" (p. 353) is not likely, if left to itself, to do as much to favor a gross and atheistic materialism as the philosophy of Seneca favored the cant of a useless and selfish sentimentality. Christianity occupies an independent position. Its watchwords are Glory to God and Good-will towards men — the devotional and the useful — the highest love of the soul turned to the most practical service of man.

* Essay on Lord Bacon.

In reading *Ecce Homo* our chief dissatisfaction arose from the fact that the author did not recognize the mystery of the Incarnation. Although he speaks on the second page of "the predestined Founder," yet the whole argument of the book is constructed without any reference to the pre-incarnate life of Christ, a life to which Christ himself makes repeated allusion, in his prayers especially. The first sentence in *Ecce Homo* illustrates this — "The Christian Church sprang from a movement which was not begun by Christ." In the very lowest and weakest possible sense, if in any sense at all, can this be true, but according to a complete collation of the facts it is false. The Christian writings give us to understand that before the world began God had a great purpose in relation to the history of man, and that the outworking of that purpose underlay and interpenetrated all human history. There may be influence without manifestation. Christ was as able to conduct the movement anterior to his Incarnation, as he is now able (in the author's own words) to "visit his people for the future only in refreshing inspirations and great acts of providential justice" (p. 119). If he can return, could he not precede? By regarding the Incarnation as part of a continuous development of a divine purpose we are saved from the unprofitable task of studying an unconnected page or a detached limb, and are also saved from the perils of detail by having to work on a vast body of evidence which is homogeneous, cumulative, and self-explanatory. From this point of view we escape the pain of regarding Christ as being hesitant or uncertain in his movements; and the words and actions which transcend our plane of criticism or comprehension are referable to the mysteriousness of his descent or the vastness of a design which can be only fractionally disclosed. It may be answered that the author did not intend to traverse so wide a ground as that which is opened by the question of Jesus Christ's pre-existence: this plea, however, is futile, for though he might not be prepared to traverse the ground, he was not at liberty to ignore the *fact*. He was not called upon to write a theological treatise, but he was called upon to recognize the clear and repeated declarations of Jesus Christ as to his procession from the Father. Given a Jew who unexpectedly took upon himself to do what Christ did, and we shall have one line of interpretation and judgment; but given the Son of God who from unbeginning time determined to do a certain work upon the earth, and we shall have a line of interpretation and judgment peculiar to itself. Is there no difference between the start-points? No author is at liberty to join Christ as " simply a young man of promise, popular with those who knew him, and appearing to enjoy the Divine favor." If he does so "place himself in imagination," he will be in danger of bending the facts to the theory, instead of taking the mould of the theory from the facts. We submit with all due deference that while the author of *Ecce Homo* was at liberty to determine the point from which his "survey" should be taken, he was bound to remember that there were circumstances narrated in the very documents out of which he gets his facts which give significance to every phase of Christ's life, and without which that life is incongruous as a narrative, and powerless as a redemption. The gardener is at liberty to view the earth in patches and neatly enclosed fractions, but the astronomer must view it as part of a system; and the danger to which some inquirers are exposed, and into which we believe the author of *Ecce Homo* has fallen, is that of mistaking gardening for astronomy. Look at Christ as "simply a young man of promise," and then regard him as begotten of the Holy Ghost, and the most contrary conclusions will be reached. In the one case, he will come up out of the earth with all its ignorance and imperfection; in the other, he will descend upon it from heaven with a divine purpose to reveal and establish. Now what is Christ's own testimony? — "I proceeded forth and came from God; neither came I of myself, but he sent me." We are therefore not at liberty to examine the life of such a speaker, as though he had appeared under the usual conditions of human existence. Accepting this account as correct, the mission of such a man must be fundamental; his most emphatic words will be unequal to the expression of all his thought, and his morality will be marked by characteristics of its own. Critics who have been able to hold equal fellowship with Plato and Aristotle, Socrates and Cicero, will realize the impassable distance which separates the earthly from the heavenly; they will feel the "astonishment" which filled the doctors in the Temple, and even when unwilling to submit they will feel unable to reply.

It may be suggested that the author does not accept the Christian writings in their entirety. Then he was bound, we submit, to indicate his principle of eclecticism. He quotes largely from the first three Gospels, and makes one or two reserved references to the fourth. Now by what law does he make choice? If the writings are authoritative on points of fact, wherein are they defective on points of doctrine? Without pressing him to an answer, we do protest against being invited to conduct an inquiry upon unequal terms. Before we start we must know each other's canons of criticism, and be agreed on common principles of interpretation; at all events we must know the precise sphere of inquiry — how much is included, how much is rejected. We cannot, if the investigation is to be mutual, allow the author to indorse or invalidate documents without distinctly telling us on what principle he is proceeding.

The author's proposal to discuss the morality in contradistinction to the theology of Jesus Christ, we cannot but regard as unsatisfactory. Are the morality and the theology separable? If for the sake of convenience a division be made, we submit that the theology should stand first, for the sufficient reason that it lies at the basis of the morality. By theology, as used in this connection, cannot of course be meant the formal science which now passes under that name (a science which has probably originated three fourths of the speculative scepticism of the age), but *the idea of the Father* which was ever present to the mind of Jesus Christ, and which regulated the whole course and tone of his teaching. Morality was not discussed by Jesus Christ as it was discussed by Aristotle, and we still maintain, as was stated in the thirteenth chapter, that the difference between Aristotle's teaching and Christ's teaching is the difference between an Investigation and a Revelation. By regarding Jesus Christ's morality as the practical side of his theology, we escape the errors into which, as it appears to us, the author has fallen respecting the incompleteness of Christ's moral teaching. When man's ideas of God are rectified and enlarged, his ideas of practical life will become correspondingly pure and noble. In other words, when a man loves God, he will love his brother also, but not until then: as Christ puts it, the question is one of cause and effect; and though he might have made a more imposing exhibition of ethical speculation and instruction, so far as mere words are concerned, yet, according to his idea of the Father, he would have been working at the wrong end, coloring the fruit from the outside instead of renewing and strengthening the root, merely removing withered leaves instead of vitalizing the juices. According to the nature of the fall must be the nature of the restoration: the fall was between man and God, not between man and man; so the restoration must be towards God, and the best proof of its reality will be found in constant exhibitions of good-will towards men. It may be true, as the author of *Ecce Homo* forcibly says, that " the most lost cynic will get a new heart by learning thoroughly to believe in the virtue of one man " (p. 177), but, if comparisons in truth be allowed, it is more deeply and sublimely true that man can never become a cynic until he has lost the right idea of God. The Fatherhood of God is the strongest defence against cynicism. Reverting to the Fall, as the true start-point from which to view all proposed remedial systems, it is to be noted as a singular fact that the Fall did not take place in an advanced condition of society, when civilization had effeminated manhood, or when bad management had disorganized social relations; it took place before a single city was built, before human society, as it is now understood, was founded; it was not a failure in speculative ethics, it was simply a misunderstanding of God — a lowering of his authority — a misconception of his nature — and *thus* a terrible immorality. It is important to remember this, because from the prevention theory it might be inferred that human depravity was simply a question of adulterated food, bad drainage, overcrowded dwellings, and impure air. It is forgotten that not one of these unfavorable conditions existed in the days of Adam and Eve. Nature was in its purest state, and yet, unless we throw the sacred writings out of court, the Fall took place amid the very brightness and beauty of the garden of Eden. So that, if the prevention theorists were so far to succeed in their work as actually to get back to the pure food, the pure air, and the pure light of Paradise, they would still have to grapple with a deeper problem than can be solved by negative philosophy. That problem is the *moral nature of man.* How can he retain his power to commit sin, but lose the disposition? Does he need restraint or regeneration? We are aware that these inquiries open upon a sphere of impenetrable mystery; but we are also aware that to shirk them is not to escape difficulty. The choice is between the mystery of light and the mystery of darkness. Immediately before us is the fact that *man is not at rest;* how can he recover his balance? By pure air, by good food, by ample dwelling-room? Where is the congruity between the question and the answer?

It has been urged that *Ecce Homo* is a fragment. A fragment of what? It may be a fragment of a larger work, but is not therefore of necessity a fragment of the life of Jesus Christ. If it has ignored, for all practical purposes, the interpretative value of the Incarnation, it is not a fragment; it may be an unfinished theory, but not being of the nature of the integer, it is not, it cannot be, in the proper sense of the term, a fragment of the life of Christ. A man might write a treatise on astronomy, but if he began by declaring that the earth was the centre of the universe, or that it described no orbit round the sun, he would not be allowed to shelter himself under the plea that his work was a fragment; it might be a fragment of his manuscript, but viewed in the light of facts, it would not be, nor could it ever be made, a fragment of the geometry of creation. *Ecce Homo* treats Christ as if he had no ancestry; fails to take any account of Christ's own claim to pre-incarnate life, and ignores those peculiar conditions which are themselves the best explanation of the mysteries of his doctrine, and which, we venture to think, cannot be ignored without moving the whole life out of its plane, and so mistaking its fundamental and sovereign purpose.

Not until the present writer had written thus far had he an opportunity of reading the Preface to the fifth edition of *Ecce Homo*. It is to be regretted, he ventures to think, that a portion of it was not given in the original Preface, particularly the following paragraph: " He was concerned with four writers who, in nearness to the events they record, and probable means of acquiring information, belong to the better class of historical witnesses, but whose veracity has been strongly impeached by critics, both on the ground of internal discrepancies, and of the intrinsic improbability of their story. Out of these four writers he desired, not to extract a life of Christ, not to find out all that can be known about him, but to form such a rudimentary conception of his general character and objects as it may be possible to form while the vexed critical questions remain in abeyance. The detection of discrepancies in the documents establishes a certain degree of independence in them, and thus gives weight to their agreements; in particular, the wide divergence in tone and subject-matter of the fourth Gospel from the other three, affords a strong presumption in favor of all statements in which it coincides with them. The rudiment of certainty which the writer sought, he accordingly expected to find in the consent of all the witnesses. If the statements unanimously attested should prove numerous enough to afford any outline of Christ's life, however meagre, he proposed to rest content with this." It is due to the author of *Ecce Homo* that he should thus be allowed, on the pages of his critic, to put his own case in his own way. No doubt a literary man may be at liberty to select a criterion by which to guide his inquiries, but how far he is at liberty to describe a book written on the above principle as "a Survey of the Life and Work of Jesus Christ," may be a question on which the author and the reader might differ. It would appear, too, that the author must have exceeded his own design, for certainly the twenty propositions which he deduces from Mark's Gospel include many of the "vexed critical questions" and "intrinsic improbabilities" which he wished to remain in abeyance, such as the power of forgiving sins, the working of miracles, the claim to be the Messiah, and the promise of the Holy Ghost. The author conceives himself to have found "the rudiment of certainty" when all the four evangelists agree in the same statement; that is to say, if any incident or doctrine be found in all the four Gospels it may be accepted as a basis of argument. This is an extraordinary canon in scriptural criticism; it at once throws a degree of discredit upon each of the witnesses; his testimony is not accepted until it is confirmed; if one evangelist confirms it, it is not enough; if two confirm the statement, the evidence is still incomplete; all the four must agree, without "discrepancy" or "improbability," otherwise, "the rudiment of certainty" is not found. But this rule of criticism is either too great or too small. Why should four be the number of witnesses selected? What answer could be returned to the objector who carried the author's rule a little farther by rejecting the testimony of four writers, on the ground that all the eleven disciples should have written independent histories? If the question turn upon the number of witnesses, it is clear that after all we must get "the rudiment of certainty" out of the testimony of the minority; and if out of the minority at all, why not out of the minority of those who have written, allowing for such differences as must attach to individuality of mind and habits of observation? And if the four witnesses agree in the twenty comprehensive propositions which have been deduced from Mark's Gospel, so comprehensive as to include almost the whole of Christianity, why may they not have arranged to palm off the story upon the world? But if it was impossible for them to have so agreed, why should their points of difference be points of doubt? On the author's principle, any four men may combine in the production of a book, and if they only take care to agree in their statements they may rely upon a general acceptance of their testimony. Is "the rudiment of certainty" not to be found by a higher method? Is the higher appeal not to what is known of God, to human consciousness, and to the "fruits" of that which is spoken? And when these methods of judgment are exhausted, what if the supernatural should transcend reason and appeal to faith? What if the universe be larger than we had conceived? Four men undertake to write a life; we are not aware who appointed them, or to what secret resource, if any, they had access; we have the results of their labor before us; shall we reject one because he is a little more or less minute than the others? The author himself, under the influence of some such consideration as this inquiry suggests, seems to have modified the plan which he laid down with such precision, for he allows that "evidence inferior to the best may have very great probability, and there are certain obvious criteria by which this probability may be estimated." Certainly; but if we accept a man's testimony when it agrees with the testimony of another man, is that not a reason for accepting it when he speaks upon subjects to which the other man does not refer? But we need not all this pleading on behalf of the Gospels: their *spirit* is one; the whole tone is self-consistent; and the moral energy of the doctrine renders it an easy responsibility to accept all the statements which relate to matters of fact.

All that the author has said does not touch the starting-point, viz., the Incarnation. Even on his own principle of accrediting evidence it is not easy to see how he has overlooked this fact, for three out of four of the evangelists distinctly point out the supernatural descent of Jesus Christ, and Mark himself introduces him at once as "the Son of God." The "rudiment of certainty" is surely here, even upon the author's own showing; so that, without imputing any intentions to the author, we cannot but feel surprised that he has not found in Christ's Incarnation some explanation of Christ's life and work. We feel this the more because the writer has not been faithful to his own principle of interpretation. On the twelfth page of his Preface he speaks of himself as " resting upon a basis of absolutely uniform testimony," yet in the course of his work he reverts again and again, either by elaborate statement or distinct allusion, to cases which are not supported by any such testimony.

He lays down a principle, and immediately departs from it. For example, he refers to the Sermon on the Mount; but where is the " basis of absolutely uniform testimony" in this case? The Sermon is reported by two only of the four evangelists. The author draws a beautiful picture of the circumstances connected with the woman taken in adultery; but where is the "basis of absolutely uniform testimony" in her case? The instance is related by one only of the four evangelists. So also in the case of Zaccheus, which the author brings into special prominence, we have the testimony of one evangelist only; yet the author speaks of "resting upon a basis of absolutely uniform testimony." The same remark applies to Nicodemus, on whose case the author remarks. What we have to complain of is, that the writer of *Ecce Homo* has laid down a principle and then practically abandoned it. He has, indeed, referred to what he terms "inferior evidence," but this does not touch the ground of complaint. For example, he says that "the account of the woman taken in adultery has scarcely any external authority, but it seems to derive great probability from the fact that the conduct attributed to Christ in it is left half explained, so that, as it stands, it does not satisfy the impulses which lead to the invention and reception of fictitious stories." It would seem, then, that a case needs only to be "half explained" in order to get credit for "great probability," and if the inventor be unable to finish his fiction, so much more likely is he to be accepted as an honest man. If the author's principle of eclecticism was sound, he ought not to have departed from it; if he departed from it at all, he should have given preference to the greater, and not to the minuter incidents, — to such an event as the Incarnation in preference to the invitation which the guests refused; but his principle failed in its practical application, so that "absolutely uniform testimony" has been supplemented by cases which rest upon individual authority.

No formal epilogue is attempted. We thought that the dual element that was in Jesus Christ was of great significance; so great, indeed, that apart from it his life could not be interpreted. Throughout the whole inquiry this has been kept steadily in view; with what advantage it is for others to determine. We have endeavored to find out God, through a study of his Son. We understand what this means in human life; if we would know any man of deep character, who is not immediately self-revealing, we shall make the surest progress by carefully studying the disposition and habits of the child who most resembles him. To study the father through the child is like studying a foreign language alphabetically, grammatically, and analytically, — not catching it in common conversation so as to be able merely to express an opinion or a want, but penetrating it philosophically, and so becoming master of it. To get through the wrinkles and folds of the father's mature character may be impossible, but the child is open, simple, legible in every letter; — from him we get the father's own start-point, and from the father we get the other extreme point. With the extremes before us, we may proceed to analysis and interpretation. Is it not much the same with Jesus Christ? Emphatically, he was the brightness of the Father's glory and the express image of his person; he was the Son only-begotten and well-beloved. To study him is to study God in his most legible aspect; so to speak, the letters are large, and so formed as to arrest untrained eyes; — mighty deeds, mightier words, and still mightier prayers. We see there how far God can come down on the human side, — how far he can be man without ceasing to be God; and it was so far, that he who had seen the Son had actually seen the Father!

To-day the great question that is stirring men's hearts to their very depths is, Who is this Jesus Christ? His life is becoming to us a new life, as if we had never seen a word of it. There is round about us an influence so strange, so penetrating, so subtle, yet so mighty, that we are obliged to ask the great heaving world of time to be silent for a while, that we may see just what we are and where we are. That influence is the life of Jesus Christ. We cannot get clear of it; we hear it in the tones of joy, we feel it stealing across the darkness of sorrow, — we see it where we least expect it, — even men who have travelled farthest from it seem only to have come round to it again; and while they have been undervaluing the inner worth of Jesus Christ, they have actually been living on the virtue which came out of his garment's hem. Yes; it seems we must touch him either at the hem or the heart, — if we will not have him for the soul, we must have him for the body. What if men reject him altogether? Then, as of old, there is no choice for them but Barabbas, and Barabbas is a robber. We see the alternative. Pilate still puts the question — "Whom will ye that I release unto you? Barabbas, or Jesus which is called Christ?" The voice of the people was once for the robber; it will yet be lifted up, never more to change, for the Son of God.

www.ingramcontent.com/pod-product-compliance
Lightning Source LLC
Chambersburg PA
CBHW020323240426
43673CB00039B/897